Also of interest from Saybrook

Rollo May
My Quest for Beauty

Roger Sperry, John Eccles, and others
Nobel Prize Conversations

Roy Laurens
Fully Alive

POLITICS
and
INNOCENCE

A Humanistic Debate

ROLLO MAY
CARL ROGERS
ABRAHAM MASLOW

and other humanistic psychologists

Saybrook
Publishers

Library of Congress Cataloging-in-Publication Data

May, Rollo
    Politics and innocence.
    Bibliography: p.223
    1. Political psychology — Addresses, essays, lectures.
    2. Political ethics — Addresses, essays, lectures.
    3. Humanistic psychology — Addresses, essays, lectures.
    I. Rogers, Carl R. (Carl Ransom), 1902-
    II. Maslow, Abraham, 1907-
    JA74.5.M39 1986   320.973'019   85-155385
    ISBN 0-933071-00-0

Saybrook Publishers
4223 Cole Avenue, Suite Four, Dallas, TX 75205

Printed in the United States of America

Distributed by W.W. Norton & Company
500 Fifth Avenue, New York, NY 10110

About *Politics and Innocence*

This book is the result of a happy interaction between Saybrook Institute of San Francisco and the Association for Humanistic Psychology. Particularly responsible for the inception of the book were Dennis Jaffe and Don Polkinghorne.

Most of the essays in *Politics and Innocence* first appeared, in slightly different form, in the *Journal of Humanistic Psychology.* A note on "Sources" at the end of this volume identifies each essay's original time and place of publication. Under the title *American Politics and Humanistic Psychology,* this book was published in a limited edition for the twenty-fifth anniversary conference of the Association for Humanistic Psychology held in March, 1985, in San Francisco.

CONTENTS

Foreword

I   GOOD AND EVIL

II   INNOCENCE AND GROWING UP

III   THE PROBLEM OF A POLITICAL ELITE

IV THE END OF INNOCENCE

FOREWORD

"Can we make America better by passing better laws or by becoming better people?" We have discovered that humane laws do not necessarily have humane political results. But can we save America and save our world by becoming better people? Three further questions then emerge: "What is 'better'?", "How do we get better?", and "How many of us would have to get better before America and our world get better?"

The humanistic movement in psychology is turning its attention to such political issues as war and peace, liberty, justice and equality, the ecology of our physical environment and the ecology of our social and spiritual environments. The following quote from Abraham Maslow is an example of one psychological approach to a humane politics:

> The empirical fact is that self-actualizing people, our best experiencers, are also our most compassionate, our great improvers and reformers of society, our most effective fighters against injustice, inequality, slavery, cruelty, exploitation (and also our best fighters for

excellence, effectiveness and competence). And it also becomes clearer amd clearer that the best 'helpers' are the most fully human persons. What I may call the bodhisattvic path is our integration of self improvement and social zeal . . . normative zeal is not incompatible with scientific objectivity but can be integrated with it.

There is a groundswell in America and throughout the world of concern for personal values and ethics in politics. To quote Mark Satin on these kinds of events in another part of the world,

Most Polish Solidarity activists felt — very strongly — that personal and socio-political change are interconnected and interdependent . . . They went so far as to say that consciousness ultimately determines society — standing Marxism completely on its head.

This book concentrates on four issues basic to the contribution that "raising" personal consciousness can make to a more humane politics for both America and our larger world.

In the first section, "Good and Evil," Carl Rogers and Rollo May struggle with the problem of good and evil, attempting to answer a problem posed at the the beginning of this introduction, "If we want to get better, what is 'better'?"

In the second section, "Innocence and Growing Up," Marilyn Ferguson and Michael Marien confront each other over Marilyn Ferguson's contention that people are, right now, making the world better politcally by making themselves better.

In the third section, "The Problem of a Political Elite," Maslow's self-actualizing person is considered in terms of an elite, "How many of us have to get better before America and our world get better?"

The fourth section, "The End of Innocence," details specific ways in which a humanistic psychology can and does contribute to a more humane politics.

Most of the pieces in this book appeared first in the *Journal of Humanistic Psychology*. As editor of the journal since 1971, I have been in a position to see the ways humanistic psychologists have progressed toward more sophisticated and responsible engagement with political issues. This development is also reflected in the evolving programs of the Association for Humanistic Psychology. Under the direction of Francis Macy, it has launched a Soviet-American exchange program, and its conferences increasingly express AHP's commitment to grappling with national and global concerns. I am pleased to present this book as a collection of some of the best thinking in humanistic psychology and as a stimulus for continued contributions to progress.

Tom Greening
Editor, *Journal of Humanistic Psychology*

POLITICS
and
INNOCENCE

I

GOOD AND EVIL

Standing in the long historical shadows behind the interaction of politics and modern psychology is the fourth-century figure of St. Augustine, Christian bishop of Hippo near the ancient city of Carthage in North Africa. Augustine's *Confessions*, a literary classic, was perhaps the first truly "psychological" piece of autobiography in the West. A journey inward, an intensely personal scrutiny of his psyche's depths and heights, the *Confessions* waver between self-accusation and gratitude for divine mercy. Augustine's assessment of human nature is negative. Humans, he concluded, are not merely fragile or wounded, they are debased, wicked and ruined. Only an act of divine power can save them from utter and eternal destruction.

Quite clearly, Augustine was no proponent of "human potential" or of happy prospects for self-development. But it is worth noting that no less a figure than Freud held views similar to Augustine's vision of human nat-ure. Like the ancient bishop, Freud was pessimistic about our ability to find real happiness, to behave selflessly, or to use freedom effectively. There is a wide gap between Freud's pessimism and say, Abraham Maslow's portrait of self-actualizing persons who are free from cultural conventions and can act altruistically on behalf of others. And there is a huge difference as well between the strict Freudian vision of human nature and the one outlined in the works of Carl Rogers. Rogers is convinced of the fundamental goodness of human persons, of their power and strength to choose change, to achieve authentic freedom and to internalize positive values.

Rollo May, on the other hand, does not share this Rogerian optimism. In "The Destiny of America," May summarizes major political events in recent American history — the Nixonian presidency, the hostage crisis in Iran, Soviet aggression in Afghanistan, the speeding nuclear juggernaut — and concludes that we can no longer live with our badly suppressed despair. Decades of dishonesty, exploitation of nature and eco-nomic repression, May argues, have now come full circle, and we are faced with a worldwide crisis parallel to the one described in the biblical story of the flood. Much of our "morality" has been mere hypocrisy, our myths of progress are bankrupt, and the American Dream is as dead as Gatsby.

These two contrasting essays, with their profoundly different implica-tions for a view of human nature, serve as a prelude to the direct exchange between Carl Rogers and Rollo May which follows. The exchange first appeared in the 1982 volume of the *Journal of Humanistic Psychology.* Rogers opens with some "Notes on Rollo May" originally written for a special issue of Perspectives (journal of the Humanistic Psychology Insti-tute in San Francisco) in 1981. The major difference between himself and May, Rogers writes, "is around the nature of the human individual." May's interest in "the demonic as a basic element in the human make-up" suggests that evil is inherent in human nature.

In a long open letter to Carl Rogers on "The Problem of Evil," Rollo May replies to the accusation that he views human nature as basically evil. First, he notes, the term daimonic — not demonic — is morally neutral. The daimonic urge in humans creates a potential for both constructive and destructive impulses. "If," May notes, "the daimonic urge is integrated into the personality (which is, to my mind, the purpose of psychotherapy) it results in creativity, that is, it is constructive." Destructive activity results when the daimonic is not integrated. It then expresses itself in violent rage, collective paranoia, compulsive sex and the like.

May proceeds with a denial that "culture" is the enemy which causes humans to behave badly. Culture cannot be given an existence independent of the selves who comprise it, since "there is no self except in interaction with a culture, and no culture that is not made up of selves." We must look elsewhere, May contends, for an explanation of the evil humans do and suffer.

Rogers himself does not, of course, ignore the cultural problems that confront us as we face the future. In his piece on "Social Concerns," he addresses several of these, including over-population, urban congestion, marriage and human relationships, and racism. In the original form of Rogers's essay, other issues in American life were also addressed, such as police brutality against protesters and the war in Vietnam. These sections are omitted from the version printed here, since they reflect conditions that have changed over the past ten to fifteen years.

Finally, Maurice Friedman enters the dialogue about "the nature of human nature" with a reflection on "The Hidden Human Image." Using the nuclear threat as a point of departure, Friedman notes that for Freud, war is inevitable, while for Einstein war is avoidable because we humans can choose for change. Here once again it is the question of good and evil which underlies the discussion. Calling on the classic mythological figure of Prometheus and the biblical character of Job, Friedman argues that humans are polar, suspended between the powerful tug of goodness in one direction and the stinging experience of evil in the other. We are not either/or beings; our life and experience are more complex than that.

The dialogue about good and evil, as it touches the political life of both America and the world, begins with Carl Rogers.

❧   ❧   ❧

CARL ROGERS, *The Person*

> *Carl Rogers writes me: "I regret that in this*
> *paper, written some years ago, I used 'he' as the*

*generic term. I hope my feminine readers will for-
give me. I have learned better since." — Editor.*

In 1978, in Spain, we had a workshop of 170 people from 22 different nations. It was a very exciting workshop, with differences in language, differences in culture; differences in religion and sharp differences in economic views. It was a workshop that had to be conducted in two languages, with other languages frequently being used also. The participants included an ardent group of Marxists and at the other extreme, conservative businessmen, such as the foreign manager for *Reader's Digest.*

In the early portion of the workshop, the Marxists were sure that a humanistic, person-centered, client-centered approach would surely be turned into a tool of exploitation of the workers; it would reduce their anger, and would defuse the Revolution. They called a special political meeting which I attended, where I learned a good deal. Toward the end of the meeting, they asked that I make clear my own political stance. I said that I would like them to give me until morning because I would prefer to give them a written statement to avoid misunderstanding or being misquoted. So here, with a little editing, is that same statement.

"I have been very much involved in the politics of the workshops we have conducted in recent years, workshops numbering from 65 to 220. Increasingly, I and the staff have been able to implement our political views in those groups, which have lasted from one to three weeks. Let me state in summarized form what I mean by politics. To me, politics involves the question of where power is located, who makes the choices and decisions, who carries out or enforces those decisions, and who has the knowledge or data regarding the consequences of those decisions. It means the strategies involved in the taking of power, the distribution of power, the holding of power, and the sharing or relinquishing of power. I've often listened in these workshops and elsewhere to fluent and articulate discussions on political issues. Yet almost never do I hear any discussion of the politics of the family, of marriage, of the school, and only rarely the politics of the workplace. Yet when a father decides what is proper behavior for the family members, when the teacher tells students what subjects they're to learn and how rapidly to learn them, when the director or manager of an organization personally makes the policies for that organization, these, to me, are political acts. They are also political acts that deny the rights of the individual.

"I believe that my own political views are best exemplified in the way that I and my colleagues have conducted ourselves in the workshops I've mentioned. Applicants are told in advance that the program will be developed by all of us, including the staff, when they arrive. They are asked to set their own tuition. They are told the estimated expenses per person that must be covered if the workshop is to be held; they are asked to consider this in relation to their own financial situation and what they can afford; then they decide what they will pay. In a recent two-week workshop, the estimated cost per person was $300. Some people paid nothing, most paid from $100 to $400. Some paid much more, and one person paid $1,200. Thus far, we've always broken even financially. I've described this at some length because it illustrates how, in regard to a most fundamental economic issue, the person makes his or her own responsible decision.

"When participants arrive, it continues to be our aim to keep with the individual the power that he or she has, or potentially has, for decision-making. Thus they choose their own rooms, and whether they wish to use a unisex or co-educational bathroom. And they meet as a total group to decide how they wish to invest their time in the workshop. These meetings are often initially confused and chaotic. The purposes and needs sometimes run at cross purposes. The staff experiences and lives this confusion with the group as equal persons, and as facilitative persons. Gradually each participant realizes this is "our" workshop. I have influence on it. I am an important part of it. Tentative plans emerge. People take initiative in forming small groups or meeting their needs in the large group. An organic process takes place and the workshop finds its suitable form. Thus persons retain their own power and become aware of their inner strength that they had not realized. It's sometimes a frightening thing to realize: I have a chance here to make a decision for myself.

"Consequently, participants at first often accuse the staff of not having done enough planning, showing that the group is eager to relinquish its power to the staff. Then they realize their own power; sometimes some of them begin to use that power as weapons against others. They make choices they regret. Every consequence of my use of my power and your use of your power is evident and out in the open. We realize how incredibly diverse are the demands and needs of individuals. yet gradually there takes place a process which, to me, is extremely elegant, like a beautiful piece of craftsmanship. The group moves closer to making decisions which take into account the needs and desires of every individual. It is not compromise, but willing, mutual accommodation. In one workshop, one decision was taken by a vote, which, of course, left the minority dissatisfied. But the group never did that again. Always the group tends to move away from oppressing anyone. This applies in major decisions, and then in such troublesome minor issues as smoking during community meetings. Various ingenious solutions have been worked out in this latter situation in ways which work hardships on neither smokers nor non-smokers. To draw a political example such as these from workshops may seem trivial, but, I believe, our political ideology is best demonstrated in our small behaviors, not in our party labels nor in highly intellectual abstractions.

"Let me summarize my own political ideology, if you will, in a very few words. I find that for myself, I am most satisfied politically when every person is helped to become aware of his or her own power and strength; when each person participates fully and responsibly in every decison which affects him or her; when group members learn that the sharing of power is more satisfying than endeavoring to use power to control others; when the group finds ways of making decisons which accommodate the needs and desires of each person; when every person of the group is aware of the consequences of a decision on its members and on the external world; when each person enforces the group decision through self-control of his or her own behavior; when each person feels increasingly empowered and strengthened; and when each person and the group as a whole is flexible, open to change, and regards previous decisions as being always open for reconsideration.

That's my platform. I suspect that some of you regard these statements as hopelessly idealistic. But in my experience, especially when a facilitative climate is provided for a group, the members choose to move in somewhat the ways that I have described. In some of my writing, particularly in my recent book on personal power, I have given examples showing the effectiveness of this kind of politics in the marriage relationship, in the family, in schools, in workshops, in the managements of business. I don't know of any political party or government which operates fully on this basis, but I do believe there is a movement toward more participation in government, and a growing distrust of authoritarian institutions of every kind. So I do not despair.

This political creed of mine does not grow out of any political tract, or any general ideology. It developed out of my own experience in which I discovered how richly rewarding it was to entrust persons with power, with support for my views in the most diverse places. I find these views reinforced by the so-called experimental plants of Proctor and Gamble Corporation, where workers are trusted to make decisions and to be responsible. I don't think the heads of that corporation understand what's going on, but they have permitted a remarkable development. I have read carefully the exploits of Carlsen's Raiders in World War II and I had myself interviewed bomber crews in that same war. In each case the most astonishing achievements came where hierarchical authority was shelved, and each person was made responsible for contributing all he could to the enterprise. I read of the remarkble leap in creativity and productivity in the early days of the People's Republic of China, under Mao Tsetung, and I had a chance to observe that where trust was placed in the peasants and workers, and they were given a great deal of autonomy, the results were remarkable.

It appears to be true, in my experience and that of others, that persons have enormous capacities for learning, for achievement, for creative problem solving, for disciplined effort toward a goal. All these capacities appear to be released in the political atmosphere I have described. My political stance is idealistic, and radical, but in my experience, and that of others, amazingly constructive potentials come into fruition when persons are able, even partially, to put these political principles into operation.

🌳　　　🌳　　　🌳

ROLLO MAY, *The Destiny of America*

It is always wonderful to promote human potential, to discuss noble ideals and make great plans for the future. I wonder if some of our concern about these noble things is possibly a defense against our own despair about the possibility of nuclear war. We have seen in the past few years how close we are to a nuclear war, how we could slide down the toboggan — we have already begun to slide down — into an atomic conflagration. And if there is any war at all among the big powers, we can be sure it will be a nuclear war.

It is firmly established that the United States government more than 30 years ago intervened to overthrow the people's government of Iran and that Allen Dulles took the Shah to Teheran in his private plane to make him an absolute ruler of that nation and to protect the profits of the big oil companies. Is it any wonder that the people of Iran hate us and regard us as their enemy? I began to puzzle about why we made this gross mistake of letting the Shah come to New York; he could have gone to France or Mexico or to a number of other places. It turns out that because he had been a friend of the U.S., and particularly a friend of David Rockfeller, and whose billions Rockefeller takes care of, and of Henry Kissinger, who had used the Shah in his Near Eastern plans, we let him in. There seems to be a very simplistic morality going on; that kind of morality led to the endangering of the lives of 50 hostages, to a great upset in this country and to the Russian aggression in Afghanistan. The Russians would not have moved into Afghanistan except that we were preoccupied in Iran. It led to the rearming of the U.S.; and it led us from these many different angles to the verge of a nuclear war.

Politics is the art of the possible, and the possible has certainly become the great problem in recent years.

The simplistic morality that we in the U.S. have been known for covers up the absence of a profound morality in our nation which we desperately need. Whatever moral structure we had in this nation was partly eroded by Ford's pardon of Nixon before any trial, eroded by the tragic immorality of the Vietnam war, and also partially eroded by a speech that President Carter made some years ago on our loss of confidence. Is that the confidence that our oil supplies will soon be restored? It is the confidence in the stock market? Is it the confidence in the political party? Is it the confidence that the United States will always remain the most powerful nation in the world? No one seems to realize that it is precisely these confidences that have led us into the state of malaise we're now in, into the state of despair that many of us feel and a great number of us repress.

The American Dream is dead, there's no doubt about that. The Horatio Alger myth that Americans can change a little bit here and change a little bit there and everything is going to be fine, the Horatio Alger dream that we can marry the boss's daughter, become wealthy, and become anything we wish — this is now dead, and we might as well face this fact. The requiem for it was the tremendously significant book of F. Scott Fitzgerald's — *The Great Gatsby*. Gatsby's life exemplifies this American dream. Anybody can change and can become anything he wants to. He can marry his sweetheart, live happily ever after. Gatsby, you will recall, changed his name, he changed his accent by going to Oxford, he changed his clothes, he bought a big house on Long Island and he made a lot of money bootlegging. Then comes the tragic ending. The fabulous dance orchestras are silent. Gatsby's big house is empty. Daisy has gone back to a rich husband and Gatsby's body lies floating in his own swimming pool. This occurs about three-quarters of the way through the novel, and Fitzgerald spends the rest of the pages talking about the consciousness of America, indicating that the American dream which he has been portraying is now gone. On this last page there come these words "Gatsby had come a long way to this blue lawn, and his dream must have seemed so close that he could hardly fail to grasp it. He did not know that it was already behind him, somewhere back in that vast obscurity beyond the city, where the dark fields of the republic rolled on under the night. Gatsby believed in the green light, the orgiastic future that year-by-year recedes before us. It eluded us then, but that's no matter. Tomorrow we will run faster, stretch out our arms farther and one fine morning . . . So we beat on, boats against the current, borne back ceaselessly into the past."

This tragedy ends with the myth of Sisyphus. We beat on, always pushed back into the past. This tragedy is what happens when a human being or a nation denies its destiny. No amount of sweetness and light is going to solve our political problems or is going to keep us out of nuclear war. We forget that vast numbers of people subconsciously want war because war then gives a focus for their hatred, gives some place for this repressed despair to go to. I think that Pogo shows considerably more wisdom: "We have met the enemy and he is us."

We in the 20th century require new myths on which to found our nation. I use the word myths not at all as meaning its deteriorated form — falsehood. Myth is the non-material structure on which society is based, and from which we draw our morality. We must replace the myth of American military might with the myth of the integration of all the people of the earth. As Don Michael so well puts it — even the use of the word "country" is already an anachronism. We need to see that the myth of our economic structure, our economic system based on free enteprise, is now bankrupt, and we must replace it with the myth that depicts the resources of the world — whether it be oil under the ground, or diamonds under a mountain, or gold mineral from the earth — that this belongs to all the people on the earth. And thirdly we must readjust or reform our myth of Horatio Alger which says each man for himself, and the devil take the hindmost. This must be replaced by some myths of community. We need a new myth of nature, in which we will no longer see nature as something to exploit, as in atomic power, but will be a cooperation with nature. We need to look more deeply and see that much of what we call honesty among ourselves is really hypocrisy. That might help us to develop a moral empathy with the other nations less gifted than our land, less gifted with a land as lush as ours.

There are signs that we in America are entering a time when we can no longer camouflage or repress our despair, and many of us are worried about that. But we know in therapy that the times of despair are essential to the discovery on the part of the client of his or her hidden capacities and basic assets. The function of despair is to wipe away our superficial ideals, our simplistic political morality. It acts like the flood in the Old Testament, it washes away and requires us to give up our self-centered demands on the universe. It means letting go in the zen sense. As I consider that there may be another flood and this flood may well be the atomic war, I hope with every drop of blood in my body that this can be avoided. But the dark night of the soul, as it is often put, and as John Bunyan put it, the slough of despondency, are necessary to go through if one is to arrive at any better system.

Joe Campbell points out that the hero must confront death. He must confront dismemberment. He must be willing to confront those things if he is ever to find the treasure. After the Augean stables are cleansed by our despair, the one thing left is possibility.

We all stand on the edge of life, each moment comprising that edge and before us is only possibility. I profoundly hope that we use this possibility not only to fight each battle politically, according to our own ethics, to stand for what we believe, as certainly we must do, but even more, that we anticipate the death of this society and the birth of a new myth on which a new society can be born. Perhaps we shall re-discover the meaning of the proclamation 28 centuries ago: Let justice roll down as waters and righteousness as a mighty stream.

CARL ROGERS, *Notes on Rollo May*

I think of Rollo as the leading scholar of humanistic psychology. He is well read, deeply informed, and has developed a wisdom which is evident in his writings.

He has always been critical of trends in humanistic psychology which lead toward trivial or unexamined goals. He has wanted the field to have depth, and to be respected for a high quality of philosophical and theoretical thought. In pursuit of this purpose he was one of the initiators of the Tuscon conference on theory in humanistic psychology in 1975. This proved to be a stimulating conference for those present, and Rollo was one of its leading figures. It is almost impossible to evaluate the long-range impact of such a conference. During the experience I felt there was a moderate amount of "one-upsmanship," and not too much clarity of communication. But the highly diverse points of view from such individuals as Gregory Bateson, Jonas Salk, Huston Smith, have, I know, left their mark on me, and this is doubtless true of the others present. Rollo deserves much credit for this enterprise.

I remember with pleasure the seminar Rollo conducted for the Department of Psychiatry at the University of Wisconsin, about 1960, when I was a member of that department. It was part of a series of sessions, each extending over several days, in which we became acquainted with the person, the theories, and the therapeutic practice of a number of different leaders in the field. Rollo did not disappoint us, and it was a pleasure for me to have him stay in my home.

I suppose my major difference with Rollo is around the question of the nature of the human individual. He sees the demonic as a basic element in the human makeup, and dwells upon this in his writing. For myself, though I am very well aware of the incredible amount of destructive, cruel, malevolent behavior in today's world — from the threats of war to the senseless violence in the streets — I do not find that this evil is inherent in human nature. In a psychological climate which is nurturant of growth and choice, I have never known an individual to choose the cruel or destructive path. Choice always seems to be in the direction of greater socialization, improved relationships with others. So my experience leads me to believe that it is cultural influences which are the major factor in our evil behaviors. The rough manner of childbirth, the infant's mixed experience with the parents, the constricting, destructive influence of our educational system, the injustice of our distribution of wealth, our cultivated prejudices against individuals who are different — all these elements and many others, warp the human organism in directions which are antisocial. So I see members of the human species, like members of other species, as *essentially* constructive in their fundamental nature, but damaged by their experience. The life of the individual is also partially shaped by his or her choices, and as we can readily observe, those choices may be in the direction of inflicting hurt on others or on the self. Nevertheless, if we can provide a growth-promoting climate, the choices prove to be, quite freely and spontaneously, in a socially constructive direction. I cannot see how this could be true if human nature contained an inherently evil element. So Rollo and I continue to differ on this point.

One of Rollo's major contributions has been his bringing of existential philosophy and psychotherapy into the realm of American psychology. In doing so he challenged conventional psychoanalysis and its mode of therapy. He also was one the first to undercut the thinking of the logical positivism which at that time was so important in psychological science. His book, *Existence* (1958), was a most significant volume, and the best chapters in it were not those of the European existentialists, but the presentation and interpretation of that point of view by Rollo himself.

ROLLO MAY, *The Problem of Evil: An Open Letter to Carl Rogers*

Dear Carl:

Your notes discussed my contribution to humanistic psychology, and I very much appreciate what you wrote. You do me honor in many ways.

You also went on to point out your major differences with me concerning the problem of evil.

As you rightly say, the presence of terrorism, hostility, and aggression are urgent in our day. I would add that the importance of our confronting these issues is crucial. Central among these destructive forces is the possibility — or probability, as many people believe — of nuclear war and the related threat of nuclear radiation. A recent Gallup poll shows that seven out of ten people in this country believe a nuclear war will actually occur, or that there is a good chance that it will occur, within the next ten years. It seems obvious that if we cannot deal constructively with the threat in atomic power and the terrorism that goes with it, our civilization will die like those of the ancient Romans, Assyrians, Egyptians, and the Greeks.

You wrote, Rollo "sees the demonic as a basic element in the human makeup and dwells upon this in his writing." You contrasted this with your own view, "that it is cultural influences which are the major factor in our evil behaviors . . . So I see members of the human species . . . as *essentially* constructive in their fundamental nature, but damaged by their experience."

It is difficult to write this letter because of my affection for you and our long friendship. But the problem of evil is so crucial that it is imperative that we see it clearly. I shall therefore try to clarify my own position not only for our personal purposes but to help readers confront these problems themselves, for the sake not only of ourselves but our children and our future world. I agree with the statement of Edmund Burke: "The only thing necessary for the triumph of evil is for good men to do nothing."

In the first place, I never use the word demonic, except to say that this is *not* what I mean. My term is daimonic, which is critically different. I quote from *Love and Will,* the book in which I write most on this topic:

> The daimonic is the urge in every being to affirm itself,
> assert itself, perpetuate and increase itself . . . (the
> reverse side) of the same affirmation is what empowers
> our creativity.

Thus I am stating that I see the human being as an organized bundle of potentialities. These potentialities, driven by the daimonic urge, are the source *both* of our constructive and destructive impulses. If the daimonic urge is integrated into the personality (which is, to my mind, the purpose of psychotherapy) it results in creativity, that is, it is constructive. If the daimonic is not integrated, it can take over the total personality, as it does in violent rage or collective paranoia in time of war or compulsive sex or oppressive behavior. Destructive activity is then the result.

You and I have seen many cases in therapy with adolescents who are accused by their parents of being destructive when they are really only trying to establish their own independence, their own self-assertion, and indeed their own right. If we undercut the daimonic, as many therapists do, we do a disservice to our clients. I believe Rilke was right when he wrote, "If my devils are to leave me, I am afraid my angels will take flight as well."

It is true that the concept of the daimonic gives a rationale for demonic activity just as it gives a rationale for creativity. This may be why you describe me (I think wrongly) as writing about the demonic.

In your letter you ackowledge the evil surrounding us. You say, "I am very well aware of the incredible amount of destructive, cruel, malevolent behavior in today's world — from the threats of war to the senseless violence in the streets." But you say that you "believe that it is cultural influences which are the major factor in our evil behaviors."

This makes culture the enemy. But who makes up the culture except persons like you and me? You write about "the destructive influence of our educational system, the injustice of our distribution of wealth." But who is responsible for this destructive influence and injustice, except you and me and people like us? The culture is not something made by fate and foisted upon us.

Obviously the culture is a great boon as well as a source of evil. We could say, as well, that the fact that we have an educational system at all and the fact that we have an economic system at all are themselves results of our culture. It takes culture to create self and self to create culture; they are the yin and yang of being human. There is no self except in interaction with a culture, and no culture that is not made up of selves.

True, any group does exert a conformist tendency toward those within it by virtue of the mutual expectations it establishes that make it a group. But this is only one element and it cannot account for the fact that human beings individually and en masse are able to turn into warmongers and individual or collective assassins. I propose that the evil in our culture is also the reflection of evil in oursleves, and vice versa.

You also write, in another context but on the same theme: "The persons of tomorrow . . . will be the ones capable of living in this new world, the outlines of which are still only dimly visible. But unless we blow ourselves up, that new world is inevitably coming, transforming our culture." But this very culture which you see as being "transformed" is what you also say may blow us up. The 7 out of 10 people who believe in the likelihood of nuclear war are also the "persons of tomorrow," but they have a quite different point of view. They obviously do not believe in a new world "inevitably" coming, "transforming our culture." They see other facts: Some of them are aware that a single nuclear bomb dropped on Chicago would result in the deaths of 200,000 people. The United States at the end of a year will have approximately 2,400 more nuclear explosives than it did at the beginning of the year, at a cost of billions of dollars. Norman Cousins, reviewing these facts, states: "A mammoth and deadly illiteracy has seized us." I would call it a collective psychosis, which has got us all in its lethal grip, and we find it attractive enough to participate in it. There is no preordained reason our society should "inevitably" survive or disintegrate as did Rome and Greece and Egypt. What about the "good" in their members? Whether we survive or not depends upon whether you and I and millions like us can and will act to change our destructive directions.

The culture is evil as well as good because we, the human beings who constitute it, are evil as well as good. Our culture is partially destructive because we, as human beings who live in it, are partially destructive, whether we be Russians or Japanese or Germans or Americans.

You have also written on the new world toward which you believe we are moving:

> This new world will be more human and humane. It will explore and develop the richness and capacities of the human mind and spirit. It will produce individuals who are more integrated and whole . . . It will be a more natural world, with a renewed love and respect for nature . . . Its technology will be aimed at the enhancing, rather than the exploitation, of persons and nature. It will release creativity, as individuals sense their power, their capacities, their freedom.

> The winds of scientific, social and cultural change
> are blowing strongly. They will envelop us in this new
> world . . . We may choose it, but whether we choose it
> or not, it appears that to some degree it is inexorably
> moving to change our culture.

You paint a seductive and enticing picture, and anyone would like to believe it. But I recall the words of Warren Bennis in the film of you and him, when he characterized your viewpoint as "devilishly innocent."

How do you square this "human and humane" world you predict with the fact that the suicide rate in this country has gone up 171% in the last 30 years? Most of this great increase is among young people in their teens and early 20s; how can one tell them that their world explores the richness and capacities of the human mind and spirit?

I wonder also how you square your statements with the famous Milgram experiments at Yale? You recall the Milgram took subjects from every walk of life (they answered an ad and were paid $4.00 an hour). The purpose of the experiment, as stated to each subject, was to teach the "learner" behind a glass partition by means of giving him electric shocks when he gave the wrong response. But the experiment was actually designed to see how far human beings would go in increasing the voltage to punish the learner for his mistakes. Subjects were told by Milgram to increase the voltage as they went through the experiment.

The results, which shocked Milgram as well as the rest of us who read about them, were that over 60% of the people willingly turned the electric current up to a voltage that they knew would kill the person the other side of the glass partition. Milgram writes that his studies "are principally concerned with ordinary and routine destruction carried out by everyday people following orders." Milgram points out that his results are similar to the phenomena uncovered in the trial of Lt. Calley for his actions at My Lai in the Vietnam war, when women, children, and old men were slaughtered in cold blood by American soldiers when commanded to do so by Lt. Calley.

How also do you deal with Philip Zimbardo's 1971 "prison" experiment at Stanford? You will remember that Zimbardo and his associates divided his psychology class of students into "guards" and "inmates" and had them go through a prison period, planned to last two weeks, in the basement of a building. He found that the "prisoners" began to taunt the "guards" and that the guards would taunt back, and soon the guards were striking the prisoners with clubs. The real violence became so destructive that Zimbardo, to his surprise and chagrin, had to stop the experiments after one week.

These students had no particular enmity toward each other to begin with. They were middle-class persons like you and me and our colleagues, and they certainly would have fit your category of "people of tomorrow." But they had a capacity for destructiveness that became, without much provocation, an evil acted out in reality. The evil possibilities were just beneath the surface. Philip Zimbardo, like Stanley Milgram, is a psychologist of stature who was simply trying to find out the possibilities in human beings for destructiveness and self-control.

Yes, the culture admittedly has powerful effects upon us. But it could not have these effects were these tendencies not already present in us, for, I repeat, we constitute the culture. When we project our tendencies toward evil on the culture — as we do when we repress the daimonic — the evil becomes the culture's fault, not ours. Then we don't experience the blow to our narcissism that owning our own evil would entail.

If you conclude that the trouble lies in the fact that human beings are so susceptible to influence by their culture, so obedient to orders they are given, so pliable to their environment, then you are making the most devastating of all judgments on evil in human beings. In such a case we are all sheep, dependent upon whoever is the shepherd; and Fred Skinner is right. But I do not think you believe that and neither do I.

True, I could cite as many incidents of heroic and altruistic behavior. I am not arguing that we human beings are only evil. I am arguing that we are bundles of both evil and good potentialities.

Let us turn to the question of evil as we experience it in our own field, that of psychotherapy. You will recall your own important experiment, continuing over three years, on client-centered therapy with schizophrenics at the Veterans Administration Hospital in Madison, Wisconsin, some twenty years ago. You will also recall that I was chosen as one of the twelve judges, who were experienced and practicing therapists, to assess that therapy.

After listening to the tapes you sent me, I reported that, while I felt the therapy was good on the whole, there was one glaring omission. This was that the client-centered therapists did not (or could not) deal with the angry, hostile, negative — that is, evil — feelings of the clients. It turned out that the other judges, by and large, pointed out the same thing. I quote from the summary written by you and your colleagues of this whole experiment:

> Particularly striking was the observation by all the theorists that the client-centered process of therapy somehow avoids the expected and usual patient expressions of negative, hostile, or aggressive feelings. The clear implication is that the client-centered therapist for some reason seems less open to receiving negative, hostile, or aggressive feelings. Is it that the therapists have little respect for, or understanding of their own negative, hostile, or aggressive feelings, and are thus unable to receive these feelings from the patient? Do they simply "not believe in" the importance of negative feelings?

One of your students, Nathaniel Raskin, quotes my report as it was discussed in that book:

> Rollo May, as one of the outside experts in the Wisconsin study, "sometimes got the feeling there were not two people in the room . . . A consequence of a misuse of the reflecting techniques . *. (is) that we get only an amorphous kind of identity rather than two subjects interacting *in a world in which both participate, and in which love and hate, trust and doubt, conflicts and dependence, come out and can be understood and assimulated.*" May was concerned that the therapist's over-identification with the patient could "take away the patient's opportunity to experience himself as a subject in his own right, to take a stand against the therapist, to experience being in the interpersonal world.

In spite of the fact that "client-centered therapists, both individually and collectively, have advocated openness and freedom in the therapeutic relationship," the outside judges focused "upon what they perceive as the therapist's rigid and controlling nature which closes him off to many of his own as well as the the patients experiences."

This same student, who has since become a therapist in his own right, adds some notes about his own experience. I realize that our students develop in their own way, and you and I cannot be responsible for them. But Raskin's comments on his own experience are so relevant to the issues here that I ask your permission to quote it:

> I used the early concept of the client-centered therapist to bolster the inhibition of my anger, my aggression etc. I got some feedback at that time that it was difficult for people, because I was so nice, to tell me things that were *not* nice, and that it was hard for people to get angry at *me*.

He then goes on to say that he needed to find some new ways within the client-centered approach to take in other phenomena, which I have called the "negative, hostile and aggressive feelings."

I find it important in therapy that the patient be able to take a stand against me, the therapist. This is in accord with what Raskin said, that he realized he was taking something away from the patient when he was "too nice, too much identifying with the other person." What he was taking away was the patient's possibility of becoming independent. Patient's anger is an essential part of their motivation in their assertion of individual steps toward psychological health. The anger of the therapist can also be a powerful aid in helping patients experience what effect their behavior has on their relationships in general.

This means that aspects of evil — anger, hostility against the therapist, destructiveness — need to be brought out in therapy. Personal autonomy occurs not by avoiding evil, but by directly confronting it. Therapists need to be able to perceive and admit their own evil — hostility, aggression, anger — if they are to be able to see and accept these experiences in clients.

I am quite ready to believe that it would be impossible for anybody to sit down in a therapeutic hour with you and not be affected for good by it. But every patient does have the possibility to destroy himself or herself, and some patients will destroy themselves no matter how much or how well you and I work with them.

I want to return to the question of inevitable cultural transformation. You write that this "new world" that you describe is "inevitably coming,"

and later you remark that the new world is "inexorably moving to change our culture." How can you be so certain? There are countless scenarios that can be written as predictions of our future. The persons who committed suicide, mentioned above, lived and died in entirely different scenarios from yours, and the polls indicate that the majority of citizens in our country would also write very different predictions. The scenarios I take seriously are those that see the evil in humankind's development as well as the good.

You also write that "we may choose (this cultural change), but whether we choose it or not, it will still happen." Do you mean it will take place regardless of whether we do anything about it? This sounds like Fred Skinner again: The environment will force us into this brave new world whether we want it or not!

As with Skinner's viewpoint, your statement that it will come regardless of what we humans do about it cuts the nerve of social action. A danger of which I am very aware is that people, hypnotically seduced by rosy predictions of the future, will conclude that it requires no effort from them and will sit back and do nothing. This, as Edmund Burke said so well, is the quickest way for evil to triumph.

There are innumerable issues that cry out for our awareness and our energies, quite in addition to the imminence of nuclear war. There is, for one, the food crunch and the problem of hunger. The President's Commission on World Hunger, 1980, stated that there are more ill-fed people on our planet than ever before, amounting to 800,000,000 (not counting the communist countries). The number is growing and, as the available food lessens, will approach panic proportions by the year 2000. This includes hundreds of thousands of children who are starving and millions more who go to bed every night hungry. This includes fathers who walk the streets, their self-esteem eroded because they are unable to find work. It also includes despairing mothers who can do nothing but watch their children starve, as we've seen happening in Ethiopia.

If we do get to a new world, it will only be by solving these problems first. If we don't we will not have the new world you see coming: The price in human suffering will be too high.

In *Love and Will* I also wrote:

> It (the daimonic) constitutes a profound blow to our narcissim. We are the "nice" people and, like the cultivated citizens of Athens in Socrates' time, we don't like to be publicly reminded, whether we secretly admit it to ourselves or not, that we are motivated even in our love by lust for power, anger and revenge. While the daimonic cannot be said to be evil in itself, it confronts us with the troublesome dilemma of whether it is to be used with awareness, a sense of responsiblitily and and the significance of life, or blindly and rashly . . . When the daimonic is repressed, it tends to *erupt* in some form — its extreme forms being assassination, the psychopathological tortures of the murders on the moors and other horrors we know only too well in this century.
>
> "Although we may recoil in horror," writes the British psychiatrist Anthony Storr, "when we read in newspapers or history books of the atrocities committed by man upon man, we know in our hearts that each one of us harbors within himself those same savage impulses which lead to murder, to torture and to war."

I am pleading for a realistic approach to human evil. A colleague tells me that when you had a discussion with Martin Buber in Michigan you said, "Man is basically good," and Buber answered, "Man is basically good — and evil." I am arguing that we must include a view of the evil in our world and in ourselves no matter how much that evil offends our narcissism.

When we can deal with this evil, then and only then what we say about goodness will have power and cogency. Then we can speak in ways that will genuinely affect our culture, in contrast to the miniscule number of people we see in our therapeutic offices.

You and I have often affirmed the capacities of human beings to be autonomous to some extent, to make decisions, to assert some freedom of choice in interrelationship with their destiny and their culture. These capacities put an added responsibility upon us to affirm realistically the anxiety involved, the precarious and limited nature of this freedom, and the fact that our belief in the human being can work for good only when the individual can face the world with all its inner and outer cruelty, its failure, and its tragedy.

The issue of evil — or rather, the issue of not confronting evil — has profound, and to my mind adverse, effects on humanistic psychology. I believe it is the most important error in the humanistic movement. Thus Yankelovich can say, in his book *New Rules* (which is concerned, as you and I are, with the persons of tomorrow), that humanistic psychology is the narcissism of our culture. I believe he is right. The narcissists are persons who are turned inward rather than outward, who are so lost in self-love that they cannot see and relate to the reality outside themselves, including other human beings. Some people who join and lead the humanistic movement do so in order to find a haven, a port in the storm, a community of like-minded persons who also are playing possum to the evils about us. I, for one, choose to be part of the minority that seeks to make the Association for Humanistic Psychology an organization that commits itself actively to confronting the issues of evil and good in ourselves, our society, and our world.

In my experience, our human adventures from cradle to grave take on a zest, a challenge, an attractiveness when we see and affirm this human potentiality of both good and evil. The joy we experience will have, as its other pole, the self-assertion, the hostility, the negative possibilities that I have been talking about. In my experience it is this polarity, this dialectical interaction, this oscillation between positive and negative that gives the dynamism and the depth to human life. Life, to me, is not a requirement to live out a preordained pattern of goodness, but a challenge coming down through the centuries out of the fact that each of us can throw the lever toward good or toward evil. This seems to me to require the age-old religious truths of mercy and forgiveness and (here I am sure you would agree with me) it leaves no place for moral superiority or self-righteousness.

I recall that in my younger days in the middle 1930s I had a position as counselor at a midwestern college. The vocal portion of the students at this college were pacifists. We believed in the League of Nations and we felt certain that we needed only to outlaw war for the world to have peace. I remember looking at a professor who said there would be another war as though he were a pariah. How wrong my colleagues and I were! We could not even believe what we read in the papers about the persecution of the Jews in Germany, just as people nowadays cannot believe what they read in the newspapers about nuclear bombs. The important point of this story is that Hitler capitalized on our noble but unrealistic ideals, and this, I believe, contributed to or at least hastened World War II. This is why I wrote in *Love and Will*:

> Not to recognize the daimonic itself turns out to be daimonic; it makes us accomplices on the side of the destructive possession.

I am not predicting doom. But I am stating that if we ignore evil, we will move closer to doom, and the growth and triumph of evil may well result.

I am not a pessimist. Yes, I believe in tragedy, as Shakespeare's dramas and Eugene O'Neill and others portray it, because I perceive tragedy as showing the nobility of human existence. Without it life would be pallid, uninteresting, and flat. I smile when I note, in conversations with some of my so-called optimistic friends, that when we get down to fundamental issues such as the possibilities of atomic war or the coming food crunch, or the fact that this planet itself will in all probability be wiped out in a finite number of years, their optimism turns out to be a reaction formation to their hopelessness; and I turn out to be more hopeful than they. This is because, it seems to me, one needs a philosophy for oneself that can stand regardless of failure in our actions or temporary despair.

All of this goes to demonstrate again that the terms "optimism" and "pessimism" refer to the state of one's digestion, and have nothing whatever to do with truth.

I write this letter, dear Carl, with profound respect for you and your contribution in the past to all of us. If I speak strongly, it is because I believe strongly.

> Yours,
> Rollo May

CARL ROGERS, *Some Social Issues Which Concern Me*

> *Carl Rogers writes: "I regret that in this paper, written 14 years ago, I used 'he' as the generic term. I hope my feminine readers will forgive me. I have learned better since." — Editor.*

All my professional life I have preferred to work in the areas in which I have competence, endeavoring to bring about constructive change in those areas. I have been a revolutionary with a narrow focus. Thus I flatter myself that I have helped to cause healthy change in the field of counseling and psychotherapy, in the conduct of encounter groups, and perhaps most broadly, in our educational institutions. But I have never before spoken out on the broad spectrum of social issues which face our society.

Now, however, I believe our culture is facing a life and death crisis on many fronts, and that I have an obligation as a citizen to speak out. I am frightened about our destiny as a people, as a nation. So I want to take as clear a stand as I can on a variety of issues. I recognize very well that I am no expert in most of the fields I shall mention, but I shall simply voice the attitudes and views of one deeply concerned person.

There is one other preliminary comment I wish to make. I have never been fond of those who do no more than "point with alarm." It is easy enough, for example, to stir up emotions by picturing the many millions on this planet who do not have enough to eat. But I do not have a high regard for those who point this out, unless their "pointing with alarm" is accompanied by some statement of the means which would move us toward ending the tragedy. Consequently, I will discuss only those issues for which we have much of the know-how, or technology, or funds to solve. What seems to be lacking in each case is the choice, in intent, the purpose, the determination to work toward resolving it. These are issues which, in every case, we could move toward solving if we had the individual and collective *will*.

Enough of these provisos and qualifications. I want to move on to some of the problems which give me great concern. I regard it as desperately necessary that we rethink our priorities and our allocation funds.

One of the most astonishing sights I know is to see the graph of world population since the beginning of recorded history. For centuries and millennia it remained almost flat, creeping upward very, very slowly. Then, with the advent of scientific medicine and the reduction of the death rate, the curve begins to sweep upward and off the chart with currently an almost straight upward climb. It is not just this astonishing curve that I would like to comment on, but what it means for us.

Take an example from an underdeveloped country which is typical of many — India. That country has made astonishing strides. In agriculture improved high-yield rice and grain have been developed; in industry the rapid expansion of all kinds of manufacturing plants have enormously increased production. And what is the result? On the average, each person in India is closer to starvation, less well supplied with the necessities of life than he was before these programs started. In spite of significant government encouragement of birth control, the population increase has been so great that it more than eats up every gain that has been made. Running with tremendous energy, India cannot even stay where it is, but is tragically slipping backward.

The noted demographer, Philip Hauser, gives figures which predict that, by a conservative estimate, the population of the more developed countries will increase by 90% in the next 50 years, but that the underdeveloped world — Asia, Africa, Latin America — will increase by 240%. Thus the heaviest burden will fall on those least able to bear it. All the projections indicate that in the coming decades, the developed countries will become richer and richer because they will be able to handle their population problem, while the underdeveloped countries will have less and less food and material goods for each citizen. It will be a world of affluent "haves" and increasingly needy, frustrated, bitter "have-nots." For more than half the world to be populated with largely unwanted, often unloved, certainly ill-fed and poorly cared for persons, looking enviously over the fence at our affluence, or surviving on our charity, is not a pretty picture.

One reason we often fail to see the urgency of the situation is that we fail to visualize the consequences. We speak of population doubling in 20, 30, 40 years, depending on the country. But we often fail to realize what that means. Even to hold on to their meager standards, there must be twice as much food, twice as many homes, twice as many schools, twice as many highways, twice as many buses or trains or planes, twice as many doctors and hospitals — and on and on and on. And how can an underdeveloped country meet this tremendous demand? It cannot!

I haven't given so many statistics in years! I'll stop. But I do want to bring home the point that this is a desperate social problem though by and large in this country we do not yet recognize it. In less developed countries it defeats every effort at reform or improvement of the quality of life. Since writing the foregoing, I have received a letter from a friend who has been in India. Two sentences will suffice. ". . . They have doubled food production in the last 5 years, but population is still out-pacing growth of resources. Life is still cheap."

In spite of all this, population increase is a problem which we have the technology to solve, and that technology is improving all the time. The pill and the intrauterine device will soon be superseded by better methods. Psychologically it is no longer a taboo subject. One would expect to find psychologists and educators actively at work, studying the attitudes which promote large families, the religious and other reasons which still stand as barriers to population control. We would expect to find educators, beginning at least with high school, providing materials which point up the urgency of the problem and making certain that every young person not only knows all the latest birth control devices, but has easy access to them. But no, neither the professionals nor the laymen have yet made the choice to move in such directions. We do not give it nearly the priority given to the B-1 bomber, as indicated by the funds allocated. Yet the problem is definitely more pressing than our so-called defense, the B-1.

Our great cities concern me deeply, but the facts are well known and I will not bore you with them. Our large urban centers are seemingly ungovernable, choking on their own traffic, becoming insufferable garbage-littered ghettos, and are rapidly becoming financially as well as psychologically bankrupt. All that is known. Yet, according to Barbara Ward, British economist, by the year 2000, 80% of us will be living in such cities. Chances are that over 200 million people will be living in — a new term — megalopolis. One will be the eastern seaboard, Boston to Washington, D.C., one will be the western coast, from San Diego to San Francisco; one will be in the middle west, stretching from Chicago to Pittsburgh. Others may develop in the South, as well.

In this incredible influx into the cities, it might be well to consider some lessons learned from a study of rats. (Imagine me invoking a rat study!) A number of years ago, John Calhoun carried on a cleverly designed experiment with a rather large number of rats. I won't go into details. Some portions of the experimental area had narrow entrances, and one dominant male rat could keep any others from entering. But the central area was available to all and could not be dominated. All the rats in every area had sufficient food and water (privileges not extended to our city dwellers) and were free to breed as they wished. A few findings give me pause.

The rats multiplied, of course, but in the areas controlled by a dominant male, overcrowding was not excessive and life was reasonably normal. In the central, uncontrolled area, there was serious overcrowding and this was accompanied by poor mothering, poor nest building, high infant mortality, bizarre sexual behavior, canniblism, and often complete alienation, some rats behaving like zombies, paying no attention to others and coming out of their solitary burrows only for food.

More ominous still, the central area, with all its bad conditions, had a certain magnetic pull. Calhoun called it a behavioral sink. The rats crowded together in it. A feeder would be ignored unless there were other rats eating at it. The more rats at a feeder, the more others would crowd in. Females in heat would leave the protected areas and head for the central area, sometimes not returning at all.

The resemblance to human behavior is frightening. In humans we see poor family relationships, the lack of caring, the complete alienation, the magnetic attraction of overcrowding, the lack of involvement which is so great that it permits people to watch a long drawn out murder without so much as calling the police — perhaps all city dwellers are inhabitants of a behavioral sink, cannibalism and all.

We have not availed ourselves of the alternatives, which are known and feasible. Corporations are, in considerable numbers, moving their offices out of spots like Manhattan, but that could simply mean making big-city slums out of places like Greenwich, Connecticut. What we need is to turn loose some of our city planners, or better yet, unleash creative innovators like Buckminster Fuller, scrap our obsolete building codes, and instruct these gentlemen to build small urban centers, designing them for human beings and human life, not simply for profit. We could build smaller cities with great park and garden areas, with neighborhoods of all races, all economic levels, which would promote humanization, not dehumanization. It would have to be such an attractive place for human beings that it would overcome the magnetism of the behavioral sink. The schools, for example, could be built along totally new lines, not only informal seating and pleasant surroundings, but planned from the first on the basis that most learning will go on either in the community, or as a result of self-directed and self-initiated learning on the part of the student.

To be sure, there would be frictions between races, ethnic groups, between persons with very different value systems, in these human cities. But the behavioral scientist could help to meet that challenge with communication workshops, with encouragement of learning from the distinctive contributions of each group to the others. We could help people to listen — and to understand. The human planning — both before and during the building of such a community — would be fully as important and as well financed as the architectural planning. It would involve the families, the schools, the recreational facilities, and would be a crucial and continuing aspect.

We know how to carry out every aspect of what I have proposed in regard to our cities. The only element lacking is the passionate determination which says, "Our cities are inhuman. They are ruining lives and mental and physical health at a devastating rate. We are going to change this, even if it costs us money!"

There are two issues which do concern me about marriage. The first is the incredible lack of any attempt at education in the field of interpersonal relationships, which would help young people to face realistically the problems they will meet. I was interviewing a young couple recently, both of whom had attended college. They had lived together for three years and then married. I was curious as to the elements in this decision. I learned that this was the story. They quarrelled all of one evening — a rather common occurrence — and finally the man told her to pack up her things and leave. She said, "I will not! I belong here as much as you do." He paused a moment and then said challengingly, "Well, then do you want to get married?" to which she replied, "O.K." It developed that there was a rationale of sorts behind this bizarre decision. He believed that if they married, marriage would be the miracle which would resolve all their difficulties. He was surprised that it had not, and only during the interview did it seem to dawn on him that perhaps achieving a satisfactory marriage might take time and effort! It angers me that neither of these young people had received the slightest education in man-woman relationships, though naturally they had learned the *valuable* things like mathematics and foreign language. Here again we have all the necessary know-how, but we define education so narrowly that it excludes everything about living.

Education is the one field in which feedback from "the consumer" is utterly disregarded. Our educational institutions were born at a time when intellectual stimulation was terribly important, since ordinary life supplied all the other ingredients of learning. But school has increasingly *become* life, and education which operates only "from the neck up" is becoming irrelevant to real learning. But psychologists are the last to listen, in their headlong (and futile) race to become a "hard science." Hence the thought of education oriented toward human relationships, toward marriage partnerships, is anathema to most psychologists, although this would seem to be the very field in which they might and should contribute.

The other issue regarding marriage which troubles me is that we have been both unimaginative and irresponsible regarding children, particularly children of divorced parents. First the child is torn by the stresses between his mother and father, and has no extended family to which to turn. Then he finds that we usually label one parent guilty. Next we shuttle the child back and forth between the two warring adults. Small wonder that psychological problems develop. Yet we know, quite accurately, what children need — continuing love and caring, a sense of stability, several sources of support and care, and a feeling of being trusted. We have experiments like the kibbutzim to observe and from which to learn. We *know* enough. We have just never made the decision that we wish to *act* on behalf of the welfare of our children. We prefer, as a nation, to spend our money on war and preparation for war.

Running like a fever through all of our culture are the attitudes we hold, mostly at the unconscious level, toward blacks, chicanos, Indians, and other minorities, including women, who while not a statistical minority, are treated as one. We know something of how to attack the roots of this problem. I have learned enormously from the few black-white encounter groups I have facilitated, and have learned that the bitterness and rage which exists can be expressed and prove constructive. I have learned even more from the much more extensive experience of two of our staff members, Dr. Norman Chambers, a black, and Dr. Lawrence Carlin, a blond Nordic if I ever saw one. They have worked with many black-white groups and with some chicano-anglo groups. They have found most helpful a simulation game they invented called "Pleasantville." Pleasantville is the home of a new industry which is employing many black workers new to the town. Everyone is given roles, the whites usually being assigned more conservative roles than they would normally play — the head of the real estate board, the local union leader, the school superintendent, the president of the women's club. It's just a game — everyone knows that. But the whites are astonished at the ease with which they can express the most bitter anger toward the invading blacks. They have gotten in touch with unknown aspects of themselves. "I never knew I had such feelings," is a very common reaction. Meanwhile, the game gives the blacks permission to voice their rage, and the polarization is out in the open for all to see.

The outcomes are an experiential, gut-level learning of racist attitudes on the part of the whites, and a rare opportunity for honest confrontation on the part of the blacks. The surprising finale is that they tend to become persons to each other, and can talk openly and freely of things they dislike and like about each other without reference to stereotypes or skin color. It becomes a much more direct, honest dealing with one another as individuals. They tend to leave the game experience feeling deeply educated.

I describe this because I happen to know of it directly. It is not the only approach which could be made, but it is a start. Carried out with black and white community leaders it would lead first to direct dealing, and then to mutually agreed decisions, which, because they were personal and real, would be carried out. Isn't this worth the price of the scores of our nuclear weapons? I believe that programs of this sort should be expanded a thousand-fold.

In 1969 I gave a talk on "The Person of Tomorrow" spelling out some of the characteristics of the new, powerful person emerging in our culture, and the vital, different set of values he both maintains and lives. I stressed his hatred of phoniness; his opposition to all rigidly structured institutions; his desire for intimacy, closeness, and community; his willingness to live by new and relative moral and ethical standards; his searching quality, his openness to his own and others' feeling, his spontaneity; his activism; and his determination to translate his ideals into reality. I have had no reason since to materially change that picture, except that for a time I feared that he was turning toward violence, which I see as the road to the annihilation of all hope for change, or toward drugs, which would essentially be escape. But those fears have recently diminished.

I have been strongly criticized for the views contained in that talk. I feel some of the criticisms are from people who simply hate to face what is occurring in the lives of our people. They prefer to get angry and "point with alarm." But some of the criticism is based on the fact that my description of the person of tomorrow applied to only a very small minority of the young, and to only a minute proportion of their elders. I have thought seriously about that criticism, and I believe it is correct. I am talking about what is, numerically, a relatively small number of people. But I believe, intuitively if you wish, that these people constitute the change agents of the future.

What research evidence can I bring to bear to justify this view? Frankly none. But historically it has been shown again and again that a small group of individuals, believing deeply in a new set of values, or a new picture of what the culture might be, has an impact far beyond its numbers. One could name the 12 disciples, the small dedicated group of early communists in China or Russia, the early organizers of the labor union movement in this country, or Martin Luther King and the black woman who sat in the front seat of the bus in Montgomery. When some part of a culture is decayed at the core, a small group with new views, new convictions, and a willingness to live in new ways, is a ferment which cannot be stopped.

I have even felt this in my own professional career. The time was evidently ripe for the idea that the resources for health lay in the client, not in the therapist, and only needed the proper psychological climate to be released and utilized for growth. No man or small group could have possibly wrought the changes which have since occurred. The view of the therapist as the expert was already beginning to decay, and the new view — like a surfer catching a wave at the right time and right angle — swept along into other areas far removed from therapy, and having an impact such as I could not possibly have dreamed.

I have exactly the same feeling about the person of tomorrow that I have had about the civil right leaders, or about my own central thesis of 40 years ago. I feel very sure that his values will prevail. The person of tomorrow is the wave of the future. Take such a small example as the astonishing changes in the armed forces personnel regulations. Did the military brass undergo a liberal conversion? Of course not. But they are realists. They recognize that no one can govern for any length of time, not even a military commander with theoretically unlimited power, without the *consent* of the governed.

I believe that our American way of life will be radically altered by the growth of a new value system, a new culture in which feelings and subjectivity and openness (rather than hypocrisy) have a prominent place, alongside intelligence. We are going to have a new America, in my judgment, an America of change and flow, of people rather than objects. We have the know-how, the skills, to bring about this new America. And now, in an increasing number of significant persons, mostly young but also older, we have the determination and the will to bring it into being. I think it is not unrealistic to believe that there will come into being a portion of the global community, residing on this North American continent, of which we will no longer be ashamed, but in which we will feel a quiet, peaceful pride.

❦   ❦   ❦

MAURICE FRIEDMAN, *The Nuclear Threat and The Hidden Human Image*

The nuclear threat is both cause and effect of the hiding of the human image. The revealing of the hidden human image can take place in response to the challenge of the nuclear threat and is perhaps the *only* way in which we can hope to overcome that threat.

In the context of the English civil war in the seventeenth century, the political philosopher Thomas Hobbes held man to be evil and life in nature to be nasty, raw, brutish, and short, a war of all against all. In the eighteenth century, in the contexts of the deteriorating French monarchy and the need to point toward the revolution which he helped at least indirectly to set in motion, Jean-Jacques Rousseau, exactly the opposite to Hobbes, held that man is good but that it is civilization that has changed him and made him evil.

Sigmund Freud, the father of depth psychology, took a position between these two. He held that civilization produces individual and collective neuroses and "discontents." But he also held in his later thinking that along with eros — the love instinct — there is thanatos — a death instinct. This means that people are aggressive and destructive, not as a secondary result of frustration of the libidinal drive, but rather as a primary given of humankind; that they would take advantage of others, that the more helpless others were, the more they would inevitably do them in without even thinking of their own advantage in so doing. "Homo homine lupus," Freud concluded — man is a wolf to man. Who in the face of recorded history and his or her own experience would have the courage to deny it? In the years since Freud said that, as much new evidence has accumulated to support his thesis as in the whole of recorded history up to that time.

This double attitude toward civilization and individuals led Freud to hold that war is inevitable in his classic exchange of letters with Albert Einstein half a century ago. Albert Einstein, the pacifist, the man of peace, the idealist, the universalist, held in contrast that war is not inevitable, that we can and should do things that will lead to surpassing war, an attitude Einstein retained until his death. Yet, with the discovery of relativity in 1905, Einstein ushered in the age of atomic physics and thereby also the nuclear age in which we now find ourselves. It was Einstein whose name led the others in warning President Roosevelt that the Nazis were probably making an atomic bomb, thus setting this country on the road to making one. On President Roosevelt's desk, at the time of his death, was a letter from Einstein and other nuclear physicists begging him not to use the atomic bomb that had been created partly as a result of Einstein's own initiative. Martin Buber told me that Einstein could have had an operation that would have saved his life but that he was so depressed and discouraged about the consequences of the nuclear arms that he did not have that operation. Einstein stands as a tragic figure — a pacifist who ushers in our nuclear age and is all too humanly aware of its catastrophic possibilities.

A quarter of a century ago I moderated a dialogue between Martin Buber, the late Jewish philosoper, and Carl Rogers, the noted American psychologist who has been very active in recent years in the fight against nuclear arms. One of the subjects that was central in that dialogue was that same question of Hobbes and Rousseau, of Freud and Einstein — the question of what we humans *are*. In conscious contrast to Sigmund Freud, Carl Rogers held that people are not evil by nature but good. If a person

should be accepted, for example, by his or her therapist, with unconditional positive regard, what would result would be that which was socially
constructive, that which could be trusted. Martin Buber, in response to
Carl Rogers, suggested a third position: that people are polar. That which
you say can be most trusted in people can be also least trusted in them. By
this Buber meant that we have a movement toward direction and we have a
refusal to take direction, a yes and a no, and that both are part of every
person. This is why Buber could not agree with Rogers, who equated
accepting persons and confirming them.

In the Summer 1982 issue of the *Journal of Humanistic Psychology*,
there was an exchange between Carl Rogers and Rollo May on the question
of good and evil in human nature. Rogers saw Rollo May as concerned
with the demonic and put him in the camp of Freud. Rogers's thought
seemed to be based on two alternatives: either you hold that people are evil
in themselves, which he felt that Rollo May did, or you hold that people are
good and that the effects of destructive authoritarian or otherwise uncon-
ducive environment, schooling, society make them what they are. Rollo
May in his reply said that he dealt with the "d-a-i-m-o-n-i-c" and rejected
the idea that he saw people as simply evil. May took a postiion very similar
to that which Buber took in his dialogue with Rogers twenty-five years
before; namely, that the daimonic needs to be directed and that if we do not
direct it we promote the destructiveness in ourselves.

The chief illustration that Rollo May used in his argument with Carl
Rogers was the probability that there will be nuclear war, and he asked
how in the face of that Rogers could so confidently talk about moving forward into the future. It seemed to May a dangerous innocence. Now the
interesting thing is that you didn't have, as in the dialogue between Einstein and Freud, any difference on this issue. Rogers said, "We are
entirely in agreement on the nuclear issue." It is well known that Rogers
has been very active on this matter.

Rogers told how his granddaughter, teaching a group of troubled adolescents, asked them what they thought of five years, ten years, hence.
The majority of them thought that they weren't even going to be alive five
years hence because of the threat of thermonuclear war. Asked by the Sen-
ate Committee, in January 1982, if he thought there would be a nuclear
war, Admiral Hyman Rickover said, "Yes, and perhaps then a worthier

race will come after we are all destroyed!" That's a new sort of image of the human. Sadly enough there is little hope even of that, because the world will not be habitable for an indefinite future after a nuclear war.

The classic way of looking at what we have been talking about is the question, Is human nature good or is human nature evil? Modern philosophical anthropology, in contrast, does not imagine, as Hobbes and Rousseau did, that you can tell what the human being is in nature minus the world in which he or she lives. Philosophical anthropology looks to the wholeness and uniqueness of the human as someone who is set in certain conditions, who has possibility, who knows that she or he will die, and who is a social being.

To go a step beyond philosophical anthropology, or rather to make it more concrete, we must look at the image of the human as something that is not a concept nor even an analysis of the existential conditions of human existence, but the image of what it is, can, and should mean to be a human being. I have published three books on this subject. The first, *Problematic Rebel: Melville, Dostoievsky, Kafka, Camus,* goes back to the Greek, biblical, renaissance images of the human, the modern exile and alienation, the problematic or modern man, and then discusses two types of rebellion against that exile — the Modern Promethean and the Modern Job. The second, *To Deny Our Nothingness: Contemporary Images of Man,* deals with the absence today of a meaningful image of the human. The image of the human is not a mere description, neither is it an ideal: It is a direction of movement of meaningful personal and social existence. In the absence of such an image, many people have tried to create a direction of movement or at least to point to one by various images. Therefore I deal in that book with Psychological Man, The Modern Pragmatist, The Modern Gnostic, The Existentialist, and the Absurd Man. In the third, *The Hidden Human Image,* I tried to apply the conclusions of *Problematic Rebel* and *To Deny Our Nothingness* on various topics, including nonviolence and violence and the threat of nuclear war. Now I have written a fourth human image book: *Contemporary Psychology: Revealing and Obscuring the Human.*

Prometheus was a Titan, one of the earth gods who was conquered by the Olympian sky god. Prometheus rebelled against Zeus, the most powerful god in the Greek pantheon, and he had knowledge and foresight with which to do so. Prometheus has come down to us as a great symbol of someone who is a proud rebel, who defies in the name of the human, and who helped to expand the realm of the human in the face of the jealousy of Zeus, so each successive generation could have greater and greater possibility and hope. What we tend to forget, however, is that Prometheus was also a tragic figure. He did not rebel against the order; he rebelled on the basis of it, because he was a god, he was immortal, and he had foreknowledge that Zeus did not have. As the sly, cunning god who gave man civilizing tools, Prometheus is indeed the father of modern science. Yet, if we go back to the Greek origins, we can also understand the ambiguity of that science. It not only wrests a place for humans in the teeth of the hostility of Zeus, but it also leads to *hubris*, the Greek notion of people bringing on their own destruction through overstepping limits. This became a realistic possibility at the point where the atomic bomb, the possibilities of nuclear war, were created. We now stand at the place where Prometheus can simultaneously bring us forward to the most undreamt-of advances of science and destroy the human in doing so.

When we look at that we have to look again critically at the Renaissance creed of Francis Bacon: that the way to the realization of one's humanity is through the knowledge that gives one power over nature. Today we stand precisely at the point where our humanity is endangered through that very power over nature. As Einstein put it, that atomic age has changed everything but our way of thinking; therefore we are in danger of destroying ourselves. Perhaps that is why Captain Ahab in Melville's "Moby Dick" throws the quadrant down on the deck and says, "Science, curse thou vain toy." It no longer does for him what it was supposed to have done.

If we look at the figure that I call the Modern Promethean, we find the carrying forward, not of the god — there is no god anymore — not of the immortality of the original Prometheus, not of the foreknowledge, but of that desire to give people something, to rebel in the name of people — a heroic, even romantic rebellion under which I suspect often lies desperation and despair. This expresses itself again and again, as I have pointed out in these three books, in an either/or stance. We now know ourselves not in a secure order like that of the middle ages, but face-to-face with the infinity that terrified Pascal, the infinite spaces between the stars. We feel it will destroy us, and so we have to destroy it. We say what Nietzsche says in *Thus Spake Zarathustra:* "If there were gods how could I bear to be no god; therefore there are no gods." With Captain Ahab we feel the White Whale is the incarnation of all evil, an evil that destroys not just Ahab but all humankind. If Ahab can destroy Moby Dick, he imagines that he will automatically establish good. In the process he becomes evil and destroys himself and all the crew except Ishmael, who is saved just to tell the story.

As the head of the most powerful nation on earth, with probably the largest stockpile of nuclear weapons that can many times over destroy the earth and us, Reagan represents the ambiguity of science. But he also represents that either/or of the Modern Promethean, even if not quite so heroic or grand as Captain Ahab. The Soviet union is the repository of all evil, Reagan asserted. The real question is not whether they are that, or whether we are all good, as Reagan imagines, but whether we can move forward to any sort of existence, coexistence, without some form of dialogue with them, which he resolutely pushes away by saying "I will *not.*" The poor are going to get poorer and poorer, the employment lines greater and greater, but we will not cut one item in our defense budget.

The image of the human is a basic attitude, a way of responding. I won't ever be St. Francis, Albert Camus, or Lincoln, but my dialogue with them can enter into the way I respond to situations they did not face. Man, said Nietzsche's Zarathustra, is a valuing animal: Without valuing, the nut of existence is hollow. We have to make choices. We have to hold in tension an unexplored future. We need, therefore, an image of the human, to go beyond the potentialism of the human potential movement and discover what the human being can be in each one of us, and in every family, community, and society. This human image underlies all the sciences, the social sciences, psychology, and the law, including the most important difference between schools of psychology. This human image stands in need of revelation. Like a face, it both conceals and reveals, and it must be revealed anew in every situation. The human image is hidden: It can never be revealed once for all, because what the human can be will only be discovered anew in each new situation.

But there is another meaning of the hiddenness of the human image in our time. That is the obliteration of the human, the eclipse of the human, the destruction of the human image which we have witnessed in Auschwitz, in Hiroshima, in Biafra, in the millions who were killed in the Soviet slave labor camps, the Gulag Archipelago.

The nineteenth century was the century of the death of God, said Erich Fromm; the twentieth century is that of the death of man. But both are the same thing. For death of God is the loss of any basis for movement, for living, for values in our life. The death of man is a consequence of that, the loss and destruction of the human image. I agree with Elie Wiesel that the Holocaust, the extermination of six million Jews and five million others by the Nazis, paved the way for the nuclear holocaust. In *One Generation After* Elie Wiesel writes, "if the human race should perish by the nuclear bomb, this will be the punishment for Auschwitz, where in the ashes the hope of man was extinguished. At Auschwitz not only man died, but also the idea of man" (or, I would say, the image of man). The Nazi Holocaust was the first great scientific extermination of people. No one ever protested effectively or tried to stop it. No plane ever bombed the train tracks to Auschwitz to save 10,000 lives a day. The possibility arose that the human image would indeed disintegrate.

When we try to anticipate concretely what it will be like when a nuclear bomb hits San Francisco or Leningrad, it is abundantly clear how the nuclear threat is a cause of the hiding of the human image in our time. But I think it is also an effect of the human image in the sense of the attitude of the Modern Promethean. The nuclear war threatens hope, it threatens the present, it threatens the image of the human, it threatens our very communication, which makes us human beings. In our day, more than ever before, there is the *death* of dialogue in which language is simply used and perverted. The latest nuclear bomb is called a "peacemaker," and all our language betrays a massive denial, a massive self-deception, a massive deception of others.

There is an alternative — a response to the challenge of the nuclear threat that would bring about a decisive change in our image of the human. What is the direction of that change, and how would that in turn help overcome the nuclear threat?

In the era of the "death of God," the era of alienation and of exile, there have been two types of rebellion: that of the Modern Promethean and that of the Modern Job. An unprejudiced reading of the Book of Job shows not the submissive, humble, figure that people always imagine Job is, but on the contrary, perhaps the person in all religious history who issues the strongest challenge to God. Job combines trust and contending within the dialogue with God. This is no blind faith. "It is all one, I despise my life. Therefore I say, he mocks at the calamity of the guiltless, if it be not he then who is it?" The attitude of Job can remain in the Modern Job even if that person, like Albert Camus, is an atheist. That attitude of openness, of readiness to enter the dialogue, of contending within the dialogue — this is the response to the challenge of the nuclear threat that could help to overcome it, and perhaps the only thing that could. It could be a revelation of the hidden human image in a time when the Dialogue with the Absurd may be our most meaningful stance. We must contend with the absurdity of trying to live and move and prepare for the future when for the first time in human history there may be no future. Even the small nations in the future will have the atomic bomb and be able to hurl the world into nuclear war and total destruction. Then too there is the absurdity of statements such as Reagan made, that it is possible to win a nuclear war, or the incredible denial that underlies the whole notion that there could be meaningful civil defense for Los Angeles of San Diego or San Francisco.

So what is this possibility, applied concretely? It is what Martin Buber called dialogue and confirmation. When Buber received the peace prize at the German Book Trade, He said the alternative to war is meaningful dialogue, in which you certainly cannot overcome human conflict entirely, but you can meaningfully arbitrate it by confirming the others even in opposing them. The Modern Promethean stance is to say *Carthago delanda est:* The Soviet Union is evil and must be destroyed; we can do it and we can survive with 35% of our population and become rich like Reagan. The alternative of the Modern Job is to say we live together in this world, for better and worse. It doesn't even matter whether the Soviets are good or evil, the real question is, "how can we live together?" There is no meaningful ethic of self-interest any more, and there is no meaningful ethic of nationalism. Human conflict must be arbitrated through the very dialogue that combines trust and contending. This is the true alternative to the either/or of the Modern Promethean.

Let me conclude by putting this in a different, yet related language — that of my book *The Confirmation of Otherness: In Family, Community, and Society.* This book begins with Martin Buber's idea that we become ourselves, we become human beings, with other selves. We need to be confirmed by them, to be made present by them in our uniqueness, in order to become ourselves. Only this and not our relation to ourselves induces our inmost self-becoming. But we are often confirmed only with strings attached. Instead of unconditional confirmation, we are often offered only a contract that reads, "We will confirm you if you will think and act in ways of which we approve."

This difference in confirmation leads to two types of community: the "community of like-mindedness," or "affininty," and the "community of otherness." Community of like-mindedness is made up of people who huddle together for security — sons or daughters of the American Revolution, or Communists, or Jews, or Catholics, or Protestants, or born-again Christians. They imagine that they are safe and secure because they use the same slogans and the same language, even though they may not have much real relation with one another. It's the "Godfather" mentality, which led Laing to say, "The family is a protection racket." Communities too are often protection rackets, and so are nations. Nonetheless, it is always ultimately false community; for it is only concerned with that coloration that makes these people feel secure because they are so afraid of conflict, of opposition.

Once I led a comparative religion workshop of young people from 35 nations brought by the *New York Herald Tribune* to Sarah Lawrence College, and it really was very meaningful to compare their different religions. But the woman who had been the wife of a U.N. diplomat killed with Dag Hammarskjöld told me, "I'm going to take four of them on the T.V. and do the same thing you did." But, of course, she would not allow any issues to arise. We have the curious notion that if we all drink Coca-Cola or Pepsi there will be no war, there will be no conflict. That is, of course, the way *to* conflict. We do not confirm others by pretending to be the same as them. This community of affinity is revealed in caricature in our day. The Reagan administration reflects the attitude of a great many American people, too — the fear of otherness, the xenophobia, the mutual mistrust, and the denial of the reality of the the nuclear threat, the self-deception and the deception of others — these are all part of the community of affinity.

The community of otherness is no mere ideal. It is a direction of movement, one for which we discover the resources in each new situation. The community of otherness means the recognition that any community is really made up of the people who are there, even if two friends, a husband and wife, a family. If the members of any such group claim that there is just one point of view, then there is a collusion where people are *pretending* not to have more. Marriage is the exemplary bond, says Buber, because in it we learn that the other has not just an opinion or point of view but a different touch from the regions of existence, a different soil, a different faith. It is this otherness that has to be confirmed for us to become human and for us to find a way forward. This is not at all a matter of individualism; on the contrary, it is a matter of the only way the community can be made real. That has to begin with friendship; it has to begin in the family; it has to begin also when people have what they used to call, quite euphemistically, the "blended family" (it was usually more like an explosion). It has to move to communities in terms of the workers, the women, the aged, the diversity of cultures; but it has to move beyond that too, to the dialogue between nations.

The community of otherness is not where people are alike but where they have a common concern. When we recognize that common concern to be a moving forward that is possible only if we halt, stop, overcome, and obliterate the piling up of nuclear weapons, then we could have a hard-headed coming together, which could distinguish between the *propaganda* that we put out (1) for home consumption and (2) to keep people in power by obscuring the economic depression that is upon us on the one hand, and the real needs and the possibilities, on the other. It is not easy, but it is a direction of movement. If instead of spending our billions in piling up ever greater, more redundant nuclear arms we should put energy in the direction of building a community of otherness among the nations, we would discover what the possibilities are. Again, this is not an ideal; there are tragic situations, but we don't *know* the possibilities until we find them. The great Protestant theologian Reinhold Niebuhr said to Martin Buber that it is not possible to have justice in society, only between persons. "I can't know how much justice is possible in this situation until I go out and my head hits the wall and hurts, and then I know I've reached the limit. But if I hadn't gone on until my head hit the wall, I wouldn't know."

Now we haven't even begun to move in that direction. We haven't even begun to do what President Kennedy did many years ago when he unilaterally stopped testing nuclear bombs, and Kruschev did the same. We haven't even begun to explore that; we've settled down to the thesis that there can be no dialogue. This is the thesis of the community of affinity, of likemindedness. It is quite comparable to what was true in our culture twenty, thirty, maybe even just ten years ago, in the attitude toward death. That is, there seemed to be a conspiracy in American culture not to look at death. People simply "pass on"; they don't die. The people who are dying in the hospitals are no longer the true province of the nurses or the doctors because they don't offer the hope for which the people became nurses and doctors. Now we have hospices, and people are really facing this in "Conscious Living and Dying" and other organizations. So far from being a morbid and somber thing, as it might seem, it gives life — the joy that can come with realistically facing the fact that this *is* a part of life.

It would be a lot better if all of us worked together discovering the limits of the possibility of dialogue, the ability within the community of otherness of pointing to this Modern Job, of revealing the human image at a time when perhaps *only* this nuclear threat could bring this about. The eighteenth century theorists imagined that they could get a universality of all humanity by overlooking all the particulars. This proved to be a terrible illusion. But the nineteenth and twentieth century nationalists have shown the mutually self-defeating effect of a nationalism that is only for itself. The step beyond is one we are forced to take by the fact that we cannot even continue to exist if we do not move in this direction. Therefore, the hiding of the human image is both cause and effect of the nuclear threat. The nuclear threat is the challenge that can evoke the response of creating a new image of the human, one that is closer to the Modern Job, to contending and trust within the dialogue of the community of otherness. That, in turn, is the only way forward to the overcoming of the nuclear threat.

❦   ❦   ❦

II

INNOCENCE

AND GROWING UP

Among the numerous testaments to the peace-activism, sexual freedom and long-haired egalitarianism of the 1960s was the folk-rock musical "Hair," a celebration of the "dawning of the Age of Aquarius." Marilyn Ferguson's 1980 book "The Aquarian Conspiracy" has inspired reactions as vigorous, if not as colorful, as "Hair" did more than fifteen years ago. Ferguson's thesis is that a quiet revolution is presently at work, a revolution in values that is leading to a new kind of society, to a move away from "big things" toward more humanized living, to a new spirit of cooperation in the resolution of global problems. This "benign conspiracy," Ferguson argues, is triggering "the most rapid cultural realignment in history." It will result in transformation at every level, personal and social, and will necessitate our relinquishing outmoded perceptions of national identity, political allegiance and international alliances. Above all, the "Aquarian Conspiracy" is a revolution in our awareness that alternatives to our present way of living are possible and that we have the potential to better the quality of our lives.

In his "The Transformation as Sandbox Syndrome," Michael Marien accuses Ferguson and other promoters of the Aquarian transformation of having a sandbox mentality. The dynamics of this mentality, as Marien explains them, are easily understood: the sandbox is "an enclosed area where children safely play, while adults carry on undisturbed, in their normal wicked ways. Two complementary forces promote this condition: adults place children in the sandbox to get rid of them, and children volunteer to play there because it is fun." Continuing his indictment, Marien lists prominent characteristics of sandbox idealogy and practice. Among them are a belief in a present or immanent cosmic change; a confusion of goals with results; the use of vapid jargon ("futuring;" "networking"); instantaneous "equality" that ignores the real differences between rich and poor.

Marilyn Ferguson replied to Marien's charges against the Aquarian view in a short piece entitled "Transformations as Rough Draft." There she argues that a society's future hinges on its dominant image of that future. "A new sense of what is possible," Ferguson writes, "is the necessary though not sufficient, prerequisite for action." If public awareness of the potential for change is not raised, she continues, a society suffers hopelessness and cannot act. Transformationist visions are thus needed as "rough drafts" to raise awareness and encourage hope — in much the same way that arms-freeze proposals are needed to lift the public's consciousness out of its despair over the prospects of a nuclear holocaust.

When this exchange first appeared in the *Journal for Humanistic Psychology* (1983), Marilyn Ferguson was invited to respond again to Marien's questions and charges. As I reported in the JHP,

> I invited Marilyn Ferguson to respond to this piece by Michael Marien. She declined, saying that she did not believe it was worthwhile to prolong the exchange. Also, in her capacity as a member of the JHP Board of Editors, she recommended against publishing this piece, and decided to resign if I chose to publish it. I certainly did not want to prolong what some might regard as a fruitless controversy, nor did I want to lose a

valued member of the Board of Editors. Such are the
decisions that make an editor's work difficult. After
several readings of Michael Marien's piece, and after
careful consideration of other opinions, I decided to
publish it, and to risk erring in the direction of continued open discussion. I hope that readers will see
Michael's critical analysis of the alleged Transformation as a valuable part of a dialectical transformational
process, rather than a counter-productive attack on it. I
regret losing Marilyn Ferguson as a member of the
Board of Editors, and wish to acknowledge her substantial contributions to JHP and humanistic psychology in general.

At the root of the discussion between Marien and Ferguson is, of
course, a question which flows throughout all the essays collected in this
book: Does psychology — specifically, the psychology identified with
the "human potential movement" — have any real contribution to make to
politics? This question is not easily answered, as James Lafferty indicates
in the piece which opens this section. Participation in therapy can produce
enormous personal benefits, he notes, without necessarily awakening clients to the need for political responsibility.

JAMES LAFFERTY, *Political Responsibility and the Human Potential
Movement*

At age 34 I entered therapy at a large growth center on the outskirts of
Detroit, Michigan. The center primarily utilized group therapy and its
therapeutic modality was eclectic (i.e., employing techniques of gestalt,
TA, encounter, psychodrama, and primal therapy.)

The clinic leaders, many of whom were "non-credentialed" therapists, fostered the development, within each therapy group, of "sub-
communities" which were to act as "surrogate families" and were to
provide group support and "re-parenting." The entire clinic population
was thought of as a broader community of the whole.

The dominant emphasis was "emotive" as opposed to "intellectual."
There was a great deal of physical stroking and physical closeness between
patient and patient and between patient and therapist.

It was a therapy setting in which therapists were also in therapy with their patients; a clinic where "duality" was fostered as a desired norm and not viewed as presenting any ethical problems.

In short, it was a growth center which was part of the human potential movement and which employed an approach to therapy familiar to many humanistically oriented people.

Much could be written about many aspects of the seven year history of this clinic. However, this article focuses on a political question which, it seems to me, is raised by the employment of the humanistic, self-actualization growth center approach common to much of the clinical work being done today.

I can best introduce and, at the same time, summarize my political question, by reference to an actual question I asked of my group members and therapist shortly after I began therapy. I was greatly moved by the sincere and open displays of love and affection that I encountered during my initial therapeutic sessions. Three months into my therapy I informed my group that I would be gone for two weeks, as I was going to be in Washington, D.C., helping to organize the anti-war demonstration planned to coincide with former President Nixon's inauguration. This was met with much criticism and resistance; not due to political opposition to my anti-war work, but due to the fact that they felt my first responsibility was to myself and the group. I responded with a question: "If the love and caring I have seen in this room does not translate to a commitment to take that love and caring into the world at large, then what is the ultimate value of that love?"

I should, perhaps, also acquaint the reader with a few pertinent facts of my own life. At the time I entered therapy I was an attorney who specialized in civil rights and selective service law. Additionally, I spent approximately fifty percent of my time as a political organizer, organizing with the civil rights movement in the early 60's and the anti-Vietnam war movement in the late 60's. At the time I entered therapy I was the head of a Detroit anti-war office and one of five coordinators, on the National level, of the National Peace Action Coalition which, among other activities, organized the massive anti-war demonstrations in Washington, D.C. and elsewhere.

My personal life, however, was in total disarray and most unsatisfying. My marriage of thirteen years was dead if not yet buried; and virtually no personal emotional responses were available to me. When asked if I was "happy," my sincere response was "happiness!" — what's happiness? People aren't put on earth to be happy, but only to struggle and to try and leave the world a bit better than they found it.

I should add that my nearly seven years of humanistic therapy eventually produced profound and highly rewarding personal results: I ended my unfulfilling marriage; I acquired the ability to be easily "in touch with my feelings"; I learned how to give and receive love and comfort; I developed a new and highly satisfying love relationship with a woman who is now my wife; I developed the ability to have close, loving relationships with my daughter and friends; and I learned how to strike a more personally satisfying balance between "taking care of myself" and helping to make life a bit more just and humane for my fellow man and woman. In short, I left therapy a much happier man than when I began.

However, at the end of my therapy, as at the beginning, I continued to feel that humanistic psychology or the human potential movement, however one may choose to label it, falls short as an answer to the broader social questions with which I and my political comrades were wrestling.

To put the matter yet a different way: the people with whom I now enjoy the closest and most intimate relationships are those friends whom I met in therapy. They make up my present day, "extended family." And yet, only one of those individuals shares my commitment to political action. In fact, of the approximately 600 patients who formed the therapeutic community at the clinic I described above, only two or three are involved today in political work and they, like I, were so involved before their therapy experience.

Virginia Satir has written that:

> For me, anything that gives new hope, new possibilities and new positive feelings about ourselves will make us more whole people and thus more human, real and loving in our relationships with others. *If enough of this happens, the world will become a better place for all of us.*

According to Rollo May:

> Care is important because it is what is missing in our
> day. [There] is the seeping, creeping conviction that
> nothing matters; the prevailing feeling that one can't
> do anything. *The threat is apathy, uninvolvement, the
> grasping for external stimulants. Care is a necessary
> antidote for this.*

Fritz Perls stated:

> While the conflict between the individual and society
> is obvious and known to everybody, while the conflict
> between selling out to society and making one's own
> bed is nothing new, while the division between com-
> pliers and rebels remains unchanged throughout the
> ages, *yet little is known of the internalizing of those
> conflicts, and how to go about finding an integrative
> solution.*

And twenty years ago, Eric Berne wrote:

> For certain fortunate people there is something which
> transcends all classifications of behavior, and that is
> awareness; something which rises above the program-
> ming of the past, and that is spontaneity; and some-
> thing that is more rewarding than games, and that is
> intimacy. But all three of these may be frightening and
> even perilous to the unprepared. *Perhaps they are bet-
> ter off as they are, seeking their solutions in popular
> techniques of social action, such as "togetherness."
> This may mean that there is no hope for the human
> race, but there is hope for individual members of it.*

In short, although I have read, with eager expectancy, much of the primary literature in the field of humanistic psychology, and although I have
discovered several fine articles on humanism and political action in various journals, including the *Journal of Humanistic Psychology,* I have been
disappointed with the failure of many humanistic writers and thinkers to
speak to the need for social change and the application of humanistic psychology to such a task.

There are, of course, notable exceptions to my disappointment
expressed above. Anderson states the problem clearly when he says:

Now, it is undoubtedly true that, so far, the emphasis in humanistic psychology has been upon individual, personal growth, and that when humanistic psychologists have addressed themselves to the possibility of bringing about widespread social change, they have often tended to emphasize the incremental results of individual growth (such as the cumulative effect of many people undergoing some kind of personal transformation through therapy or encounter group experience). *There has been less of an inclination to consider the possible ways of changing institutions or to understand institutional change as a way of facilitating personal growth for great numbers of people.*

And, Anderson does suggest the direction we should follow:

If we should choose to make the highest development of human beings a deliberate social goal, then the task before us is to think about the growth possibilities of all people, at all social and economic levels, and also to understand fully what it means when a species begins to become responsible for its own evolution.

In 1979, humanistic psychologists issued this call:

We are perhaps in the midst of a major evolutionary transformation of civilization. The Future may bring the unfolding of an awesome and joyous new vision of human nature. It is also equally possible that it will bring disasters and great crises: economic, social, political, ecological.

What happens tomorrow will be the result of what we do today: how we live, work, play, think and feel. Awareness of this brings a sense of responsibility; we reevaluate our lifestyles, explore alternatives, and consider our resources for directing change consciously and collectively.

This is all well and good. But why couldn't the matter have been put more clearly and forthrightly? I would have written this portion of the call as follows:

America today is experiencing a major evolutionary and revolutionary transformation. We are committed to an America based on a new, loving vision of human

> nature. For this to transpire we must strive to seek out
> and eliminate racism and sexism and economic repres-
> sion which stunt the growth of this new human nature.
> What happens tomorrow will be the result of what
> we do today. Therefore, we will strive to find new ways
> to apply our collective energy to eliminate the unjust,
> repressive and disease producing vestiges of the past;
> we will commit ourselves to collectively bringing
> about through action, a new socio-political order in
> which the humanism we preach and teach will be trans-
> lated into a societal structure where humanism will
> truly be the realizable birth right of all.
> We invite you to join us in our work.

I appreciate the fact that the AHP is not a political organization. And
yet, if we are an organization committed to finding solutions to the human
problems of our clients or patients, then can we fail to have a political
thrust to our organizational work? If we recognize that the problems our
patients and clients present are often, in whole or in part, a result of the
way our nation is now governed and structured, can we fail to address
those broader, external, political issues?

I also appreciate the fact that the AHP has spoken out and taken positions on various questions of broad societal concern. What I am suggesting, however, is that the organization's political work be labeled as such
and be made a dominant and announced part of the organizational structure and program of AHP.

My point is that it is simply not enough to suggest, as Satir does above,
that if everyone would light one little candle the world would "become a
better place for all of us." The plain fact is that some people can't afford
candles, some people won't light a candle unless persuaded and urged to
do so by others, and some people spend their lives blowing out other people's candles. Only an organized, active, and militant political movement
will truly make the world a "better place for all of us."

My impression is that humanistic therapy is generally viewed as complete or at least successful, if one leaves with an enhanced feeling of self-
esteem and finds oneself more "centered" in the world in which one lives.

An emphasis in the therapeutic community in which I participated was
on getting out of the "child position" vis-à-vis one's mate, or friends, or
employer, or parents. Certainly, I have no quarrel with such a goal.

But, the communities in which our clients and patients live are not comprised solely of mates or friends, or employers or parents. All people live in a much broader community of men and women and what happens to any one member of that community affects us all.

My "brothers and sisters" are not only those men and women who now occupy my immediate life space and constitute my "extended family," but rather include all men and all women everywhere who constitute a vast family of humankind.

Thus, if the government and other institutions in America operate so as to repress my often distant brothers and sisters, do I not have a responsibility, if I am truly "adult," to assume an "adult position" vis-à-vis that government and those institutions?

Put yet another way: If I will no longer interface as a child with my mother and will not tolerate repressive, hurtful behavior on her part, can I tolerate the repressive and hurtful actions of my government and still call myself an "adult"?

I think not. If I sit quietly by while the government or institutional forces in this society operate in ways which perpetuate racism, or sexism, or wage unjust wars in my name, or create economic repression for masses of my brothers and sisters, then I am behaving as a "child" in my relationship with the "parent-government" or "parent-society".

I believe that it is incumbent upon every humanistically oriented therapist, or workshop leader, or growth center facilitator, to help his or her clients to recognize the ways in which society is causing or contributing to their "illness." In short, to encourage their patients or clients to assume an adult stance not only in terms of their dealings with friends and associates, but in their dealings with society itself.

I do not believe it is the prerogative of the practitioner to propagandize on behalf of his or her personal political ideology, but only to deal forthrightly with the fact that political institutions do affect the quality of each and every person and that all people are inextricably related by the very fact that society is organized and operates upon us all in ways which are psycho-political in nature.

In summary: to be an "adult" must come to mean that each person will take responsibility not only for his or her own private life, but will also take responsibility for insuring that what transpires in the broader family of humankind will not be dictated by the parent-government at City Hall, or in the State capitals, or in Washington, but will transpire as a result of the active intervention of each man and woman.

Correspondingly, we in the human potential movement must actively intervene in the affairs of state to ensure that "society" or the parent-government does not produce patients or clients at a faster rate than we can ever hope, on an individual basis, to treat.

To quote, again, from Anderson:

> As we consider such questions, the humanistic per-
> spective becomes not merely psychological, but politi-
> cal; we are not talking about principles of research or
> therapy, but about principles of social action and insti-
> tutional change. Our new vision of the possibilities of
> human existence becomes a set of guidelines for build-
> ing a human community. It is no longer the concern
> merely of writers and clinicians and social scientists
> but a *res publica,* a public thing.

MICHAEL MARIEN, *The Transformation as Sandbox Syndrome*

At the outset, I want to emphasize three beliefs that I share with many others:

> —Peace, freedom, equality, justice, community,
> love, truth, health, beauty, frugality, self-reliance, and
> self-fulfillment — despite frequent conflicts with each
> other — are all worthy goals, and should be pursued
> for all people worldwide.
> —The old paradigms or ways of thought are obso-
> lete; new and broader paradigms offer more promise
> for the intelligent conduct of human affairs.
> —Hyperindustrialized societies are in deep trou-
> ble, as are "developing" countries seeking to follow
> their example; major changes will be necessary if we
> are to survive in any dignified fashion.

Although a transformation in values, perceptions, and institutions is desirable, it is far from inevitable. Despite an urgent need, change in a humanly desirable direction may not be taking place at all, or may be taking place at such a miniscule rate so as to be irrelevant. Indeed, I strongly suspect that the widespread belief in a transformation that *is* happening in fact keeps it from happening. We need reasonable hopes, of course. But making a religion out of social change — developing a body of unquestioned belief, derived from concern for the human condition and hope for a better world — only serves to deflect energies away from the hard work that must be done.

To illustrate, imagine that you are an agent of the FBI or CIA. You are called into the office of the Big Chief and informed that there may be a subversive movement afoot — some call it the Aquarian Conspiracy. It threatens the American way of life by seeking to disarm the U.S. and make peace with the Soviet Union, by redefining national security, by weakening the nation-state in favor of global peacekeeping, by weakening the global economy in favor of national and local self-reliance, by slackening U.S. participation in world competition for high-technology leadership, by encouraging individuals to be more self-reliant and not to consume as much, by promoting environmentalism at the expense of commerce, and by decentralizing economic and political power through wider participation in corporate and community decision making. This is clearly subversive. Your mission is to stop it. What should an effective agent do?

Being wise in the ways of the world, you realize that the 1950s strategy of fighting the Red Menace will no longer work in the sophisticated 1980s. In our age of infoglut, why give valuable publicity to the Green Menace, when the movement, at least in the United States, is largely invisible? Rather, you would exploit the widespread tendency of the movement, such as it is, to render itself politically impotent. You understand the dynamics of the sandbox: an enclosed area where children safely play, while adults carry on, undisturbed, in their usual wicked ways. Two complementary forces promote this condition: Adults place children in the sandbox to get rid of them, and children volunteer to play there because it is fun.

To stop the potential subversion of America, all you have to do is go with the flow and promote the Sandbox Syndrome. It's easy. Here are some tips:

(1)Encourage Belief in Success. Promote the view that cosmic change is coming, or taking place. Similar to the fundamentalist Christians, who

believe that Armageddon is about to take place, to be followed by a millenium for those who are saved, preach that the Transformation, or the Third Wave, is happening now — that we have reached the turning point, and that people are now seeing that we can't continue the old ways. Don't attempt to offer evidence for this change, other than a one-time 1977 Harris Poll based on leading questions, or some fuzzily estimated data sanctified by association with Stanford Research International. Anything else would involve left-brain quantifying — an artifact of Consciousness II.

(2)Confuse Goals and Results. It feels good, and it won't hurt anyone's feelings, to proclaim that we are working for peace, we are changing minds, we are healing. Perhaps we are; perhaps we aren't. The intention and the process are primary, not the outcome. Any hint of a managerial, performance-oriented approach is fascistic.

(3)Don't Criticize. That's related to asking embarrassing questions about results. Just let it be. Being peaceful, loving, supportive, and cooperative means treating everyone equally and saying ill of no one. After all, everyone means well. Prickly questions are hostile and best ignored, or met with a hug.

(4)Add a Dose of Hubris. Stand on the leading edge, the crest of the Third Wave, amidst the New Age. You're superior to those unliberated, linear cluckheads out there. You know; they don't. Write a guidebook to networking or bartering, the magic processes of the alternative culture — but don't acknowledge the networks and barters used by the rest of the world. Your folkways, too, are superior. To enhance communication, invite Them to your saunas and hot tubs — don't even think of visiting their bridle trails and tennis courts, or, among the masses, their corner bars and bowling alleys.

(5)Promote Your Own Dialect. Tired of pedantic jargon? Create your own hip language. Turn nouns to verbs such as "peacing" and "futuring." Use adjectives such as "incredible" to describe every experience. Blows the mind, but who needs it? Use positive words such as "network," "caring," "holistic," "creativity," "synergy," "foresight," "cooperation," "transcendence," "win/win," "human scale," and "human values." Don't use negative words like "competition," "corporations," "communism," or "crime." Maybe they'll go away.

(6)Extol the Informal and the Nonacademic. Your intuition is a safe guide, as is the common sense of the people. Ignore the elitist academics, with their ponderous footnotes and interminable data. Accordingly, the academic journals and commercial publishers should also be dismissed, in favor of small book publishers and honest, alternative periodicals.

(7)Get the Holistic Picture. You can acquire instant wisdom by taking the general systems point of view, or viewing whole systems. When you have the Big Picture of humanity, nature, and society, you know it all, and there is no need to learn any more. A historical perspective isn't needed because these ideas are obviously new.

(8)Create Instant Equality. Forget the rich and the poor. The rich have great power, which is too much to contemplate. So don't. The poor can't meet their basic material needs, which is also a downer, best ignored. Preach that we all have enough and that more self-help is needed. Fits nicely into the antipoverty strategy of the Reagan administration.

(9)Be Self-Centered. You have the power of the New Age in your head; change your consciousness and you can change the world. We have met the enemy and he is us. The responsibility for health, for change, for peace, is within you. All of the above — and more, no doubt, could be added — add up to the Sandbox Syndrome: a set of behaviors guaranteed to keep an individual or an organization in a childish state of innocence, content with building sand castles, instead of real-life structures. A good CIA agent would promote this simple-mindedness, rather than publicly fight the specter of the Green Menace.

But what if you read some books by Lester R. Brown, Willis Harman, Hazel Henderson, Ivan Illich, Amory Lovins, James Ogilvy, James Robertson, Theodore Roszak, Kirkpatrick Sale, Mark Satin, E. F. Schumacher, Robert Theobald, William Irwin Thompson, Alvin Toffler, and others, causing you to believe the Green Message? What if you see the necessity of a sustainable, decentralized, human-needs-oriented society — the Jeffersonian vision of America as the *real* American way of life, rather than the Hamiltonian, corporate view? With a flush of true patriotism, you decide to be a counteragent and to work for genuine ecodecentralism. What do you do? Here are some general tips:

(1)Grow Up. All of the above-mentioned positions are simplistic. An upward growth requires a broader, more subtle, and complex view:

Two Paths to Transformation

	Utopian/Puerile (The prevailing Way of the Sandbox)	*Pragmatic/Mature* (A possible pattern of the future)
1. Progress	The Transformation is happening	Weigh both successes and failures
2. Results	Goals are outcomes	Outcomes are not necessarily in accord with goals
3. Supporters	Be supportive and don't criticize; all efforts are good; no sense of evil or excellence	Constructive criticism; back winners and drop losers; evil and failure are possible
4. Opponents	Ignore or vilify; you are superior	Seek to debate opponents and learn from them; invite hard questions
5. Language	Create your own; ignore official definitions of reality	Use common language to communicate broadly; challenge ideas in power
6. Information	Favor intuition and the non-academic	Seek the best in formal and non-formal, scholarly and popular
7. Truth	Perfected wisdom through instant holism	Holism as a learning tool and unrealized ideal
8. Power	Ignore it	Acknowledge it — and its very unequal distribution
9. Self	You are central; change self to change world	You interact with nature and society; many paths to change

(a) Develop a wide range of indicators that describe both successes and failures.

(b) Don't confuse goals and results, but insist on measures of performance and on standards.

(c) Be constructively critical: Point to good work and how it can be improved — and also to work that is useless or damaging.

(d) Be humble: We all have much to learn in an age of ignorance. Identify your opponents and their arguments, and learn from them.

(e) Use the English language correctly as a tool of thought, and to enable communication with those in need of hearing your message.

(f) Seek the best thought from both academics and non-academics; use your intuition as one of many learning tools.

(g) Similarly, holism should also be used as a tool for learning, and recognized as an ideal to strive for ceaselessly both in space and time.

(h) Recognize that inequities in wealth and income are increasing, that the poor need help to help themselves, and that even good help will not necessarily help.

(i) Understand that there are many sources of problems in both individuals and society, that the two are interactive, and that individuals are often not at all responsible for their problems.

(2)Connect Some Disconnected Yins and Yangs. In advocating a Taoist framework for dealing with reality, Fritjof Capra notes that a dynamic balance between yin and yang is good, and imbalance is bad. Several balances are mentioned above (success and failure, academic and non-academic, individual and society). Several additional pairings not to be found on Capra's list are also needed:

(a) Inspiration and Perspiration. Our spirits can benefit from the uplift of preaching and cheerleading. But exhortation toward the promised land is not enough; we must work very hard to bring it about.

(b) Realism and Idealism. We need idealists with a foot on the ground of reality, as well as realists who can keep some ideal in mind. Both, in dialogue with each other, should replace the great number of utopians with no sense of reality and "realists" with no appreciation of any ideal.

(c) Cooperation and Struggle. In our age of instant gratification by video and drugs, many think that social change should be instant, painless, and non-reversible. While seeking out opportunities for cooperation, a dialectical view of struggle is also needed. Indeed, those who ostensibly share your views may not necessarily be cooperative, and your greatest struggle may be with such "movement killers."

(d) Intellect and Spirit. In trying to escape from what is seen as too much rationality in modern society, an excuse is often provided for anti-intellectualism in the name of the neglected "right brain." We need a more rational rationality, not less rationality.

(e) Critics and Lovers. As pointed out by John W. Gardner, we should avoid the extremes of unloving critics and uncritical lovers. Another way to consider more productive behavior is to note the traits of Abraham Maslow's self-actualizing people, which include fighting untruths, not needing to be loved by everyone, enjoying greater efficiency and being effective, looking at facts courageously, and avoiding illusions.

(3) Get the New Age Act Together (to Some Degree). The pervasive condition that must be faced is the fact that we live in an age of infoglut. Another book, journal, conference, or newsletter about peace, healing, or environmentalism will not necessarily help people, and might simply add to the pervasive problem of information overload and fragmentation. The transformational message must be recognized as "the world-crisis solution with a hundred names" — green revolution, human scale, person-centered society, human economy, conserver society, solar age, meta-industrial alternative, Gandhism, and so on. As long as this message is fractured into a hundred or so labelings, The Transformation, or whatever, will continue to be stillborn.

(4) . . . and Take it on the Road. Talking to the converted is sufficient for a religious organization, although even religions seek converts. If we are serious about a genuine transformation of values and perceptions, the world must know that desirable and practical alternatives exist. Despite the great volume of New Age literature, "the world-crisis solution with a hundred names" still remains invisible to mainstream culture, or is readily dismissed as "small is beautiful" romanticism. New Age literature is seldom reviewed in mainstream periodicals. It seldom enters textbooks or political campaigns. The old ways of thinking are still very much in power:

(a) One-dimensional, flat-earth politics, restricting all possibilities to "the" left-right political spectrum of liberals and conservatives, still prevails in our political analysis.

(b) One-eyed economics, ignoring the informal or household economy, continues to define "the" economy.

(c) One-directional social evolution, involving more economic growth and a service society, continues to be the only definition of progress.

(d) One-time education, assuming that an individual has completed learning upon leaving school or college, continues to inhibit adults from discovering ignorance and learning needs.

To improve on these paradigms in power, there must be widespread and genuine debate and discussion, rather than smug isolation and loose talk or paradigm change.

(5) Aim High and Don't Shoot Your Foot. There is a frequent tendency to underestimate the transformational task, while overestimating the progress that has been made. This is complicated by the use of images and ideas that are intellectually laudable but politically inept: for example, a "no-growth society," in contrast to the more attractive notion of a human-growth society. Western science is another illustration: rather than rejecting it, and creating an easy target for the charge of being antiscience, a better strategy would advocate a more scientific science — a superior world science that incorporates various scientific traditions.

This advice is for the counteragent, who would seek to promote an actual transformation. But the task is difficult. The agent, who embraces the Way of the Sandbox, follows the path of least resistance. Both the agent and the counteragent are at work. Who will win? Probably the agent. Still, the counteragent may prevail — the slender hope that prompts this essay. Whom do you want to win?

MARILYN FERGUSON, *Transformation as a Rough Draft*

I share many of Michael Marien's concerns about simplistic and extravagant claims of a New Age (a term I never use). And I agree that there is hard work to be done. Since he has tied *The Aquarian Conspiracy* into his view of "transformation as a sandbox syndrome," it seems appropriate for me to respond.

I think he has missed some important points and jumped to a few unwarranted conclusions.

● As Fred Polak pointed out in his classic *The Image of the Future*, the future is largely determined by a society's dominant vision of the future. Kenneth Boulding made the same point in *The Image*. A changing image precedes social and material change. A new sense of what is possible is the necessary, though not sufficient, prerequisite for action.

● Marien assumes that people will quit struggling if they become hopeful that a new kind of society, with new values, may be emerging. What a curiously negative view of human nature! In my experience, the opposite is true. Once people have an inkling that their ideals are *not* foolish and unfounded, once they think there's a real potential for change, they clamor for a way to contribute. What life game has higher stakes? Cynicism — not false hope — is the major excuse I hear for inaction. Fresh hope carries with it inherent impetus and responsibility.

● Just as the nuclear freeze proposals are a "rough draft" for arms reduction and a strategy for raising public awareness, transformational projects and writings are raising popular awareness of alternatives.

● Marien says that, "despite the great volume of New Age literature, 'the world-crisis solution with a hundred names' still remains invisible to mainstream culture." Within the past year, I've compared notes with dozens of spokespersons for social transformation. Without exception, they described a new openness in the society. The excitement about John Naisbitt's *Megatrends* is an example of growing establishment awareness of changing values.

Who cares? It's not just "the converted," as Marien puts it. Since *The Aquarian Conspiracy* was published in Spring 1980, I have been invited to talk about personal and social change to the World Business Council, church groups, IBM, Digital Equipment Corporation, the American Hospital Association, the American Council of Life Insurance, farm wives in Canada, hotel and restaurant executives, members of the U.S. Congress (twice), business leaders in Sweden, educators in England, communications technology specialists in Switzerland, and university audiences in Vienna, Hamburg, London, Oxford, and Cologne.

Among the readers of *The Aquarian Conspiracy* are leaders of the Solidarity Movement in Poland (they ordered ten copies), the late Anwar Sadat, the president of the Sociological Association of the USSR, governors, senators, and a White House staff member. Maybe some of these people are just checking it out, as in Marien's CIA scenario, to kill the movement. Seems unlikely, though.

There are *Aquarian Conspiracy* discussion groups in nursing homes, prisons, universities, churches, and government agencies. Recently a reader called from Tokyo to say that 75 people had met the night before to form a network. The book is now out in French, Swedish, German (it was a Number 2 bestseller in Switzerland), Spanish, Portuguese, Dutch, and Japanese.

● Marien urges that we "connect some disconnected yins and yangs." I could not agree more. This is a crucial point, one we emphasize in our newsletters. I have written at length of the power of the "radical center." The Transformational Platform drafted by the New World Alliance urged balance and synthesis. Everywhere I hear people quoting Rene Dubos: "Think globally, act locally."

Marien concludes that there is only a "slender hope" that the Way of the Sandbox will not prevail. I wish he could meet the hundreds of thousands of hardworking visionary people I've met in the past two and a half years. If he were to "take it on the road," as he recommends, he might have more hope — *realistic* hope that incites to action.

MICHAEL MARIEN, *Further Thoughts on the Two Paths to Transformation: A Reply to Ferguson*

I am pleased that Marilyn Ferguson was able to take time from her busy globe-hopping schedule to respond to my exploratory essay on "Transformation as Sandbox Syndrome" in her reply, "Transformation as a Rough Draft." Unfortunately, the Great Conspirator offers no evidence that she has actually read the essay, or, if she did, that she understands it. Although I am tempted to ignore her seemingly hasty response, Ferguson's empty claim that I have "missed some important points and jumped to a few unwarranted conclusions" should not go unanswered. There may be some truth in the statement, in that my paper was originally prepared as a mere ten-minute presentation and the subject is highly speculative, but Ferguson fails to introduce any point that I missed or explain any unwarranted conclusions (which are really only hypotheses). Moreover, she serves to illustrate my main arguments, as I shall demonstrate, although this surely was not her intention. This occasion also provides an opportunity to extend slightly my inchoate argument, and to state it in an alternative "straight forward" dimension, in that humor is sometimes not seen as the mask for utter seriousness that it often is.

My essay, in brief, attempted to outline two "paths" to a transformation in values, perceptions, and institutions, leading to a society that is sustainable, decentralized, ecologically conscious, peaceful, healthy, just, and oriented to human needs of all people.

The first path (or Transformation I or T-I, to try a new labeling) is characterized as the utopian/puerile path, or the prevailing "Way of the Sandbox." The sandbox is an enclosed area where children safely play, while adults carry on their usual activities undisturbed. Children volunteer to play in the sandbox because it is fun, and adults seek to place children in the sandbox to get rid of them. Politically, much of the behavior now associated with "The Transformation" can be described as the sandbox syndrome: it has little or no impact, and is not taken seriously. Examples of this childlike behavior includes a religious belief in imminent success (e.g., to cite Ferguson, "A leaderless but powerful network is working to bring about radical change in the United States"), the confusion of goals and results, an acritical stance toward "transformational" efforts, hubris and exaggeration (to cite Ferguson again, "Broader than reform, deeper than revolution, this benign conspiracy has triggered the most rapid cultural realignment in history"), an incapacitating dialect, pseudo-holism, self-centeredness, and middle-class egalitarian blinders that ignore the growing gap between rich and poor. In sum, it is much well-meaning noise but little result, or, to cite Marien's Iron Law of Cosmic Balderdash, actual change is inversely correlated with the heat and height of the rhetoric.

Transformation II (or T-II) is an attempt to grow up politically, and to deal effectively with the real world. In terms of the inner-directed lifestyles described by Arnold Mitchell, it is the difference between the immature "I-Am-Me" group along with the youthful "Experiential" group, and the mission-oriented "Societally Conscious" group combined with the psychologically mature "Integrateds." A more mature or pragmatic approach does not abandon ideals, but teaches us to work effectively toward these ideals in a society of massive institutions, modern technologies, information glut, and many competing interests. T-II behavior would acknowledge both successes and failures in "the movement," insist on measures of performance rather than confusing goals with results, consistently engage in constructive criticism, learn from the arguments of those with whom they disagree, communicate concisely in proper English, and promote effective organization.

There are several ways to present this notion of two paths to transformation. I chose at the outset to make a humorous analogy, imagining what a CIA agent might do to stop the Green Menace — go with the flow and promote the thoughtless and unproductive behaviors of the sandbox syndrome — and what a counteragent might do to work for a genuine neo-Jeffersonian vision of America. Another way to present this idea would be to proclaim that a profound and historic transition from Transformation I to Transformation II *is* taking place. This prophetic stance would be hypocritical, though, because such hortatory statements are characteristic of the T-I style. Still another form of presentation, which I am now employing, is to state cautiously that a transition from T-I to T-II may take place and certainly ought to take place; however, there is little or no evidence to suggest that such a maturation is taking place yet. This would reflect the T-II style, which does not assume that progress toward the goal of transformation is necessarily being made by those individuals who claim to be working for peace, justice, humanity, etc.

Consider another analogy of swimming to China. At the risk of seeming idealistic about human potential, I believe that it is possible to swim to China — if one is in superb physical condition, if one has the necessary support team, and if one punctuates the journey with appropriate periods of rest (that's cheating a bit, but let's put this matter aside). The problem with the T-I worldview is that it has no sense whatsoever of the task at hand, and it ignores history. It is as if a swimmer steps into the California surf, swims out for a hundred yards, and proclaims that, "I'm swimming to China." This is followed by mastering an additional 150 yards, and the progress statement that, "I've more than doubled the distance traveled." Both of these statements are true. Yet the swimmer soon drops into the murky depths, similar to the countless movements in American history that have pursued cosmic ends with miniscule means. And new swimmers continue to step into the surf without asking whatever happened to the previous swimmers.

The T-II approach would entail careful planning for a long and rigorous trip, and would require actual cooperation rather than merely talking about it. As argued by Theodore Caplow, a greatly improved society might be within our present grasp if projects of social improvement involved a recognition of seven essential parts: a description of existing conditions, a careful and honest statement of the end condition to be achieved, dividing the project into successive stages, designing methods for getting from one stage to the next, an estimate of time and resources, devising procedures for measuring goal attainment, and attempting to detect unanticipated results. A similar formulation is offered by the *Resource Manual for a Living Revolution,* which advocates developing a theory of change, acquiring a sufficient understanding of the workings of our economic and political system (otherwise, actions may go wide of the mark and even aggravate problems), planning a strategy, building communities of support and organizational strength, preparing for action, and evaluating action (a necessary beginning that is often forgotten). Such a thoughtful approach, however, appears to be the exception rather than the rule. And this is why I think that it is important to distinguish between T-I and T-II behavior.

With these comments as an introduction, I will now proceed to consider each of the five points that Ferguson purports to make.

(1) *Who Has What Image of the Future?* Ferguson begins her response to my essay by throwing the book at me, or in this case the pair of books: Polak's *The Image of the Future* and Boulding's *The Image,* which both emphasize the importance of a society's dominant image of the future. Obviously. The important question that Ferguson does not consider is who has what image of the future and how the alternative images are changing relative to the dominant images of society. I suggested in my

article that the "transformational" image of the future is fragmented into "the world-crisis solution with a hundred names," and I have since documented all one hundred of them, although there are doubtless more. Even if this babble of banners is not divisive — if those who follow the Green Perspective, the Solar Age, the Conserver Society, the Communications Era, etc. can all easily relate to each other's titlings — how many people in all does this entail? Is this group of Aquarians, Decentralists, Greens, or whatever growing (as we are led to believe), remaining essentially the same, or shrinking? My entire essay was addressed to what is needed to make the alternative image dominant. So where is the missed point or unwarranted conclusion?

(2) *Hope and Struggle.* The second charge is "Marien assumes that people will quit struggling if they become hopeful that a new kind of society may be emerging." I am puzzled as to how Ferguson infers this from my argument, but it is not a statement with which I would concur. Some people devote their lives to a quixotic pursuit of the Promised Land. But most people will quit struggling if their expectations are set unreasonably high, and the resulting actions fall far short of this ideal. As noted by Hadley Cantril, "A vision of a brighter future will lead only to despair or will be given up entirely unless there are some ways to start making the vision come true." The awakening of hope can be the first step in social change, but too many of our transformational leaders seem to specialize only in the awakening of hope, rather than pointing to the entire range of needed actions. Might it be time for the transformers to transform themselves?

(3) *Transformational Projects Are Raising Awareness?* Ferguson's third point makes no reference to my article, but simply states the goal that "transformational projects and writings are raising popular awareness of alternatives." This, of course, nicely illustrates the T-I trait of equating intentions with results. Some transformational projects and writings are doubtlessly raising popular awareness of alternatives, while others may have no result or the counterproductive result of turning people away from alternatives. I don't know which ones are working or are not working, although I entertain suspicions (i.e., hypotheses). Overall, I suspect that much of the transformational effort is preaching to the convinced, and thus

a waste of scarce human resources — exactly what the mythical CIA agent would seek to promote. Where is the evidence of any recent shifts in public opinion? And if there are any shifts, can they be reasonably attributed to transformational efforts?

(4) *Other Spokespersons, Naisbitt's Success, and Ferguson's Travels.* Finally we get to the "evidence," such as it is. To illustrate that the transformation is taking place, Ferguson offers the opinions of her fellow spokespersons for social transformation, the success of John Naisbitt's *Megatrends,* and the worldwide travels of Ferguson herself combined with the success for her book. But, alas, all are pseudo-indicators.

I thought that Ferguson was kidding when she pronounced that, after comparing notes of dozens of spokespersons, "without exception, they described a new openness in society" (whatever that means). I read the statement several times, wondering why she would provide such a splendid illustration of the inbred Sandbox mentality. I guess that she truly believes it. But there are many other believers in other beliefs. We could get unanimous consent from dozens of tub-thumping evangelists that Jesus is coming. And all of the advisors to the President would surely be convinced that Reaganomics is improving the economy. The generals in the Pentagon plan our future based on the belief that the Soviets are well ahead of us in the arms race. A convention of computer salespeople would fully agree that a worldwide information revolution is taking place. So why are the cheerleaders for the transformation any more correct than the self-interested adherents of any other cause?

The second putative indicator of success is the "excitement" about John Naisbitt's *Megatrends,* which became a bestseller. Does this indicate "growing establishment awareness of changing values," as Ferguson asserts? Not necessarily. Naisbitt's fluffy book is a triumph of packaging, presenting an easily-digested upbeat collection of good news to a public that is starved for it.

Naisbitt doesn't tell us how a transformation can take place, but in typical T-I fashion proclaims in the subtitle of the book that the ten megatrends — and only this magic number — are New Directions Transforming Our Lives. Here are the new shibboleths to replace Mom, and apple pie: an information society (never mind our Age of Infoglut), high tech conveniently balanced by high touch (never mind any lags in humanized response), an interdependent world economy (never mind any imminent collapse), long-term planning, (never mind for what), decentralization in government and business (never mind unemployment and low wages), self-help and self-employment, (never mind lack of capital), egalitarian networking (never mind establishment networking), the trend to multiple options (never mind whether the options are meaningful), and the population shift from Snowbelt to Sunbelt (never mind the Sunbelt water problems).

Some of the megatrends are new and some are not, some are compatible with each other and some are not, some are reversible and some are not, and some are for real and some are not. In the chapter on long-range planning, for example, no evidence is offered that there *is* any shift from short-term to long-term thinking; rather, we are merely given repeated assertions that it is the proper thing to do. As Anthony Downs observes in his critique of "exagger-books" by Naisbitt, Ferguson, and Alvin Toffler, such writers are guilty of "mega-hyping the pseudo-facts." (It might also be noted that, as an illustration of the acritical daisy-chain phenomenon among many transformational authors, Ferguson and Toffler both supply back-cover blurbs for Naisbitt's book.)

Although Naisbitt may be a tad weak in veracity, has he nevertheless been influential in changing establishment values? I doubt it, although I would welcome any real evidence to the contrary. Popularity in book sales is not necessarily related to veracity or influence. At best, we can say that Naisbitt is a good read, for people who like their nonfiction on the light side, with sugar.

Finally, we are offered the evidence of Ferguson's own book, translated into seven languages to date, and her worldwide travels to spread the good news of the Aquarian Conspiracy. Doesn't this show that Great Things Are Happening? They are surely happening to Ferguson, but not necessarily to the wider society. So Ferguson is a hot ticket on the lecture circuit. But so are Art Buchwald, Henry Kissinger and G. Gordon Liddy. The important question is whether Ferguson and the Transformationals are any more influential among the world's movers and shakers than the spokespeople for other interest groups. Indeed, are they influential at all, or merely an entertaining curiosity?

(5) *Think Globally, Act Effectively.* Ferguson's final complaint is not a complaint at all; but hearty agreement that we connect some disconnected yins and yangs. She then goes on to announce that, "Everywhere I hear people quoting Rene Dubos: 'Think globally, act locally'," which may be a disconnected yin and yang, but might better be seen as a trendy cliche, and more evidence of the prevailing Way of the Sandbox. Of course we should try to think holistically in global terms (while recognizing the difficulties in attaining this ideal); however, we should act not only in our local community, but appropriately at all levels of the global community — and in the most effective way. Rather than evidencing attempts to transcend the cliche barrier, the widespread deification of the Dubos slogan suggests that we have not yet begun to move very far from T-I to T-II.

Ferguson concludes with the wish that I could meet "the hundreds of thousands of hardworking visionary people" whom she has met in the past few years. I have little doubt that there are such numbers of fine people, just as I have no doubt at all that solar energy is abundant and could readily satisfy the world's energy needs. But we have not yet harnessed solar power in a cost-effective way, although promising developments in the price and performance of photovoltaic cells are in the offing. Similarly, the energy for widespread social change is abundant and widespread, but we have yet to harness it effectively — and the task of doing so is probably more difficult than that of harnessing solar energy, which is more readily measured and less subject to illusions. One indicator of the necessary evolution from T-I to T-II will be the moment when advocates of social change begin to speak in terms of outcomes, rather than merely the inputs of hardworking people.

Perhaps I am quite wrong. As editor of *Future Survey*, I look widely for evidence of change in the books of more than 150 publishers, several dozen general interest magazines, several newspapers, and more than 100 scholarly and professional journals. I try to look at everything, but necessarily fall far short of this ideal. Perhaps, somewhere in printed form, there is a compelling evidence that the Transformation is taking place to a substantial degree, or even some evidence of a significant change of images and paradigms that would precede such change. I invite Ferguson — or anyone else — to point out this evidence, or discuss the problems in collecting it. Perhaps the Transformation is happening, and the empirical work to supplement the intuitive pronouncements simply remains to be done. But why isn't it done? If the change is so momentous, why aren't hordes of social scientists measuring it and arguing about it? Might it be possible that the Transformation is not happening at all, but that a fair number of middle-class professionals have been led into a religious trance with the soothing idea that it *is* happening? Ferguson and others may be doing the movement for a better world more harm than good by keeping people at the T-I level, rather than pushing them up to the maturity of T-II.

To conclude with a remarkably apt verse from Kipling:

> This season's Daffodil,
> She never hears
> What change, what chance, what chill,
> Cut down last year's;
> But with bold countenance,
> And knowledge small,
> Esteems her seven days' continuence
> To be perpetual.

III

THE PROBLEM OF

A POLITICAL ELITE?

The popular American sensibility distrusts elitism, especially in politics. Although revisionist historians point to the patrician predilections of several of our Founding Fathers, the common view remains that our nation was conceived on the principles of the purest egalitarianism. (How easy to forget that the voting franchise was not fully extended to women until 1920 and that some of our citizens must still fight for their right to vote!) Any notion of a political elite — whether it be Plato's philosophers or Nietzsche's supermen — seems repugnant, not to say dangerously akin to the totalitarian regime of Nazi Germany. Still, human experience tells us that though all persons may be "created equal," history does produce figures who are clearly superior to their contemporaries and who thus gain a status and authority which merit attention and may even command our respect and obedience. Such people seem more fully "realized," more truly and completely alive — a Gandhi, for example, a Jesus or a Mozart. Such people strike us as "superior" precisely because they do not make us feel "lessened" or inferior. To meet such people is to become enriched rather than diminished.

In Abraham Maslow's phrase, these elite persons might be described as "self-actualized." Characteristically, self-actualized people have transcended self-centered concerns and ego-defenses aimed at preserving fragile identities. But if that is the case, could a self-actualized elite have any impact at all on politics? Maslow tackles this and a host of related issues in a piece entitled "Politics 3." Originally assembled and edited from Maslow's unpublished journals by Robert E. Kantor for the Educational Policy Research Center of the Stanford Research Institute, I edited "Politics 3" further for publication in the *Journal of Humanistic Psychology* (Fall, 1977). During the course of these journal-entries, Maslow makes a number of suggestions about what he calls "growth-politics." The primary task of such politics, Maslow contends, is to transcend, but not abolish, national sovereignty in favor of a more holistic, inclusive species-politics.

Along the way, "Politics 3" also offers some reflections on the good/ evil issue. Maslow chides humanistic psychologists who claim there is no instinct for evil in human nature because, as he notes, such a position forces the conclusion that all evil comes from outside human nature. This Maslow rejects as "modern Rousseauism." The truth of the matter, Maslow suggests, is that evil cannot be entirely blamed on either human nature or "culture" (technology, social conditions, etc.).

Where then do self-actualized "good people" come from? Not, Adrianne Aron argues, from Maslow's eupsychian politics. In "Maslow's Other Child," Aron wonders whether "self-actualization" is not really "self-indulgence." She is especially critical of Maslow's principle of individual sovereignty. In theory, such a principle should give rise to toleration, to heightened awareness of other's needs for freedom and self-expression. But Aron is convinced that Maslovian actualization and sovereignty lead instead to a solipsism so intense it pulls people away from larger social concerns. Her prime example of such solipsism is the Bay Area hippie culture of the 1960s.

Aron claims that Maslow influenced the hippie culture through a dualistic concept of the self. On the one hand, Aron argues, Maslow viewed the self as sovereign and inviolable. This "democratic premise" derived from his conviction that all people are equal in that they have an inviolable right to choose for themselves what they like. On the other hand, Maslow believed that some choices are superior to others. Such an "aristocratic premise" stems from his belief that some choices are more dignified and worthy — and thus implicitly more human — than others. As Aron sees it, Maslow's vision of what constitutes "good politics" is developed from this aristocratic premise, which assumes a basic inequality among people.

Not every commentator on Maslow's work agrees with Aron's critique. In a response entitled "Comment on 'Maslow's Other Child'," Charles Hampden-Turner contends that Aron's attempt to link Maslow with the Bay Area hippies constitutes "guilt by remotest of associations." Self-actualization as Maslow understood it, writes Hampden-Turner, has nothing to do with solipsistic self-interest; it was, rather, his attempt "to overcome the false dichotomies between selfish and unselfish, equality and excellence, real and ideal, inner and outer, individualism and cooperation." Maslow's conviction that some choices and values are "superior/better/more human" is, in fact, a move toward democracy rather than aristocratic elitism. For a truly superior work — in art, literature or music, for example — actually evokes our imagination and thus establishes a more democratic relation between artist and public.

The possible application of Maslow's theory of self-actualization to politics is taken up by Stephen Woolpert in his "A Comparison of Rational Choice and Self-Actualization Theories of Politics." Rational choice theory explains only political behavior; it is content simply to verify what people do. In contrast, humanistic political psychology of the sort promoted by Maslow and others insists that "the proper way to explain politics is to identify the human purposes, needs and values that make politics intelligible."

A politics that stresses humanistic values must begin with the recognition that human nature is itself in process. Far from being a fixed and finished reality, human nature is constantly created through the activity of human beings themselves. This is the argument of Walter Nord's "A Marxist Critique of Humanistic Psychology." Nord believes that psychology needs to be corrected by Marx's stress on the need for a social system in which all members develop together.

Finally, Allan R. Buss explores humanistic psychology as "liberal ideology" by examining the social-historical roots of Maslow's theory of self-actualization. As an historical movement, humanistic psychology began, Buss explains, as a liberal reaction to conservatism in both personal and political life. Unfortunately for the movement, success has led to the adoption of its language and rhetoric by government and industry. As an ironic and unintentional result, what began as "liberal" ends by maintaining the social reality from which liberation was sought. Like Nord, Buss criticizes humanistic psychology for neglecting greater social concerns. "Getting better" at the personal and individual level will not guarantee an improved social order nor will it resolve pressing global concerns like war and peace, hunger and overpopulation, racism and human rights.

As this discussion about "the problem of the political elite" begins, Abraham Maslow is being interviewed by Mildred Hardeman.

🌳   🌳   🌳

MILDRED HARDEMAN, *Dialogue with Abraham Maslow*

In the spring of 1962, Abraham Maslow came to The New School for Social Research in New York City to talk with the students in a course I was teaching. Because the news of Maslow's visit had spread, many students from other classes joined us. Before Maslow's appearance, an afternoon was set aside to prepare the students. Sheldon Lublin and I outlined Maslow's psychology, and after explanation and discussion, students were given the opportunity to write the questions they wished to ask of Maslow. The questions I ask in the dialogue were compiled from the queries of the students. The following is an edited version of the tape of the dialogue.

Bertha Maslow has graciously consented to the publication of this material. She has indicated that it will eventually be placed, along with other Maslow material, in the Archives of the History of American Psychology, University of Akron, Akron, Ohio 44325.

🌳

Question: You've made a distinction between the kind of creativeness that is the heritage of all human beings, and the special creative talent of a Spinoza or Beethoven. Would you describe further the creativity that we all potentially have?

Maslow: First of all, may I say that this is something of a pious pilgrimage. These very things that I'm talking about today really took their start here at The New School. They began when I came from the Midwest, as an experimental psychologist, to the seminars of Max Wertheimer, who all alone formed the best psychology department in the world. It was in a lecture that he called "Being and Doing," on Taoism, Lao-tze, and Zen Buddhism. I'd never even heard the words before. And this is what started me off, and a lot of other people as well.

About the creativeness, I want to be as empirical as possible. We have no maps. Still, the scientific spirit here would be the eager and humble submission to the facts.

Our universal creativeness should be called by a different name, because it is not the same as the great inborn talent in an occasional Schubert or Mozart. One source of evidence is children. It is a matter of watching children in the new type of education through art. I was so astonished — this is a personal thing, it always is — that these children could do what I couldn't do. I tried, God knows. I took classes in art and did an exercise and was very pleased with myself. Then my two little girls admired this so much that they wanted to copy it, and they went zip, zip, and made my thing look so foolish and awkward that I never touched it again. We must all recognize as a miracle the fact that they can do many things that we cannot do. For instance, if we ask children to get up on the table and make up a dance, they would do it. If I had to do it, I'd die!

This is the kind of creativeness that I could see in psychiatrically healthy people such as Max Wertheimer. They have a certain child-like quality, the same kind of easy spontaneity, this ability to adapt very easily to a problem in its own nature, the same kind of ability to improvise that young children have.

Question: Is it possible to bring about peak experiences directly?

Maslow: The data that we have are really very scrappy. "Peak experience" is a made-up word, but it is parallel to words that have been used for thousands of years, by various people under various headings: mystic experiences in the West; satori, samadhi, nirvana, and the like in the East. On the whole, the evidence from the religious investigators, and now from the beginnings of empirical investigators, is that you cannot bring about peak experiences directly. C. S. Lewis wrote a book on this called *Surprised by Joy* and that's about the way of it. It looks as if we can increase the probabilities, but can never make a certainty.

I would certainly be very wary about the possibilities of drug-induced and electrode-induced peak experiences, which apparently we can now do in white rats. Peak experiences that really change the person come about where they are earned. The person comes to some glorious insight as the result of a year of sweating on a psychoanalytic couch; or a philosopher who has been working for fifteen years at some problem comes to an illumination.

If we exclude the electrodes and drugs, then there are some possible generalizations about increasing the probabilities. For one thing, it seems clear that with greater psychological health, simply being a finer and more fully human person, peak experiences come as epiphenomena, unsought-for by-products.

Also, it is possible to choose your way of life. For example, I think a doctor delivering babies would be more likely to have peak experiences than a process server. It's easier also if you are an honest man than if you are a crook.

One of my graduate students and I have been playing around with the idea of peakers and non-peakers. We found a few people who reported that they had not had peak experiences. Also Freud, in *Civilization and Its Discontents* disavows what he called the "oceanic" experience. Some friend of his had reported that he had it, and Freud in a characteristically reductive way said, "Well, this is a childish business," and probably prescribed bicarbonate of soda.

Now we feel that all human beings have peak experiences, even feeble-minded people. Probably the non-peakers are those who are afraid of the experience and have had to renounce it. It is very understandable, because it means a giving up of normal consciousness with which we control ourselves. Borderline schizophrenics or obsessive-compulsive people, for example, are always afraid to lose control. And many laboratory scientists tend to say that if you can't quantify a thing and find it in the laboratory, it doesn't exist.

Question: How is it possible for each of us to help other people in their quest for self-actualization?

Maslow: I think this is obviously too much to attempt to say. There is a real literature on this, where one could pick up literally thousands of suggestions. In general, it looks as if the best way to help other people grow toward self-actualization is to become a good person yourself. Trying to help other people can be a way of avoiding our own troubles. I can deny that I am hostile, for example, by going and helping everybody else not to be hostile. A more humble approach is better. Clean your own doorstep first. That would guard you against hurting other people and being phony and dishonest. Also, it would automatically produce all sorts of good results because "to move toward self-actualization" means to move toward realism of perception, spontaneity, a particular kind of humor, and so on.

The writings of a whole group of people are available. It's interesting that these, some of them revolutionary documents, are a deep secret from the official world of letters. Carl Rogers' book, for instance, *On Becoming a Person,* is loaded with answers at various levels for this question. It's never been reviewed, so far as I know, except in the professional journals of the American Psychological Association, who pan it all the time because it's not laboratory work. Probably future historians will mark this era with that book and those of Erich Fromm.

I would recommend the few journals that now quite specifically try to answer that question. One is the *Journal of Humanistic Psychology,* which is the more empirical effort. And for the layman, I would recommend the magazine called *Manas.* It tries to bring to bear all the resources of contemporary knowledge on the problem of making a better society and a better human being. I have found that for about half of my freshman students and the high school kids that my daughters brought home *Manas* breaks through their blase, world-weary attitude. Of course, this world-weary outlook is a defense against their own frustrated idealism. I've been giving *Manas* to the freshman like pills.

Question: Have you any changes to suggest in adult education to help their growth toward self-actualization?

Maslow: I think that at the lower levels, at age three, four, five, and six, we're doing fine right now. I think we have failed worst in grade schools and high schools. Although it's a little too impractical, I would recommend as a kind of beginning, the book by Paul Goodman, *Growing Up Absurd*. Education needs to be more in accordance with what we know of human nature. I would hope for a college that did not grant degrees and had no compulsions of any kind, because I believe that people at the college level, if they have not been destroyed, know better what's good for their growth than the professors do.

Self-education is another story altogether, and is always possible under any circumstances. Even in college I would maintain that if you have some vision of your goals, then the means to it are easily found. Then you can use even bad instructors. I hope that some of the people now called "third force" or "humanistic" or "existential" psychologists are thinking of working up manuals for self-education, self-therapy, and self-growth.

Question: In your book, *Toward a Psychology of Being*, you indicated that pain and suffering can be conducive to growth. How is it possible to grow through pain and suffering rather than to become bitter?

Maslow: In the first place, most people become bitter. We don't generally recommend pain and suffering, not only for obvious reasons, but also because pain and suffering are apt to crack the person rather than strengthen him. But there are some fortunate people who are strengthened.

I've never thought about the question in exactly this phrasing, but what comes to me is the superficiality of our whole culture — the young people, the affluent, and spoiled people. That includes most of us at most ages. Even the more intellectual of us, the more earnest, even the nicest people, tend too much to be superficial.

The traditional religions have pretty well died, and they were the ones that used to take care of the serious problems of life. A new religion that can attract intelligent people has not yet been made. There is no official way in our culture of really being serious. The priests of the present society are really the psychoanalysts who deal with pain, anguish, dread of death, how to make a serious life for oneself, how to handle one's own evil.

We psychologists are now becoming dimly aware for the first time of what human beings can be like, and we realize that friendship and intimacy are practically absent in our society. It is often said that Americans are very friendly; but people don't ordinarily dare to look seriously at their relationships, because if they did, there would be the profoundly hurtful feeling of being utterly alone in the world as you realize that you don't have a real friend.

But it *is* possible to have very beautiful and fulfilling relationships. They happen in a fraction of one percent of the population. It may be that we'll work out techniques in the next decade or two for fostering relationships.

I think that Freud certainly was correct in his basic postulate. First face the truth, and that'll bring pain.

Question: You spoke of a possible new religion in the future. Would you clarify that?

Maslow: In three sentences, no. We don't have a vocabulary. Our words have become meaningless. I was once in a group of three professional theologians and three avowed atheists, and everybody got confused. It turned out that these very intelligent theologians had renounced the definition of God as a man with a beard and were laughing at me for fighting the 1890 picture of God. Tillich defines religion as concern with ultimate concerns, and I become puzzled because that's the way I define psychology!

People like Carl Rogers and Erich Fromm are now making a picture of human nature and life which is being seized upon by the advanced theologians. What will be coming along in a decade or so, I'm not quite sure. But certainly it will have a real respect for human nature, not regarding it as totally evil. Truth and goodness and beauty are inherent in human nature. They don't have to be given to us from outside. Well, with that kind of basic postulate, which these three theological deans agreed with, I think we have some notion of what's coming.

Question: One final question. Would you tell us what aspect of your work you're most interested in at present?

Maslow: What I'm most interested in, and what I would suggest that you be most interested in, is what I've been calling the psychology of Being. In an article called "Notes on Being-Psychology," I tried to lay the groundwork for the research that must come next.

The psychology of Being is defined there as the study of ends rather than means, and the study of the human being insofar as he is an end, not insofar as he is useful. It is the study of those situations which produce in us "end" experiences, which are valid in themselves — just good because they're good. Nobody has ever studied them in a scientific way. For the first time in human history, if we can manage it, we would begin to have an *empirical* science of ultimate value.

Our values are what give us direction in life. And so this is really the study of the directions in which we *must* go if we are to have such and such experiences which we would all like to have.

❦   ❦   ❦

ABRAHAM MASLOW, *Politics 3*

Introduction

At times it seems as though the Growth Centers and revolutionary youth both agree on discarding the worth and value of rationality. They seem to overemphasize the senses and emotions, and they exaggerate the number of people who are "up tight" in the United States and who need release from inhibitions without considering that many people need more inhibitions rather than less (impulse disorders, psychopaths, immature, feebleminded, and so forth). They often tend to be too exclusively Dionysian, regarding logic, science, education, and the like as imprisonment, with feeling and sensory experience, rather than knowledge, as the wellspring of their motivations. They stress impulsive expressiveness, mistaking it for healthy spontaneity. They agree in mistrusting power and authority, defining them both in an extremely low way (i.e., as dominating, and not recognizing that authority and power can be humanistic and transcendent). They believe that if one lifts the restraints and allows absolute freedom that only good will result, which means (implies) an unfounded faith in basic human goodness and an implied belief that evil comes only from social restraints and inhibitions. They do not have enough respect for the profound instinctive needs of safety, security, law, order, keeping the peace; and they do not realize that without these needs, freedom is impossible. They think of power as evil, not realizing that they must temper, restrain, and control the forces of inhumanity and chaos within the human soul. They agree in lacking intimacy and a sense of community, and keep on seeking it unconsciously. They tend to be short-term, here-now, impatient, and they do not realize that education, persuasion, becoming a good person, and developing a good society, are all lifetime tasks requiring a large segment in time.

The problem with compassion, charity, agapean love, understanding, patience, and so forth, especially in its U.S. liberal version (the weak liberals, that is), is that some persons identify it with weakness, a lack of force, and a rejection of force. But my theory of evil at this point says that force, aggression, indignation, and so forth, can be healthy as well as unhealthy, and that they can be used well, or used badly, and that one could be the kindest man in the world and also be firm, strong, and decisive in the face of evil and not give in at all. This is humanistic realism at the B-level, accepting and understanding human nature as it is at its various levels of development. And it seems precisely the self-actualizing person who can most cathartically let loose the full force of his or her anger with the least amount of guilt, conflict, and ambivalence.

However, we can learn from history about the danger of the philosopher-king, the one who is so superior, so aggrandizing, and so competent, that other people become dehumanized, overprotected, enfeebled, and do not develop their own teeth and claws and muscles. Any humanistic leader has to take as part of his job the fullest development of the potentialities, strength, leadership, and self-actualization of everybody.

We accept that growth must be with the consent of the population, which means education in the broadest sense, including "education" for the retarded, the immature, and so forth. This may require, for example, talking in parables that the simplest man can understand at some level, but which are also true at the highest level. Thus, the skills of the humanistic politician must include approaches that go beyond those of the scholars and scientists. He must know how to reach and educate the feebleminded, the prejudiced, the racist, the militant, the violent, and the fearful.

If we recognize as a basic value the consent of the governed by all levels of education, then we must be prepared also to learn and teach patient waiting, and recognize that educating for the revolution and evolution of man must be slow because education is slow, and therapy is slow.

Politics 3 asserts that the real problem is of personal goodness, that is, of producing good human beings. We should now consider ourselves self-evolvers. This is a new age, a new era in the history of mankind, because now we can decide ourselves what we are to become. It is not nature of evolution or anything else that will decide. We must decide, and we must evolve ourselves, shape ourselves, grow ourselves; we must be conscious of our goals, values, ethics, and the direction in which we want to go.

That raises questions of: How do we measure these things? Is it possible to measure? What are the indicators of growing goodness in the population? What is the technology of becoming good? What are the strategy and tactics of growing better human beings? There are Gallup-type tests that would indicate the social, moral, and spiritual states of the population — whether it is going up or down, and so forth. There are also experimental methods, like the "lost letter" technique to test whether people would bother to go to the mailbox to mail it; or strewing beer cans around the picnic area to see how many people would pick them up to put them into the garbage can.

There is some evidence that the extreme right and the extreme left, and a lot of other people in between, share many of the same ultimate goals. We need to explore and develop this sharing into a universalistic value system; no peace and no world law is possible until we have a stated, shared value system. And there are good examples of it: conservatives would probably agree with so-called New Left people on such values as individualism and maximum freedom for self-actualization of the individual. They and the humanistic politicians would agree also on as much local self-determination as possible; as much decentralization as possible; and as much sense of involvement, achievement, and effectiveness from the grass roots as possible. One could go further eventually with this and try to establish a way of building a representative democracy, and ask the question: Is it possible to start with intimacy groups — T-groups for instance — or communities small enough to have town hall meetings, and then to have such groups on a face-to-face basis elect a representative to the next hierarchy of, let us say, the 5,000 people level which, in turn, would elect to the next higher level, and so forth?

This might be another branch of our present government, to supplement it. Or it might, one day, work toward a direction as a way of electing our senators, and the president. It might be helpful to obtain the Boy Scout oath, the New Left platform, the SDS Manifesto, the Ayn Rand manifestos, the Goldwater programs, and so forth to show how much these are similar. This method could be a start of trying to write down the universalistic ethics.

Politics 3 stands with Aldous Huxley when he declares:

> . . . that everlastingly possible psychological condition, which is the individual's *metanoia*, or change of mind, out of the temporal into the eternal order. And to my mind there is not the faintest prospect of any enduring improvement in human affairs until a larger minority than at present, or in the past, decides that it is worthwhile to bring about the change of mind within itself. The most one can hope to do by means of social reform and rearrangement of economic and political and educational patterns is to remove some of the standing temptations towards remaining with mind unchanged. We pray to be delivered from temptation, because experience shows that, if we are tempted often and strongly enough, we almost inevitably fall. A social rearrangement which shall remove some of the current temptations towards power-lust, covetousness, emotional incontinence, mental distraction, uncharitableness and pride will make it a little easier for the individual man and woman to achieve their final end. The social function of the artist or intellectual, as I see it, is to suggest means for mitigating the strength of the temptations which, now and in the past, the social order has forced upon the individual, luring him away from his true end towards other, necessarily self-stultifying and destructive goals.

One must be careful to reject here most of the talk about the technological problems of lengthening life, improving medical care, promoting ecology, reducing poverty, improving food quality, and so forth, by stressing as strongly as possible that these are amoral questions in the sense that these questions could just as easily have been raised in Hitler's cabinet if he had won the war. Longer life spans, better fabrics, better shoes, and the like are purely technological problems that have nothing to do with ultimate values, morals, and ethics.

The following thoughts were presented by Daniel Patrick Moynihan in his article, "Politics as the Art of the Impossible."

> What is it that government cannot provide? It cannot provide values to persons who have none, or who have lost those they had. It cannot provide a meaning to life.

> It cannot provide inner peace. It can provide moral
> energies, but it cannot create those energies. In partic-
> ular, government cannot cope with the crisis in values
> that is sweeping the western world . . . To the con-
> trary, politics is an expression of morality: a form of
> morality. But it cannot create moral values any more
> than a steel mill can create iron ore . . . It would seem
> that what we have to do is to create a secular morality,
> acceptable to the non-religious, that accommodates
> itself to what man will actually do, which is to say, per-
> sists in the face of imperfection.

In effect, what Moynihan is saying is that the job of providing values
and the secular morality belongs to people other than the politicians. I
would rather say that this problem belongs to everybody, but especially the
psychologists and philosophers. One can describe Politics 3, ideal politics, as part of the creation of a secular morality. That is, the Eusychian
ideal of society as a fostering of human fulfillment is part of the secular
morality. The two main problems of creating the good person and the good
society are interwoven inextricably. Only a clear vision of these interwoven goals can serve as the basis for a secular morality and, therefore, for a
political and social philosophy that will tell what direction to go, what to
do, how to do it, and what needs to be done.

Secular morality helps get the work of the world done, below the level
of government. It allows the decision-making, managerial, and unifying
roles of government to be accomplished, but it also fosters *reindividualiz-
ing,* the placing of more and more responsibilities and power on the shoul-
ders of individual people at the grass roots, making them feel like active
agents rather than pawns, and making them feel effective and heard. In this
regard, many different groups in America agree in valuing decentralization, local town hall meetings, and "power to the people." This includes
channeling responsibility for different tasks to various equipped private
institutions; to small clubs, groups, families, small foundations, and
finally to single individuals who would pursue some cause which they
themselves want to pursue. There was a saying during World War II: "If
you aren't part of the solution, you're part of the problem." Today, this
might be reversed: "If you aren't part of the problem, maybe you're part of
the solution." If you do your own job well, that is to say homeostatic politics, if you keep doing your own job well, then this is the necessary (but far

from sufficient) basis on which all growth and improvement in politics rests.

Politics 3 is against adversary justice and law; amoral science; lower need economics; jungle journalism; medicine from above; technologized nursing; separative expertness; docility education; antitranscendent religion; intrusive and non-Taoistic social work; nonpersonal psychology and sociology; nonparticipatory ethnology; merely punishing criminology and jails; selfishly antisocial advertising business and industry; business-first radio and television; health as merely survival; the use of personal talents or superiorities primarily to acquire selfish privileges; the use of other human beings without regard to their personal growth; antiquality manufacturing; noncompassionate radicalism; polarizing of relations between classes, castes, subcultures; nonsynergic salesman-customer relationships; and despair art.

Politics 3 is against all that rests on a merely evil conception of human nature or of society, or on a merely good conception of human nature or of society; despair and hopelessness; any we-they polarizing; malice, hatred, revenge; the wish for one's own death or the destruction of others, or of the world; any splitting of humankind into inherent classes, castes, or subcultures; and the assumption that any polarizations or splits which do exist are inherent and permanent.

One of the clear questions for the normative social psychologist, and one that we would now add to our Politics 3 ideas, is the necessity for integrating the advantages of bigness with the advantages of smallness while avoiding the disadvantages of both. This can be done, or at least is being attempted with more or less success, especially in the business world, and we have much to learn from it.

As a simple model, we could consider the way in which it is being worked at the college and university level. First is the Berkeley phenomenon of the huge, monster, centralized bureaucratic giant in which feedback and customer satisfaction have been lost entirely and in which there is communication only downward and not at all upward. The impersonality, the feeling of helplessness, the feeling of being a pawn rather than an agent, and the feeling of not being heard, of having no control over one's fate — these are all consequences of such an impersonalized, huge bureaucratic organization. The same was true at Columbia, perhaps even worse, where the president, the trustees, the administration in general, did not have the slightest idea of what was going on among the customers (i.e., the students) or even the faculty.

On the national political scene we can consider as models for bureaucratic monstrosity the governments of France and of Soviet Russia. In both countries, there has been total centralization with all sorts of consequent inefficiencies, stupidities, incitement of rage, feelings of helplessness, and so forth. Again the missing element is upward communication (i.e., feedback from the customers, knowledge of customer wishes). It is interesting that in both countries this system has broken down after never working well. What is being instituted is almost inevitably a greater communication upward, local control, decentralization, planning after feedback from the customers. It can all be summarized in one phrase, individual self-choice. It is important to retain at least the advantage of smallness: the individual person is given a choice from among alternatives and then expresses his own preference by his act of buying or registering in a particular class in college, or "voting" with his feet by migrating, and the like. Democratic management (Theory Y, enlightened management) can be seen from this point of view as essentially participatory, localized, decentralized democracy with consequent excellent customer feedback, with control at the individual, personal, grass roots level.

However, it is important to emphasize that this is a matter of attitude. An authoritarian system or person does not ask or listen or solicit feedback; he tells or orders, or makes pronouncements, without getting feedback evaluation, satisfaction, assessment, evaluation, or knowledge of "techmatic" consequences (i.e., of how it actually works). The democratic attitude, which goes deeply into both the individual character and the social arrangements, arises from a profound attitude of respect for other people. We might even say compassion, or agapean love, or openness to others: the willingness to listen, indeed, the eagerness to listen, with the final consequence of freely giving to the other person the opportunity for real self-choice from among real alternatives. Another name for this democratic attitude is "Taoistic respect," which arises from not shaping, manipulating, bossing, or controlling others, but rather from respecting them enough to allow them and encourage them to please themselves by expressing their preferences and choices.

The heart of this as far as humanistic politics or humanistic ethics is concerned, is the derivation of social and technological machinery from the profoundly psychologic and individual phenomenon of the democratic character structure (contrasted with the authoritarian character structure). Democratic, self-actualizing people need a political system in which they experience having an effect, being heard, being understood, making things happen, being effective agents rather than pawns. This is the opposite of feeling helpless, controlled, maneuvered, or dominated. An authoritarian system and authoritarian individuals produce the latter effects on a person; democratic systems and democratic individuals produce the former effects on individual persons. It is not difficult to understand why people, given a choice between the two, with real experiencing of the two, will practically always choose the democratic person and the democratic society. Democratic, compassionate, loving, respecting, growth-enjoying attitudes in strong persons are growth-fostering and self-fulfilling in weaker persons. In other words, political, social, and management machinery can be deduced from humanistic psychology.

Social and political mechanisms which would enhance desirable personal consequences (from the data available) are:

1. Communication upward as well as downward. People want to be heard and to feel that they are heard; they want to express their feelings and judgments about the issues, and especially about those who are closely personal (i.e., the issues that affect the running of their own lives).

2. They would like to be masters over their own fate and their own lives, as much as possible in a complex culture and contingent universe.

3. Involvement enhances these feelings. All this equals increased participation, responsibility, involvement, and numbers of choices and decisions.

All of these desiderata call for a general increase of the power at the grass roots (i.e., at the personal and local level of political organization). They call for an increase in powers, rights, duties, and responsibilities for local organizations, and a decentralization of power wherever this is functional and useful. This implies the need for more participatory democracy and less delegated or represented democracy.

Of course all this has to be functional and, therefore, there is the additional principle of social, political, and economic efficiency that needs to be considered when the decision is made about what should be centralized and what should be decentralized. That is, that should be decentralized which is best and most efficiently achieved at the face-to-face level at the local level, at the neighborhood or community level. That should be centralized which is most efficiently achieved at the state level, the national level, or the world level.

Also, there is convincing expert opinion that the stress merely and solely on "my rights and liberties" tends to produce pawns rather than active agents, dependent rather than independent individuals, boys rather than men, helpless rather than responsible self-deciders and self-choosers. There should be added to this statement about "my rights and liberties" the additional statement, integrated with the rights and liberties, "my duties and responsibilities and necessary decisions."

For grass roots psycho-political organization, my suggestion is that the most basic module of social organization (beyond the individual himself) would be the equivalent of a T-group, that is, a face-to-face group moving toward intimacy and candor, valuing self-disclosure and caring feedback. This, of course, might in various situations, be the extended (or somewhat extended) nuclear family. Perhaps one day it will be both (i.e., one day the accepted way of knitting together and extending a family will be T-group techniques). When that is so, there also will have to be these same stresses on honesty, intimacy, authenticity, self-exposure, feedback, as much trust as realistically warranted, and so forth, in all other social organizations in which the individual participates.

For instance, there is little question that much of formal education will have to be based on these techniques and these goals. Perhaps the normal class size will be about ten to twelve or fourteen students, which so far seems to be about the most desirable optimal size for achieving Eupsychian organizational ends. College dormitories, and perhaps future dormitories at lower educational levels, could be organized upward on this basic T-group-of-twelve module. Architecturally, this group can live together in such a way as to enhance T-group goals.

The same is also true for religious, semireligious, and postreligious groups, interest groups, professional groups, and most other groups. For larger political purposes, larger groups can be built up by pooling two T-groups, or three or four, ten or twenty, or whatever the case may be according to the needs of the situation. The size of the total group should again be dictated by simple efficiency (i.e., which jobs are best performed by a group of twelve, by a group of one hundred, or by a group of ten thousand, and so forth).

This leaves open the question about the participatory face-to-face groups and the larger groupings which are built out of them. How are they to choose their representatives when larger representative democracy becomes most desirable because it is most efficient? For some purposes, such as the equivalent of electing a president of a nation, one-person-one-vote would probably function best. For other purposes, however, there might well be voting only by the chosen representative of the T-group, of the hundred group, of the thousand group, etc. This, like many other things, has to be worked out experimentally and in actual experience.

Current politics at every level tend to be atomistic rather than holistic. The most important example of atomism is national sovereignty, which many scholars conceive to be *the* main condition for wars, and the certain guarantee that wars are inevitable. The main task of growth-politics is to transcend (not abolish) national sovereignty in favor of a more holistic inclusive species-politics.

The atomism, separatism, and mutual exclusiveness of national sovereignties is seen as systemic rather than symptomatic (i.e., the atomistic, separative way of cognizing, valuing, socializing, and acting is deeply embedded in the blood and bones of most, but not all, living people everywhere; in all departments of life; in all interpersonal relationships; in intrapsyhic relationships; in relations to nature and to the physical world; even in [Aristotelian] logic and [analyzing] science; even in the most common conceptions of love, marriage, friendship, and family). Often these relationships are seen unconsciously as adversary or zero-sum, counter-synergic (i.e., who dominates and who submits) or, "my advantage must be your disadvantage."

But even where this mutual exclusiveness between two individuals, or within a family, is transcended so that they become a holistic One, it is most frequently (in the world) achieved at the cost of making the group, club, or the family (clan, tribe, class, nationality, religion, or racial group) into an internally coherent, cooperative, friendly, loyal, need-pooling group by making it mutually exclusive from the rest of the world.

In the past, the main technique mankind has had for achieving amity within a group has been to see all the nongroup, the "they," as more or less an enemy. That is, atomistic people become allies because they have a common enemy, if not a threatening or dangerous enemy, then one toward whom they feel superior, righteous, contemptuous, condescending, and attacking. The ultimate absurdity is that this seems to be true for most peace and antiwar groups (with honorable exceptions). All polarizing, splitting, excluding, dominating, hurting, hating, insulting, anger-producing, vengeance-producing, put-down techniques are atomistic and antiholistic and therefore help to separate humankind into mutually hostile groups. They are countergrowth and make species-politics less possible, put off the attainment of One World Law and government, and are war-fostering and peace-delaying.

Moving toward specieshood and species politics means profound holisticizing of ourselves, each of us, of our interpersonal relationships, of subcultures, of societies and nations, of our relationships with not only our own species but with other species as well, and with nature and the cosmos as a whole. It means moving toward holism in each of our professions (e.g., away from adversary law, politics, economics, and so forth) in each of our atomistic, separate fields of knowledge. The holistic movement must occur also for each of our social institutions, religion, work and management, education, and administration of justice.

Against this overcondensed background, I wish to make one specific proposal: T-groups (encounter groups, sensitivity training, and so forth), as well as different other techniques now used in growth centers, and summarized as Esalen-type education, should be used toward holisticizing the society and eventually the world. This began already with the NTL Institute's mix-max groups (i.e., forming T-groups with people who are as diverse as possible). It seems possible, however, to accomplish more in this direction; a better example is the use of black-white confrontation groups.

The suggestion implies also a thorough re-examination of the widely accepted principle of homogamy. We have much data to indicate that, for example, the more similar people are in their background, class, caste, religion, education, national origin, race, the more likely it is that their marriage will be happy and will endure. This is assumed to be true for all interpersonal relationships, friendships, business partnerships, neighborhoods, and neighbors.

It is true that we feel more comfortable and relaxed, less tense, uneasy and uncertain, less suspicious and paranoid, less alien, less wary, with someone who has our tastes, our folkways, our prejudices, and so forth. It is easier to organize our lives to maximize contact with persons having similar interests and to minimize contact with persons having dissimilar interests.

But if the necessity for holisticizing mankind is accepted, this way of making our lives easier and more comfortable can be seen as a "cop out," a weak fleeing from confronting the uncomfortable but necessary issue: If we wish to move toward specieshood and brotherhood, how do we overcome our separative and encapsulating techniques? How do we transcend the differences that currently compartmentalize humankind into mutually exclusive, isolated groups who have nothing to do with each other? How do we make contacts across walls separating classes, religions, sexes, races, nationalities, tribes, professional groups, and IQ groups?

If we all agreed that this was a tremendous and urgent necessity requiring immediate action, we could solve the racial differences quite easily, at least in principle, by subsidizing heavily only interracial marriages. One day the emergency may be so great that even such measures may have to be tried. Already it has been suggested that the United States and USSR exchange large numbers of their children to guarantee against bombing each other.

Much more practicable, however, for the general purpose of transcending homogamy, would be the widespread use of T-groups as a holistic-political tool. There is presently enough successful experience with black-white T-groups to provide encouragement and guidelines for involving other separated groups in creative encounters.

The T-groups technique is suggested not because it is a panacea, but because it is available, widely used, and increasingly accepted. It is already functioning in educational teaching institutions, and there are trained facilitators and international contacts available.

In principle, it would be wise to keep in mind the end goal, the brotherhood of all human beings, rather than any particular single method. Any method is good that fosters communication, understanding, intimacy, trust, openness, honesty, self-exposure, feedback, awareness, compassion, tolerance, acceptance, friendliness, love, and that reduces suspicion, paranoid expectations, fear, feelings of being different, enmity, defensiveness, envy, contempt, insult, condescension, polarization, splitting, alienation, and separation.

In ideal terms, the Eupsychian State is one in which individual people left to their own devices, resources, and consciences will arrive at the same B-values and the same conclusions about the basic schema of life. Simultaneously, they will be allowed complete freedom for idiosyncracies, and differences in constitution, temperament, and the like, which fall well within the normal range of acceptable, healthy individual differences between people.

Currently, there are large numbers of value questions, both ethical and moral, that remain with the realm of individual differences, temperament, taste, judgment, constitution, personal history, cultural roots, and the like, and which are still to be left to individual conscience, taste, or judgment.

However, there are other questions that are not to be left to individual conscience (e.g., whether a baby is to be loved or not). This is an absolute for the species; babies have a right and a need to be loved. There is something of the sort also true for dignity and respect for all human beings, and certainly the same is true for the B-values. B-values are intrinsic values that are being discovered and introjected and made one's own by each person discovering and studying himself and his own depth individually and then reaching the same conclusion as other people.

For any humanistic politics, the process of reaching conclusions has to be developed carefully. It entails a kind of visual image that is like the "good way" of rearing babies and children (i.e., it is like being in an extremely large playpen that has definite limits, but has a large amount of space within the playpen in which individuality, permissiveness, Taoism, and let-be may prevail). It is the same matter of being extremely firm and unyielding about ultimate and intrinsic values while being yielding and permissive about all nonintrinsic values. This provides an area of life for individual taste and for the normal and healthy range of individual differences. It allows the individual to express his or her individuality; yet also it rejects firmly the Sartre-type relativity, which has no limits. These value limits are biological limits and come from the nature of human specieshood.

What can be said about the problem of human evil? If the humanistic psychologists say "there is no instinct for evil" or "there is no original sin," it leads to the mistake of the intellectuals in general saying that all evil must, therefore, come from outside human nature (i.e., from society, technology, other people, villains, exploiters, or whatever). This kind of modern Rousseauism is promulgated, oddly enough, by the same people who would reject Rousseauism as overoptimistic. Humanistic psychologists must face the task of explaining how human nature generates evil without itself being intrinsically evil. Perhaps we should be saying something like "all that we know about evil and human troubles and the shortcomings of people and society leads us finally to see that we can neither blame human nature entirely (as with the doctrine of original sin) nor can we blame society entirely (as with various brands of Rousseauism). But the way to handle the matter is via the bodhisattvic path, which means to say you must simultaneously and in tandem cleanse yourself and cleanse your society. The good society is useless, just as a blueprint in itself can be useless, unless there are relatively good people to implement it, carry it out, and live it through."

This permits another interpretation of current grumbles such as "this gratification did not make me happy and whole and autonomous and self-actualizing, therefore it's all a fake; it's of no importance; it's a swindle; it's evil." Such grumbles miss the point that the disillusionment was generated by illusions of which we had better rid ourselves. For instance, grumbling youngsters expect too much of the lower need gratifications, of the material life. They expect too much of sex and love, of having an auto, and money to spend, of having a house, going to school, having a degree, and so forth. But it should be made clear that all these were illusory expectations. Any humanistic psychology must make this extremely clear. The grumble theory should be developed more to show that the heaven — the nirvana; the permanent content and happiness; the permanent lack of pain, trouble, depression, and the like — must all be relinquished as expectations for human nature. There will always be grumbling, complaining, wanting, lacking, seeking, and striving. Any theory of utopia, or the good society, or the good person, must be based on this accepted fact. The fury with which some persons attack the whole society, calling it evil and horrible, and so forth, shows clearly a kind of cognitive pathology, an inability to see facts which stare us in the face. They complain loudly and bitterly, and at the same time they complain about not being able to complain (about not having free speech, for instance). Clearly these are disappointed, disillusioned people. And disillusion here clearly means that there were previous illusions; that is to say factual mistakes and unfounded beliefs or expectations.

To move ahead along our evolutionary road, there are several clear-cut steps we must take:

> The major institutions of influence must begin to characterize in their policies and practices a genuine belief in fellow men. They must show in their actions that all people can make valuable contributions to mutual growth and development. They will thereby end the process of "we will solve your problems" and begin to work together with others to solve mutual problems. Parents and teachers must begin to join with young people to grow and develop together. They must demonstrate in their actions a belief in dignity, respect, and self-affirmation for the young. These future adults will not develop or extend their inner blueprints fully through creative action until they truly believe in themselves and the beauty and goodness of their inner selves. Institutions such as mental hospitals and prisons, which should exist for the purpose of rehabilitating the occupants, must recognize the inherent dangers of their practices of "excluding" their charges. They must change to self-developmental forms of practice that recognize and use the values and goals of humanness existing in all individuals.

These are not idealistic dreams. Today there exist concrete techniques for bringing about self-understanding, expanded awareness, confluent education, and amplified use of imagination and judgment. We can catalyze the application of these techniques through a symphytic psychology which will allow people to become creators of value by means of their enhanced feelings of worth, dignity, capability, and being needed. We can begin to fill the unfulfilled promise of our greatest underdeveloped resource — humankind. As people begin to use the ethics and processes of symphysis, they will shed the artificial means of excluding a hierarchical identification to achieve growth. Since many more people will be able to develop their symphytic and creative capabilities, the desire to create artificial self-ascendancy and exploitative growth by devaluing others or by defensive banding together will be lessened.

In our search for the specific and particularized techniques for symphytic development, we can look today to those persons participating in intensive research in the development of human creativity. These techniques, aside from having made possible the discovery of the principle of symphysis, now provide tangible and immediate, if only beginning, answers to the problem of "how."

The far goal is to avoid war via One World, One Law. The precondition for this is a new image of human beings and a new image of society. Techniques of making higher persons and techniques of making higher societies have been mentioned: education, therapy, T-groups, the Eupsychian network, and the like.

As part of the scientific attitude, we suggest many schemes and experiments. Why not try all of them experimentally even at the same time? For instance why not have many colleges being run entirely by various groups such as the black militants, or the students themselves, while others could be run like military academies with complete discipline, or with extreme permissiveness, or anything in between. Then, we could watch them to observe how they function; we could try to learn from them, both the mistakes and the failures. Of course, the observing would have to be empirical in the sense of evaluation feedback, watching, evaluating, and assessing.

Let us consider the Bill of Rights as a precious psychological document, as a manifesto and a strategy of brotherly love. The Constitution, the Bill of Rights, and other documents of that kind can be seen and used as basic instruments in a revitalized technology of agapean love. They provide ways for a large heterogeneous nation to manage itself under extremely difficult conditions. It is difficult for two people to live together, let alone 200 million. Because we are different from each other and have not learned yet to accept these differences, constructing a society in a way to retain our autonomy, free choice, and permission to grow to full humanness will be difficult, and making the best possible compromise under these circumstances will never be a perfectly satisfactory compromise. We have not learned how to do that. However, I am proposing here that we conceive of politics as superordinate to other realms of thought such as authentic interpersonal relations, the authentic community, the brotherhood of man, because politics means essentially the actualization of the whole of life. In the same way, we could speak of "religionizing" the whole of life, instead of making it an atomistic, separate activity for one day of the week, occurring in one particular building and in the hands of one kind of person with the proper credentials. So too, the arrangements by which we can help each other, live with each other, and make divisions of labor might be called socializing the whole of life. Democratizing the whole of life and making a larger definition of it — the need to grow translated into the right to grow — is crucial for full humanness, for self-actualization.

🌣   🌣   🌣

ADRIANNE ARON, *Maslow's Other Child*

In his critique of Abraham Maslow's theory of self-actualization, Brewster Smith confesses that criticizing Maslow makes him feel as though he is "turning a howitzer on a butterfly." But Smith then goes on to argue that ethics and politics cannot and must not be ignored by a humanistic psychology. As he points to Maslow's neglect of these topics, the reader is led to suspect that this is perhaps no butterfly after all.
🌣

To examine some of the more menacing aspects of a pursuit of self-actualization that disregards political and ethical matters, I shall discuss here the dominant social pattern of the hippie movement in its early days. In the hippie pattern Maslow's dream of a compassionate, reciprocal, empathic, high-synergy scheme of interpersonal relations gets lost behind a reality of human exploitation. Where the theorist prescribed self-actualization the hippies produced mainly self-indulgence. Yet, I shall argue, the hippie result is not alien to the Maslovian theory, for when the relationship between self and society is left undefined and unattended by a theory of self-development, one social pattern is as likely to emerge as another. The hippie model is undoubtedly less attractive than the butterfly, but it is no stranger to the cocoon.

To the degree that Maslow anticipated a specter resembling the hippie pattern, he eschewed it. He could say, for example, of the seeker of peak experiences that:

> he may run the danger of turning away from the world
> and from other people in his search for triggers to peak

experiences, *any* triggers. In a word, instead of being temporarily self-absorbed and inwardly searching, he may become simply a selfish person, seeking his own personal salvation . . . and finally even perhaps using other people as triggers, as means to his sole end of higher states of consciousness. In a word, he may become not only selfish but also evil.

A person who winds up in this condition, Maslow observes, becomes not a psychologically healthy self-actualizer but a psychopath, with "no conscience, no guilt, no shame, no love for other people, no inhibitions, and few controls." We learn from this portrayal that there is a dramatic difference between those who achieve self-actualization and those who go astray, but we are not told what causes one seeker to succeed and another to fail, one to arrive at Eupsychia, another at the corner of Haight and Ashbury.

Although Maslow grants that "good human beings will generally need a good society in which to grow," he refuses to blame society for the perverse turns that the quest for self-actualization may take, for he believes that people can and do achieve self-actualization despite society's imperfections. But if environmental conditions play no significant part in guiding the seeker, what is the determinant of success or failure? Is the seeker himself responsible? Is the road hard to follow? Or is the cartographer to blame for not charting the course in such a way as to facilitate success? If Maslow is the cartographer, his theory the road, and the hippies the wayward travelers, what must be changed to get the seekers to their destination?

Sensible though the metaphor of cartographer may be for a theory which promises to transport people from one psychological place to another, it is suddenly apparent that Maslow left us no maps to guide us to the promised land. Neither the counselors and therapists deputized as guides to self-actualization, nor the solitary adventurers who would set out on their own, have a clear idea of how this pinnacle of human existence might be reached. Maslow describes often and at length what it looks like once one has arrived, but still he does not explain how to *get* there, so that if the hippies have floundered on the way, their error is understandable.

But to speak of the hippies as travelers in search of Maslow's happy state is to take a certain liberty with history by construing their actions as self-conscious attempts to implement Maslow's theory, when in all probability both the theory and the man were unknown to them. That the hippies should have sought the very thing that Maslow claims to have found is a mere coincidence — not a deliberate plot or self-conscious effort. But the very fact that they ventured into the realm of self-actualization means that they set foot on territory where Maslow reigns as king; and as all who enter there become *ipso facto* Maslovian subjects, it is conceptually useful, if technically inaccurate, to view the hippies as followers of Maslow. Since the hippie experience is above all a quest for the kinds of peak experiences that maslow describes, and since every person who aspires to or achieves the sort of thing that Maslow terms self-actualization moves wittingly or unwittingly onto Maslow's turf, the hippies, whether or not they know it or like it, must be considered Maslovians.

Subjects in the Maslovian realm live in a curious place which discriminates between superior and inferior human beings, higher and lower values, better and worse conditions, greater and lesser pleasures, and so on, but teaches that one learns to make these discriminations by looking inward, at the self. Here every human being becomes not only ultimate judge of the true, the good, and the beautiful, but also the author of all value. If I say to you, for example, that I wouldn't give you two cents for the Sistine Chapel, I have pronounced on its artistic quality and simultaneously fixed its worth at less than two cents. You cannot argue that it is a priceless treasure, because its value to others has nothing to do with how I felt when I looked at it, and it failed to move me. If it is worthless to me I have a right to call it worthless. If it is valuable to the art critics, the critics have a right to assign it a higher value, but that will not alter my judgment. "Only pluralistic description can serve," Maslow writes; all we can arrive at collectively is "a catalogue of all the different ways in which the word 'value' is actually used by different people."

There is a difference, Maslow declares, between good things and bad things, but each of us must make an independent decision about the nature of that distinction. "Try seeing if you can tell the difference between two brands of cigarettes with your eyes closed," he advises. "If you can't tell the difference, *there is none.*" With respect to the things that affect you, you are sovereign and infallible. With respect to the things that affect me, so am I. How, then, are we to live together in the Good Society, let alone the same household?

During the time of the heyday of the hippie movement when thousands of young people descended into the neighborhoods of San Francisco's Haight-Ashbury district and Berkeley's south campus area, this was the salient question in the hippie mind. In effect, the hippies created a social milieu in which the Maslovian notion of individual sovereignty could be given expression, with people sharing geographical space but not necessarily sharing values. To accomplish this they had to develop a social law by which to live. Thus they came to the principle of toleration, the only reliable safeguard for genuine pluralism.

Maslow himself never arrives at the doctrine of toleration which follows so logically from his premise of individual sovereignty. Nor does he arrive at some alternative social doctrine or mechanism for implementing his theory of self-actualization, though his writings indicate where his sentiments lie, and from them we can almost extrapolate a social theory. We are forced to extrapolation because although Maslow is able to tell us what the relationship between self and society ought to look like when it is good, he is unable to provide us with a blueprint for its construction. The reason for this, I think, is twofold, having to do in the first place with the thrust of his theory and in the second place with unresolved contradictions within the theory. Let us take these one at a time and examine them more closely.

Although Maslow insists that the creation of a good society is an urgent need today, what really interests him is the creation of the self-actualized person. Although he believes that the good society and the good person "develop simultaneously and in tandem," he relies for improvement more on personal growth than on social reform. The thrust of his work is toward the individual as opposed to the community, the private as opposed to the public, the interior life of the mind as opposed to the exterior life conducted in the society of others. He instructs us to look inward, yet he does not mean, as Hobbes did, that we may thus "read and know what are the thoughts and passions of all other men," in order to turn our attention more profitably to the social world. Rather, Maslow counsels introspection so that we can discover our unique identities and thus achieve full humanness through an intense affair with the self. He cites Carl Rogers, who asks with an observation reminiscent of Hobbes, "How does it happen that the deeper we go into ourselves as particular and unique, seeking for our own individual identity, the more we find the whole human species?" The point which Maslow (following Rogers) wishes to make, however, is that to discover your specieshood is to learn

> what you peculiarly are, how you are you, what your potentialities are, what your style is, what your pace is, what your tastes are, what your values are, what direction your body is going, where your personal biology is taking you, i.e., how you are *different* from others.

He adds that you will also learn how you are similar to others, but this is, of course, less interesting.

Since the thrust of Maslow's thought is inward toward the individual and the personal, social conditions fade into comparative obscurity. The task at hand for Maslow is self-actualization, and as far as social improvements are concerned,

> no social reforms, no beautiful constitutions or beautiful programs or laws will be of any consequence unless people are healthy enough, evolved enough, strong enough, good enough to understand them and to want to put them into practice in the right way.

If we should not ignore social questions altogether, we should at least postpone them until there are enough self-actualized people to give the questions cogency. What would it matter, Maslow might ask, if we achieved pure toleration but were insufficiently developed to enjoy it?

I have said that the hippie insistence on toleration follows logically from the Maslovian premise of individual sovereignty, and that Maslow's lack of interest in the social problems attendant to such a premise results in part from his deep, nearly exclusive preoccupation with personal problems. The second reason for Maslow's failure to deal with the dynamics of the self-society relationship is that he has no single coherent concept of the self from which to begin. Rather, he has two separate and irreconcilable views of the self, and though toleration is an excellent social companion for the one, it cannot co-exist with the other.

Maslow's first view of the self as sovereign and inviolable stems from what might be called his *democratic premise,* so named for its recognition of the right of every individual to his or her tastes, opinions, values, etc., and its admission to an *equality of rights* with respect to these preferences.

According to this view, each person has an uncontestable right to his unique choices, whether he prefers things which Maslow would consider bad, or things which he would approve. With respect to their right to decide for themselves what they like, all people are equal, and therefore it follows that all must be given equal opportunity to make and act on their own decisions. That is to say, there must be toleration.

The second premise, on the other hand (with its concomitant view of the self), focuses on the distinctions between good choices and bad choices, between what is lofty and what base, what superior and what inferior, what noble and what common, and admits a preference for the former in every case. Here Maslow is not content to celebrate the fact that every human being is unique and will show a unique set of preferences when allowed to make choices, but is intent on showing that some choices are better than others, and some people better choosers. Here the equality of rights advanced in the democratic premise is overtaken by a powerful *inequality of things and persons* which, while not denying the dignity and worth of the individual person, holds that some people are more dignified and worthy than others. Indeed, it goes so far as to say that some are more *human* than others, and deserve therefore to lead the rest. For this reason we may call this the *aristocratic premise*. Here we can see that the Self we met in the democratic premise stands on one side of an evolutionary branching, the other limb of which is occupied not by a sovereign individual, but by a dependent one. Opposite "the *best* specimens of intellect, creativeness, character, strength, success, etc." stand "the weak, . . . the underprivileged . . . the less capable, . . . those who need to be helped." And if the point now is to have the poor branch emulate its formidable counterpart, it would be foolish indeed to encourage repetition of bad habits and choices by instituting the practice of toleration.

In light of the second premise we can see that if the theorist were to honor his or her democratic principles by granting all people an equal right to expression through a doctrine of tolerance, the self-actualized ruling aristocracy created by the aristocratic premise would lose its mandate. Approaching Maslow's thought from this direction, we see that toleration is not a logical sequel to his theoretical premises, but is consistent with only one of them, while being anathema for the other.

In developing these two parallel but contradictory strains of thought Maslow committed an error in reasoning that cannot be rectified. One moment he will assure us that if we detect no difference between two alternatives offered to us, then there is no difference. He will invest us with the authority of a judge and make each of us a legitimate arbiter of tastes. The next moment he will assert that some forms of music are base (1950's rock) and others lofty (Beethoven), thus setting standards *for* us instead of granting us the right to rank them according to our own tastes. He justifies this switch by stating that all superior (i.e., self-actualized) people will agree that the music of Beethoven is greater than that of Elvis Presley, assuring us that if only we were self-actualized then we too would agree. Similarly, he will say when he writes on formal education that "the schools should be helping the children to look within themselves, and from this self-knowledge derive a set of values." Again we hear the idea that values originate from within, that each of us must be the supreme authority for our own lives. But again the message is contradicted, for in writing of the relationship between the "transcending" self-actualizers and "the common people," he reports that the latter have tended to revere the superior specimens and expresses his hope that this deference will facilitate designing a world "in which the most capable, the most awakened, the most idealistic would be chosen and loved as leaders, as teachers, as obviously benevolent and unselfish *authority*." In this ideal world, all ordinary people voluntarily alienate their sovereignty by relinquishing it to a class of people who, by virtue of their self-knowledge, have earned the right to final judgment on all matters and to the ordering of all values. People of this class become the authorities, and the rest of us their reverent subjects. And since the only type of conflict conceivable in this projected world is shadowboxing, or disputes with the self, the dictatorship of the self-actualized becomes absolute — as absolute as that of the Hobbesian sovereign.

Maslow develops his own ideal of the good life from the antidemocratic branch of his thought, but leaves the other, emphatically democratic, branch standing in opposition to it. Where in this wild dialectic is the *real* Maslow? Where is the great Maslovian synthesis to resolve the theoretical contradictions in self-actualization? If the model of Eupsychia were more detailed, we could perhaps look for an answer there, but it reveals only an inclination toward the aristocratic thesis, without any dis-

cussion of its antithesis or resolution of the tension between the two.
"How much tolerance for degrading, value-destroying, 'low tastes'" can
we allow in our Utopian world?'', Maslow asks. "How achieve love,
respect and gratitude for authority (policeman, judge, lawmaker, father,
captain)?" Tolerance will be limited and authority diffused, but no mention is made of a concurrent line of thought for which decrees are abhor-
rent and insupportable. No argument is offered, either, to explain how the
"highly anarchistic group" sometimes described as inhabiting Eupsychia
will be reconciled to these curtailments of freedom. No argument is
offered for how these restrictions will facilitate "a laissez-faire but loving
culture, in which people (young people too) would have much more free
choice . . . and in which . . . [people] would be much less prone to
press opinions or religions or philosophies or tastes in clothes or food or
art or women on their neighbors." Both the favored aristocratic premise
and its democratic opposite remain intact, even in Eupsychia, where they
live in eternal conflict. The antagonists appear to be irreconcilable, but if
Maslow ever recognized this he nowhere sought to correct it. He left
standing an error in reasoning that produced the dualism of the butterfly
and its less attractive twin referred to at the outset of this article. The one
was a dream world of high synergy, the other the reality of the Haight-
Ashbury with its ultimate horror, the rock concert at Altamont. And
though Maslow would claim paternity to but one, he is in fact the father of
both.

Maslow passed on to both his heirs a cluster of concerns and preoccu-
pations which, in an abbreviated and somewhat oversimplified form, consists of concern for values, behavior, self-concept, life goals, character
traits, social relations, and social orientation. By comparing his dissimilar progeny on the question of what each sees as mattering most in these
concerns, we can observe the radical differences between them. Schemat-
ically the comparison is presented on p. 104.

What must be borne in mind about this dualistic scheme is that it is the
creation of a single theorist who neither acknowledged its dualism nor
synthesized its contradictions. It is doubtful that Maslow ever understood
he was the father of twins.

In this chart, the clusters of emphases subsumed under each of the major premises are, while irreconcilable with each other, consistent within themselves. Each side forms a coherent, harmonious pattern that could be used as a template for designing a life style — a life style which of necessity would be disdained by all who elect the pattern of the other side.

CONCERN	EMPHASIS	
	Democratic Premise	Aristocratic Premise
VALUES	ORIGIN (Values must be developed from within the self)	HIERARCY (Some things are to be valued more than others)
BEHAVIOR	AUTHENTICITY ("Trust thyself; every heart vibrates to that iron string" — Emerson)	WISDOM (Learn to be a good chooser)
SELF-CONCEPT	SENSUOUSNESS (Your sensations and feelings reveal your true self)	ACHIEVEMENT (Until you have achieved self-actualization your self is incomplete)
LIFE GOALS	PEAK-EXPERIENCES (Aspire to life's highs; seize the time: Now)	VOCATIONAL COMPETENCE (Become a master in your work; defer gratification)
CHARACTER TRAITS	SELF-SATISFACTION ("Do you want to find out what you ought to be? Then find out who you are!" — Maslow)	SELF-CRITICISM ("Man is something that is to be surpassed. What have ye done to surpass man?" — Nietzsche)
SOCIAL RELATIONS	NON-INTERFERENCE (Laissez-faire; you do your thing, let me do mine)	EMULATION (When experts do their thing, novices should watch and learn)
SOCIAL ORIENTATION	TOLERANCE (A celebration of the Self: Let a hundred flowers bloom. Maximum freedom for all)	DEFERENCE (A celebration of self-actualization: Let the best step forth and the others step back. Synergy for all)

Maslow never asks which side we are on, for he seems not to have noticed that he was surrounded by warring factions of his own making. The young Americans who formed the hippie movement, though, *had* to pick sides, because they felt themselves to be surrounded by a larger society which was pushing them in directions they did not care to go. To resist its pressures was to make a declaration of position, and by accident the position they chose was the very position which follows from the democratic premise in Maslow's thought. It involved a concern with the origins of values, with authenticity of behavior, sensuousness, and peak experiences. Its self-satisfied people advocated noninterference in interpersonal relations and enforced this tenet with a law of toleration.

The early hippies sought to avoid the intolerance and interference in people's lives that they encountered in the straight world, by creating certain geographical sanctuaries where people would be allowed to do just about anything they wanted, so long as they inflicted no direct harm upon others. As is typical of social movements, this movement began as a reaction against prevailing conditions in the larger society. It was not the product of an inspiration felt while contemplating the Self. Although introspection might well have yielded the same commitment by each individual to do his or her thing, it alone could not possibly have furnished these individuals with a favorable arena for *acting out* their things. This point is significant for the contrast it affords between Maslow's narrow conception of the self (in both premises) as something which develops principally by auto-cultivation, and the wider, more complex looking-glass self understood by C. H. Cooley and others as developing by exposure to others through a process of reflection. The hippie settlements in San Francisco, Berkeley, and elsewhere not only encouraged the kind of introspection recommended by Maslow, but also provided an entire milieu to which people could relate and in which they could see themselves reflected. This had the effect of both affording comfort to those who were there and *drawing others in by its example* — something that Maslow's method could accomplish only with great difficulty, if at all. It had the further effect of providing a new source of identification for people whose associations with the dominant culture had left them feeling isolated and alienated. In identifying with a new subculture, or *counter*culture, they could dissociate themselves from those parts of the dominant culture which felt wrong, demeaning, and repressive to the self.

As a consequence of their reactiveness against the dominant culture the early hippies fixed on the theme of "do your own thing," for they perceived America as a place where everyone was under pressure to do someone *else's* thing. Thus, hippie "things" often constituted an assault on convention, so that there was no costume too bizarre for the hippie, no style too far out. Just as sexual practices outlawed or considered perverse by straight society were casually accepted, so it was possible for people to live in strangely furnished houses, eat unusual foods, smoke exotic weeds, and belong to weird religious cults, without anyone minding in the least. Sexual freedom, political freedom, religious freedom — all these were tolerated by the movement and protected by the people in it.

But the hippies carried their toleration a step beyond the civil libertarianism which grants people the right to do their various things, to the point where they acknowledged the *validity* of a multitude of "things," each of which has an equal right to free expression. At that point discrimination becomes impossible, and at that point, it will be recalled, Maslow had to abandon his democratic premise to vote for aristocracy. Maslow could not endure the proposition that pushpin is as good as Pushkin, or Presley as good as Beethoven, and had to insist that self-actualization involved the adoption of a *particular* set of values, rather than the development of *any* set of values derived from inner knowledge. (Eventually he took the position that self-actualization theory cannot exist without elitism.) For the hippies, though, the democratic premise is pursued, and not only is everybody entitled to a license to practice his thing, but each thing is entitled to respect. Consider, for example, this hippie's response to an inquiry about free love:

> Oh, that's out of sight. I think that anybody that wants to ball anybody at any time should do it, because it's okay. I don't think anyone should necessarily make a big thing out of it, it's — as long as you don't get uptight about it and other people don't get uptight about it, but if they did I'd probably respect them because that's their thing.

This young man is willing not only to tolerate, but to *respect* the "thing" of some anonymous, hypothetical people who get upset about sex in the streets. If respect is given with such abandon, what then are the criteria for withholding respect? Obviously, everybody has his own thing, and if everybody's thing is inviolable, then every thing, or *everything* is all right.

In the hippie view, true toleration demands a respect for the inviolability of each idiosyncratic way of coping with the world. This view in a general way creates a wider latitude of individual freedom and expression, but it affords no possibility for reckoning with conflict. It cannot solve the problems that arise when one individual's thing interferes with the thing of another individual, or the interest of one group threatens the well-being of another group. Choices must, at some point, be made, and with a doctrine of tolerance that outlaws only coercion and harm, the choices are all untenable. Any choice necessarily requires discrimination, and discrimination is exactly what the hippies wanted to avoid.

One of the ways the hippies hoped to eliminate intolerance was by making no judgments. It was thought that if one was nonjudgmental, broadminded, flexible, and able to adjust to other people's habits — instead of making others adjust to one's own — then all the ground work was prepared for true toleration. Hence people worked at developing flexibility and broadmindedness, unaware that suspension of judgment would inevitably lead to exploitation, either of their own trusting selves or of other seemingly free spirits. Without judgment, there was nowhere to place blame, and without blame, there was no way to assign responsibility or to differentiate between good and bad behavior. When it came time (as it did at Altamont) to make those choices between contradictory things, the hippies found themselves in a moral paralysis, which is precisely how Maslow would have found himself had he pursu d the democratic premise of his own theory of self-actualization.

In addition to the social liabilities generated by the normlessness of an "anything goes" ethos, there is also a personal tax that must be paid. The tendency to accept oneself and others unconditionally, as they are, laying no stress and placing no contingency on what they might become, is to take away from the individual incentives for struggle and personal growth. In various forms hippie interviews echo Maslow's prescription, "Do you want to find out what you ought to be? Then find out who you are!" But never do we hear Nietzche's challenge, "Man is something that is to be surpassed. What have ye done to surpass man?"

In the hippie subculture it is enough to make do, to get by, to master the technique of "Acceptance," as Maslow calls it. Drugs are a convenient shortcut to accepting the world uncritically as one finds it, but some hippies managed to accomplish this without the help of drugs. Among the latter group is Gary Hulse, a 19-year-old hippie from Indiana who was interviewed in the Haight-Ashbury during the heyday of the movement. The only area in life in which Gary does not apply the technique of acceptance is work, for he, like most hippies, would rather sell dope, collect welfare, or be kept by another person than go to work at an ungratifying job. Though they agree with Maslow's vocational principle and embrace for other occasions the technique of acceptance, the hippies will not buy his eulogies on the modern corporation or go to work in one. When Gary Hulse was interviewed he was about to move in with a woman who had offered to support him. Asked if he felt uptight about her putting the money up, he said,

> No, I don't. If I can get a job and work — a good job that I liked, one that I really wanted, I would go ahead and work and wouldn't feel bad, but if I can't, I don't mind her doing that, since she has about 2,000 bills in the bank, plus her old man gives her $150-160 a month.

Maslow contends that all self-actualized people transcend the conventional dichotomy between work and play and learn who they are by doing what they do in their chosen vocations. We must ask — for Maslow does not — how realistic it is to think that a poorly educated 19-year-old youth like Gary will ever find gratifying work in contemporary America. Despite Maslow's enthusiasm for the modern corporation, there has hardly been a flowering of self-actualization on the assembly line, which is where Gary Hulse would most probably be employed were he to go to work. Given his alternatives, Gary's chances for happiness seem more hopeful if he is kept by his friend than if he is paid, say, by a Ford assembly plant. And given his penchant for accepting what *is* and equating it with what *ought to be,* he might even learn to be "religiously awed" by this arrangement, "to the point of ecstasy."

Gary has learned much about acceptance since coming to San Francisco. He left Indiana because life there was painful for him, and not knowing about the technique of acceptance yet, his only choices were between flight and conformity. Describing what it was like for him back home he says,

> Yes, there was a lot of discrimination. Well, people would throw stuff at you and people would just be down on you — always have remarks. Yeah, just walking down the street they would call you names. I mean, you can imagine what they did!

The Haight-Ashbury offered respite from the slurs, stares, and abuses heaped upon hippies for their unconventional appearances, but the motley collection of people who inhabited the district were also very mobile. Every excursion out of the Haight put people back into the larger society, and even in relatively tolerant areas like northern California, hippies often were treated with as much unkindness as Gary experienced in Indiana. But those who became masters of Maslovian acceptance, like Gary, learned how to adjust to the abominations. Asked whether anything that used to bother him no longer does, Gary replied,

> Yeah, people staring at me. That doesn't bother me anymore. Or their calling something to me — I just laugh at them, cause they are more ignorant. They're just showing their ignorance when they laugh at any-one else, when they point at anyone else, when they say something to someone else. They are just showing their ignorance.

In Gary's opinion, conditions do not need to be changed, people do. The proper task of people is to adjust themselves to their environments, at least to the extent that they can accept them and not be distracted by them — to the extent that they can fuse fact and value through acceptance, as Maslow would put it. It does not matter that people still stare, point, laugh, and ridicule other people because of the way they look; what mat-ters is that some people are still vulnerable enough to take these insults to heart. With a resounding "metagrumble" Gary pronounces his view that American society is all right as it is, and what is needed is a populace that would be open-minded enough to ungrudgingly tolerate the status quo. As he puts it,

> There should be no new society. Society is all right except for a few things, like not being broadminded enough as a whole . . . I would say that there are very

few people in society that are broadminded. I would
say less than five per cent.

As we saw earlier, broadmindedness is considered by the hippies to be
a fundamental step in the creation of a true toleration which would put an
end to the judgment and give everyone the chance to do his thing. After
everybody stops being judgmental, it really doesn't matter what the world
looks like because there is nobody left to complain. As long as each person
is content in doing his or her private thing, it makes no difference whether
he or she is doing it amid wretchedness or magnificence, turbulence or
tranquility.

Here, then, is the end of the journey of the people who came into the
hippie movement seeking refuge from the injustices of the straight society
and a chance to pursue self-realization. They came from the provincial
Netherlands to the free-wheeling Bay Area to be among kindred spirits
whom they could count on to understand their discontent and tolerate their
idiosyncracies. They strove in this new scene to practice genuine toleration and let everybody do his or her thing without restraint. To carry it off
they cultivated broadmindedness and the art of making no judgments on
other people, turning a deaf ear to dissonance and a blind eye to ugliness.
In oblivion one is no longer affected by what is going on all around but is
fully immune to all parts of the environment save those one creates for
oneself. The journey begins in society but ends in the self.

For such a tour one might as well have stayed home, which, indeed, is
where the more sophisticated Maslovians remain. Considering that the
United States today is still producing what Maslow would call meta-
grumbles, home is perhaps not such a bad place to be, unless of course we
entertain the thought that in public places events and decisions might be
threatening the fulfillment of those things which Maslow identifies as our
basic human needs: safety, belongingness, affection, and esteem. Deeply
involved in cultivating the Self, Maslow, like his followers in the group
movement as described by Sigmund Koch, "is adept at the image-making
maneuver of evading human reality in the very process of seeking to discover and enhance it." He can by fiat transform Gary Hulse from victim
into hero, and change his situation from one of horror to one of splendor,
without ever confronting the objective social reality in which the boy
lives. With this maneuver every biography can have a happy ending, even

that of the forlorn Gary Hulse, whose ability to ignore the abuses and insults of his fellow citizens suddenly takes on the character of triumph, and whose pathetic acceptance of the status quo somehow becomes a noble, transcending act. Indeed, the whole picture is reminiscent of one that Maslow himself paints as an illustration of what we can arrive at if only we try hard enough:

> . . . *The New York Times* front-page picture in 1933 of an old Jewish man with a beard being paraded before the jeering crowd in Berlin in a garbage truck. It was my impression that he had compassion for the crowd and that he looked upon them with pity and perhaps forgiveness, thinking of them as unfortunate and sick and subhuman. Being independent of other people's evil or ignorance or stupidity or immaturity even when this is directed toward oneself is possible, though very difficult. And yet one *can,* in such a situation, gaze upon the whole situation — including oneself in the midst of the situation — as if one were looking upon it objectively, detachedly from a great and impersonal or suprapersonal height.

Maslow, by having us "transcend" a banal concern for ethics and politics, would have us "walking through the abattoir without getting bloody," never questioning whether some day we might find ourselves being led through that abattoir by a Judas goat.

CHARLES HAMPDEN-TURNER, *Comment on 'Maslow's Other Child'*

It is a pleasure to read Aron's paper, so cogently argued, so lucidly stated, and written by such an intelligent and determined critic. Humanistic psychology needs just such rigorous challenges and testings of its seminal ideas and thinkers.

Withal this pleasure, I regard Aron's critique as almost wholly mistaken. Her logic and style are fine specimens of that genre of thinking against which Maslow fought for most of his life.

To deal first with the clearest flaw, I must object to her unlovely coupling of Maslow with Bay Area hippies. She quotes Maslow as disapproving of their life style. She quotes hippies as not having heard of Maslow. She quotes mainly from Maslow's post-60s writing which could hardly have influenced the counterculture, and then she wraps the albatross of Altamont around Maslow's neck. How this small section of the nonreading public of California become "Maslovian" followers of a professor in Waltham, Massachusetts is a total mystery. It is guilt by remotest of associations. One might as logically call the Hell's Angels "Aronites" because of their critical views of the "love generation." It is "conceptually useful if technically inaccurate to view hippies as followers of Maslow" we are told. Useful to whom? Surely the test of any conceptual scheme in social science is whether it elucidates *real* events, not just the axe that one particular critic is grinding!

If one is genuinely interested in Maslow's influence, then Abbie Hoffman has traced his own revolt in part to Maslow, and Richard Flacks, an early member of S.D.S., showed some early signs of being influenced. The Canadian radical journal, *Our Generation,* cites Maslow frequently. So far from his influence being nonpolitical or lacking in social ethics, this is precisely where his influence may be the deepest and most lasting. Political scientists and ethically concerned social scientists who are advancing and broadening his work include: Walt Anderson, Christian Bay, James C. Davies, Elizabeth Simpson, Jean Knutson, Richard Peterson, John Glass, Bill Eckhardt, Elizabeth Drews, Leslie Lipson, and Bill Harman to mention but a few.

It is curiously unfair that Maslow of *all* people, who led psychology out of its hibernation in laboratories and consulting rooms should be scolded for running scared of ethics and politics. He was not very sophisticated in political affairs, but how many psychologists are knowledgeable of anything beyond a pitiful array of dependent variables, or the consciousness of a half-dozen patients from which they generalize?

I am sorry that Aron relied so heavily in her critique of a man's lifework on *The Farther Reaches of Human Nature,* which is a semimystical sequel to Maslow's major works, and considerably influenced, I suspect, by his approaching death. She seems to sense nothing of his painful preparation for a journey that all of us must make, suddenly, arbitrarily, and quite alone. There is certainly in this last book an individuation, a leave taking, a moving acceptance of what was so near. Doesn't she see that the old Jewish man in the market place was Maslow himself? Just as the old man was helpless to change the evil and ignorance around him, so Maslow in those final days was feeling helpless too.

There was so much churning inside him, so little time to say it, such a massive capacity in his audience to misunderstand. His mood was transcendent. He felt at times "above" people. But how does one die with a life's mission yet incomplete? Dying has yet to be democratized; the grave has yet to be desegregated. While Maslow lived, his mind and compassion embraced each other. Aron's article testifies to a cold divorce of these same two elements.

I regard Maslow's major work as *Motivation and Personality* along with his subsequent elucidations of the concept of synergy. It is here that Maslow answers most of the criticisms in Aron's article. I do not pretend to distill "the essential Maslow" but only write of the "Maslow-for-me," for I must confess that Maslow's very incompleteness is a pleasure for me, since it elicits my desire to contribute and participate in his formulations. He has something to teach us perhaps about "democratic theorizing."

As I understand Maslow, his idea of self-actualization seeks to overcome the false dichotomies between selfish and unselfish, equality and excellence, real and ideal, inner and outer, individualism and cooperation, on most of which Aron is demonstrably "hung up." Maslow argued that divisions and conflicts *within* the personality paralleled divisions and conflicts *between* persons and groups, hence his call to look within ourselves was *not* a retreat for social engagement but a means of resolving dichotomous structures at all levels simultaneously.

It is a falsification of Maslow to reduce and to polarize his conception of self-actualization in self-gratification. Self-actualization was a composite, synergistic formulation combining the satisfaction of self *and* others, and hence the fulfillment of self through socially significant action. In contrast, self-gratification is mere indulgence of the self in possibly exploitive ways. Nor in his earlier work did Maslow separate peak experiences from vocational competence and excellence or achievement from sensuousness. It was in dedication to such life goals that peaks (and troughs) were found. Achievement was rarely, if ever, defined by Maslow as an approximation to an *external* mark; it was actualization of that for which the sensate spirit yearned.

Aron's chart is less a criticism of Maslow than a nosology in the approved manner of "science," an Aristotelian division into A and not-A, against which Maslow consistently struggled. Aron-the-Atomizer has done a dissection job on the spurious pretext that the hiatus between the counterculture and the straight culture is "somehow" Maslovian.

There really is a distinction between a person who, in the face of bitter opposition, is one of the first to insist that any psychology worthy of the name must be holistic, human, and concerned with ecstatic experiences, and other persons who seize upon such watch words and run the whole idea into the ground! Maslow strove to put humanity into the sinews of the economy and into managerial practices, *not* to set up parasitical communities of "pure love" in Californian resorts. To criticize Maslow for trying to work with businessmen *and* to criticize him for fostering the anti-commercial passivity of middle-class drop-outs is a trifle fanciful and exceedingly ungenerous. For what disaster is he *not* responsible?

I am puzzled because Aron sees with considerable insight the pathetic error of the hippie ideology. If you tolerate everything and everyone, you ultimately prefer or value nothing. They are one-dimensional people, only it is the opposite dimension to that which Marcuse attacked. The perpetually open-minded person is not better than the perpetually closed-minded person. The first cannot make a decision; the second cannot alter a decision.

But doesn't Aron see that her polarized diagram is a similar disaster? She tells us:

> Each side (of the diagram) forms a coherent, harmonious pattern that could be used as a template for designing a life style — a life style which *of necessity* would be disdained by all who elect the pattern of the other side.

Why "of necessity?" What is "coherent" or "harmonious" about these patterns? I agree that our society has been roughly (and tragically) polarized in this way. I agree that her distinctions are cerebrally neat and typical of conventional social science. I disagree that Maslow created, desired, or approved such polar conceptions. I insist that he fought them most of his life, and I insist that *in social reality* these patterns are neither coherent nor harmonious, but quarrelsome, dangerous, and absurd. Powerless conscience evokes conscienceless power. Innocent "goodies" invite cynical "baddies." Happenings are the mere antithesis of compulsive corporate planning. The sensuousness, the authentic and the "peakers" are *never* going to prevail against the achieving, the wise, and the competent because the former is a weak pattern and the latter is a strong pattern. Repression within, and oppression without, would become a permanent feature of the dominant group.

Maslow followed the tradition of Gandhi and King in insisting that we embrace *neither* polarity, but struggle to synthesize apparent opposites. Just as King asserted himself *and* went limp, knelt *and* marched, spoke otherworldly language which had unmistakable *this*-worldly referents, so Maslow tried to humanize the corporation and told the kids who wanted to sit passively at his feet to "go make chips" (i.e., work hard and creatively).

I have left to the last Aron's best point, as I see it, that Maslow pursued twin ideals without making it sufficiently clear *how* they could be reconciled. He makes it very clear to me *that* they should be reconciled, which is why I reject the diagram of polar opposites and the language in which they are expressed as even remotely fair to Maslow.

I contend that those who present us with dualities and say "reconcile!" are going almost as far as a nonelitist social science can go. I say this because the reconciliation of opposites is an art of creative and relational synthesis. Every person or problem we encounter requires a slightly *different* combination of the opposite resources within us. That is why you cannot personify the good without creating a plastic Jesus, a kitch virgin, or a muscular Christian like Billy Graham, clean-cut, prefabricated and contrived. The good is always elusive. We can recognize it in retrospect, "*Then* I was fulfilled, happy and loved," but we cannot program it in advance for "highs" like a juke box. Maslow knew this. The hippies did not, and I'm not sure that our critic does either.

But let me go a little bit further, extending Maslow as it were, into a sphere where part of what I say is his and part mine, and I can no longer distinguish one from the other. I want to show that "Aron's polarities" are reconcilable and that the real coherence and harmony is *across* her dichotomies, not within them. (The italicized words are her polar conceptions.)

That valuing *originates within the self* does not turn all values into subjective, relative, and unqualifiably unique entities. Because all human beings are in some respects alike, all internally wrought values, *authentically* communicated, may in some respects be alike, hence comparable, hence *hierarchically* organizable and hence universally wiser than other values.

Beethoven's music could therefore be "better" than 1950's rock in a number of ways. Its structure of tune-within-tune could be more complex. It could demand more of the listener and give more to the listener. There could be more respect for the listener by the composer. More participation by the listener. I lack knowledge of music, but this principle is certainly true of literature. Good literature evokes the imagination of the reader and his or her power of discernment so that a more *democratic* relationship with the reader is enjoyed by a greater rather than a lesser literary *achievement*. It is trash magazines that tell you *exactly* what to think and feel. ("Guilty!" said the foreman, "Guilty, guilty, guilty echoed in my ears!") I suspect that rock music is similarly intrusive and bombastic. Both forms are the merchandising of an entertainment industry seeking to "hook" an audience. Popular yes! Democratic no!

Values may also be "better" or "worse" through their organizability of *other* values. For example, authentic communication is a value essential to the process of valuing itself, while a preference for strawberry ice cream is rarely, if ever, a lynch-pin of the valuing process. Maslow argued that values contributed in different degrees to synergy (i.e., to value-organization and to human organization) without which *any* viable synthesis would be impossible.

The other "irreconcilables" are even easier to synergize. *Sensuousness* was for Maslow an important guide to what was worth *achieving*. He was certainly no automatic admirer of what the world called success or achievement. Rather he was an apostle of that creativity where feeling, intellect, and pragmatism meet. I don't recall any passage where he insists that *peak-experiences* are to be enjoyed only by the *incompetent* or outside one's *competence*. That polarity is not his! He certainly believed in the widest *tolerance* and *noninterference* in the exercise of others' rights, but *emulation* can be quite voluntary and *deference* a tribute paid by one expertise to another. One does not either emulate/defer totally, or not emulate/defer at all. One can imitate an honesty and commitment, while dedicating these to a different end or "thing." The fulfillment of self-actualizers is to be emulated. This does not require a carbon copy of their particular achievement.

But I do not wish to seem to wriggle or to split hairs, so let me go to the root of Aron's rod, and its polar fallacies. At bottom she seems to assume that equality and authority are irreconcilably opposed, and neither Maslow nor I agree with her.

The fallacy is a common one and I would like to try to lay it to rest. We treat people as equals, *not* because when all is known about them that can be known, we shall value them as ourselves, *but because equality is the best way of eliciting from others the best that is in them.* When we have elicited what we can, we have to make a judgment, and that judgment could be deferential, or superior, or incomparable — but judge we do and judge we must.

Should we encounter the same person again, that we have judged inferior *or* superior to ourselves, *the "method" of equality is still the best* from the point of view of growth and learning. Why? Because the situation is now different and on this subject and occasion the other may surprise us. It is still our obligation to elicit from that person the best he or she can give! It is not more respectful to treat the other as a superior to ourselves because we thereby devalue our own capacity to confirm that person. In other words, equality shows a maximum possible respect that precedes and facilitates communication. It is a good working hypothesis, but deference or a feeling of superiority may follow communication. It is all part of a natural process, and we repress our awareness of *any* part of the process at our peril.

No one can safely say in advance how much equality should be mixed with how much authority at any particular moment. This synthesis of opposites shifts constantly. A woman goes camping with a man. One of the two is a medical student. The other falls ill. The sick one defers to the authority of the one partially educated in medicine. The boat overturns. The poor swimmer defers to the good one. They make love with almost perfect equality, but not quite because one may initiate it and arouse the other.

In any democracy the rights of individuals must be synergized in some proportion with the authority of the group and its representatives. Debate must end if action is to be taken, or we shall have marvelously articulate talkers in an impotent organization, which is a fair description of the movement that was. It never understood authority. It so hated power it emasculated itself.

According to the Greek myth, there stands at the gateway to the Aegean Sea a rock and a whirlpool known as Scylla and Charybdis. The two sides of Aron's diagram are a fair approximation of this quandary. Maslow was trying to tell us that we must make our own way between these. For most of his life he steered a brilliant path between rock-like Scientism and the whirlpool of Mysticism. Perhaps toward the end he dropped the rudder and accepted the current that was bearing him down. When my steering begins to fail, I only hope to have lived and steered as well as he, and to have critics who can feel for my dilemma as well as think about what I have written.

❦   ❦   ❦

STEPHEN WOOLPERT, *A Comparison of Rational Choice and Self-Actualization Theories of Politics*

Humanistic psychology is entering a period of increased social and political emphasis. A new political consciousness is unfolding, as links are forged between the human growth movement and movements concerned with the environment, nuclear energy, holistic health, decentralism, appropriate technology, consumerism, world peace, and other forms of political liberation.

This important and often controversial shift brings humanists face to face intellectually with a new but formidable rival theory. Mainstream political thought in this country is not based on either Freud or Skinner. The dominant approach, especially among scientifically inclined policy experts and political scholars, is called rational choice theory.

It would be hard to exaggerate the contrasts between rational choice theory and humanistic political psychology. They represent radically opposing views of both human nature and the political process. Moreover, this confrontation between humanism and conventional political thought arises at an important crossroad in human history. So this is more than just an academic debate. The kind of society we bequeath our grandchildren depends to a large degree on whether we base our current political decisions on humanistic or rational choice premises.

It is worthwhile, therefore, to compare these two political perspectives. After a brief summary of each, I will discuss the major differences between the self-interested rational actor model and the self-actualization model of politics. My purpose is to show the relationship between the humanistic vision of the possible person and a larger political vision of a humane society that promotes the growth and well-being of all its citizens.

I assume that the work of Maslow and Rogers is well known. In the last fifteen years, however, many other humanists have explored the political relevance of third-force psychology. They include Anderson, Bay, Burns, Davies, Gurtov, Hampden-Turner, Knutson, Matson, Roszak, and Satin. I will use the umbrella term "self-actualization theory" to describe the common humanist core of these political writers.

This common core assumes that politics is related to people's psychological needs. Although many political events can be rationalized after the fact, rationality alone cannot adequately explain our political life. Following Maslow's theory of human development, motives are said to have a universal structure that channels political activity in certain directions. Several versions of the need hierarchy exist, but they all begin with the lower physiological needs and end with some notion of self-actualization at the top. Human growth is generally defined as movement away from dependency and toward the fulfillment of potential.

Using this approach, politics includes all the ways that people engage with one another to meet their needs within their social environment. Political power can either benefit or harm human growth. Maslow and others have depicted a healthy ("eupsychean") society in which personal well-being and political well-being go hand in hand. Such a society encourages its citizens to be open to experience, to discover and pursue their own preferences, and to join together to achieve their common goals. Authenticity, tolerance of diversity, and interpersonal understanding are highly valued.

The political arena of such a society offers citizens both a way to increase their autonomy and a way to express it. The health of a eupsychean society stems from the fact that mature, autonomous people are naturally more sociable and democratic than deprived, dependent people.

By contrast, regimes that thwart the growth of their citizens run the risk of political decay. When people's preferences are imposed on them by others, as in authoritarian or conformist societies, the result is both personal and political alienation.

Unlike self-actualization theory, the rational choice approach to politics has its roots in utilitarian philosophy and classical economics. The core of this theory is a model of the self-interested rational actor. Riker and Ordeshook state:

> We start with people who, for our purposes, are bundles of opinions about nature and of preferences about the alternatives nature offers them. We assume that people behave as if they sort out and logically arrange the preferences in their bundles, so that when faced with a choice, they can choose as directed by their preferences.

According to this view, people's preferences are not linked to any theory of needs. Preferences are simply given, irrespective of their origin. People are predicted to choose whatever course offers them the most utility. (Utility means satisfaction, and is calculated in various ways by different writers, but the differences do not concern us here.

Rational choice theory sees politics as a game, in which participants play to win according to accepted rules. From this assumption, preferred political strategies for voting, bargaining, and coalition building are derived. For example, Riker's "size principle" is the idea that political actors "create coalitions just as large as they believe will insure winning and no larger."

The first contrast between rational choice theory and self-actualization theory has to do with the way they explain political events. There are three aspects to this issue.

The first is whether a political theory's evidence must be restricted to observations of what people do. Rational choice theory adopts the empirical approach of the physical sciences: mental states and subjective events do not count as scientific evidence. Riker and Ordeshook say:

> The only external evidence of what people want is what they do . . . When words and actions differ, which is

> to be given credence? The behaviorist position is to
> believe the inferences from action.

So rational choice theory can be verified only from the standpoint of the outside observer.

Second, rational choice theory reduces specific political events to examples of general causal laws. Like other empirical theories, it is searching for recurring patterns and regularities in politics.

Third, rational choice theory does not explain the psychological *meaning* of politics. If its hypotheses correspond to the behavioral evidence, it does not care whether they also correspond to the subjective experience of those involved.

Self-actualization theory objects to this approach on the grounds that, when dealing with political affairs, the very process of explanation is different from that used to explain nonhuman events. The differences in the subject matter of the natural and social sciences require two different kinds of knowledge: observation of casual laws versus insight into psychological meanings. The proper way to explain politics is to identify the human purposes, needs, and values that make politics intelligible.

In this sense, the self-actualization model, like most nonrational models, is less "model-like" than its rival. Its political insights are not expressed in mathematical formulae. The rigor of empirical testability is sacrificed.

In return, self-actualization theory explains political *action,* while rational choice theory explains only political *behavior.* Political behavior refers to physical movements, such as voting in an election. Political action refers to purposeful, intentional conduct: One may vote to voice approval of a candidate's entire platform, just part of it, or simply because the candidate is the lesser of two evils. Likewise, abstaining from an election may signal apathy, contentment with both candidates, or a protest against the whole political regime. Rational choice theory recognizes only two classes of behavior in these situations, voting and abstaining. And it explains decisions to vote or abstain by showing that they are rational, given the costs and benefits to the individual.

Self-actualization theory, however, finds a wide range of political conduct within the ranks of voters and abstainers. Since voting means different things to different people, a one-dimensional explanation is inadequate. By describing the motivational dynamics of politics, self-actualization theory unveils its richness and variety.

This violates the empiricist rule against considering mental states as evidence. But clearly it is impossible to reveal the inner significance of political activity without considering the purposes that people have for engaging in it.

The next major difference between rational choice and self-actualization theory concerns the source of political conduct. Some political theories explain events by pointing to the individuals involved. Court rulings, for example, are explained by referring to the skill of the attorneys, the judge's values and attitudes, and so on. Other theories explain politics in terms of social structures and institutions. Court decisions are explained by legal rules, professional training, and the like. In order to compare our two models on this matter, the question is whether they explain politics (predominantly or exclusively) in terms of personal or situational factors.

Riker and the rational choice theorists do not employ psychological explanations. The rational actor model deals exclusively with how people behave as members of political institutions such as electorates, legislatures, and political parties. It is concerned with political *roles,* not political people. To show this, it is necessary to examine Riker's treatment of motivation.

Remember that only behavior can be used as evidence of people's preferences in his theory. So if rationality were defined simply as "choosing the preferred outcome," then all choices resulting in behavior would be rational by definition. To avoid this tautology, Riker must say something specific about people's political preferences. What he does is to assume that a single motive drives all political actors:

> What the rational political man wants, I believe, is to win, a much more specific and specifiable motive than the desire for power . . . Unquestionably there are guilt-ridden and shame-conscious men who do not desire to win, who in fact desire to lose. These are the irrational ones of politics.

This appears to be a psychological theory about people in politics, but it is not. The goal of winning is built into the political system, not into human nature: "The goals specified," says Riker, "are inherent not in the character of the actors, but in the logic of the roles they play." In other words, political behavior is caused by external demands placed on people by political institutions. The desire to win is intrinsic to political *roles*, not to human beings. Riker says elsewhere:

> We need no theory of human nature — it only confuses us . . . To bring in psychological considerations . . . distracts us from our business, which is the study of what is said and done, not the study of reasons for saying and doing.

Self-actualization theory, by contrast, holds that the study of politics *requires* the study of political motives. Liberation movements, for example, are not simply attempts to win power. They are basically attempts to meet people's need for equal standing, respect, and esteem.

It is of the utmost importance to know if our political actions reveal health or pathology, autonomy or dependency. Gandhi and Nixon both sought political victory, but while the former raised both himself and his followers to a higher motivational level, Nixon debased his regime.

It is an oversimplification to say that the desire to win in politics is always rational. McGovern's strong stand against the Vietnam war in 1972 contributed to his defeat, but it may also have encouraged Nixon to end our involvement in Vietnam. Regardless of McGovern's merits as a candidate, if it is irrational to place a higher value on peacemaking than on a short-run electoral victory, then too much rationality is harmful to our political health.

It is even more inaccurate to say that political acts are the product only of external forces. Of course, social conditions do constrain our political choices. They may obstruct or support the process of human development. But politics also involves intentional choices. It reflects not only situational factors but also subjective elements, such as the needs that color a person's political style. Consequently, the responsibility for our actions rests ultimately with ourselves, not with circumstances beyond our control. Otherwise, how could we talk about political ethics or the moral justification of politics?

❧

Another issue in comparing these two models is the relationship between political and nonpolitical conduct. The basic question is whether a person's political actions can be understood without reference to the nature of the whole person.

Rational choice theory is atomistic. It seeks political explanations that are divorced from explanations of nonpolitical conduct (leaving aside the problem of defining the boundary between the two). Since rational choice theory makes no explicit psychological assertions, it is not in a position to explore the relationship between one's politics and the rest of one's life. According to this view, people are made up of separate parts, or "bundles," which are logically isolated from one another. Politics can be analyzed by one discipline, psychology by another, and economics by a third, without yielding distorted results.

On the other hand, self-actualization theory takes a global approach. As Matson says, political conduct

> is not a discrete event to be caught and studied while all else is held constant . . . It cannot be forcibly separated from the self-system of which it is a part without doing violence both to the system and to the part.

According to this view, the qualities of the whole person govern the nature of the constituent parts. There are no detachable, self-contained segments of a person's life. In an important sense, politics has to do with our personal relationships, the kind of work we do, and the way we look at the world. Each of these aspects of our identity influences how we engage with one another to satisfy our needs.

Political explanations that do not refer to the whole person are at best incomplete and at worst false. To quote Allport:

> The political nature of a man is indistinguishable from his personality as a whole, and . . . his personality as a whole is not the sum total of his specific reactions, but rather a congruent system of attitudes, each element of which is intelligible only in light of the total pattern. A man's political opinions reflect the characteristic modes of his adjustment to life.

There is much more to politics, therefore, than winning and losing. It involves all the ways in which we strive to make ourselves more fully human. This is another way of saying that politics is not purely a function of reason, but also one of psychological needs. As a holistic healer would put it, the physical well-being of the body politic cannot be treated in isolation from its emotional and spiritual dimensions.

Let us now compare the two models' positions concerning human perception. What mental processes must occur if people are to act in accordance with each theory? The answer in brief is that rational choice theory adopts the passive "Lockean" model of the mind, while self-actualization theory subscribes to the active "Leibnitzean" model. The former treats the mind as something that reacts when stimulated. The latter assumes a voluntaristic, self-propelled consciousness.

The ideal rational actor is a passive information-processor who has undistorted knowledge of an objective reality. Left-brain cognitive processes, especially logic and conceptualization, are central. Political calculations should be detached from, and uncontaminated by, the influence of needs and feelings. Otherwise, one's observations may become biased and one's logic faulty.

The self-actualizer is portrayed not as a neutral recorder but as a purposeful creature who bridges mental and material realities. Perception is a transaction between a human subject and a physical object. People construct concepts such as justice and freedom to give meaning to their political world, then they translate those abstract concepts into social institutions, such as political parties, laws, and armies. So the "objective reality" of politics is very much a product of the human mind. The idea of an external world whose existence is independent of human consciousness is rejected.

Moreover, intuitive, right-brain processes do not necessarily distort perception. The degree of cooperation between feelings and perception depends on the person's level of need gratification. Distortion of perception is greatest for those who are most dependent. Healthy people can consciously align their values and goals with the opportunities and constraints of the given situation. Their intuitive, nonrational processes provide the creativity and inspiration that a truly humane political vision requires. In addition, their superior perception of reality leads to a superior ability to reason, to perceive the truth, to come to conclusions, to be logical and cognitively efficient in general. So people's political perceptions cannot be divorced from their political motives. Both political vision and political reasoning improve with the health of the individual.

🍂

Political theories not only describe politics, but also influence it. This self-fulfilling quality of political theories is extremely important. Because people can adjust their actions in light of their expectations, political theories may modify the conduct to which they refer. For example, if we believe that another regime is hostile to ours, the way we treat that regime may encourage its hostility.

The final difference, then, between rational choice and self-actualization theory is in their impact on our society. Rational choice theory's strategies for maximizing utility can be applied to politics to increase the chances of winning. It thereby promotes certain kinds of political skills. People learn how best to achieve a given goal, but not how to rank their goals in the first place. Winning then becomes an end in itself, regardless of the effects on people's needs. Political technique displaces political vision. In addition, if people accept the notion that external forces dictate their political decisions, they tend to feel less responsible for their actions and less concerned with the inner realities from which their acts arise. Politics becomes a game — "I don't make the rules, I just play by them."

Self-actualization theory provides knowledge that is useful, not for controlling the outcome of political events, but for increasing the self-awareness of political actors. By deepening our self-understanding it frees us from external and unconscious limits on our actions. Healthy people make political decisions on the basis of consciously held values, not out of expediency or opportunism. That is why self-actualizers are less socialized and "encapsulated" than other people.

When freely chosen goals replace external demands as guides, politics becomes less predictable, but it also becomes more growth-enhancing. So by focusing on the connections between people's felt needs and their political conduct, humanistic political psychology provides an antidote to the alienation of impersonal political processes. It encourages people to feel a greater responsibility for their political decisions. This is not to deny that social conditions bring about the problems of poverty, crime, drug addiction, and so on. But it is still *psychologically* and *politically* essential for people to take personal and collective responsibility for addressing these problems. We diminish our power and our freedom by blaming social circumstances, because we make ourselves dependent on others for solutions.

Each of these two models, then, represents a major theme of our contemporary political experience. They symbolize the competing political alternatives that we confront at this juncture in history. The widespread acceptance of rational choice theory reflects the technocratic, rationalizing trend of modern society. At the same time, the new political emphasis of humanistic psychology is an expression of our increasing self-awareness. It represents a healthy reaction to the impersonal, alienating qualities of our political experience. It is this fact that gives the humanist/rational choice debate a sense of urgency; the two models' potential effects on our society are so totally different.

These two portrayals of politics are derived from essentially different models of human nature. Matson characterizes the rational actor as an "organic cash-register or pleasure machine, endlessly totting up the balance of profit and loss, of pleasures and pains." According to rational choice theory, political behavior is explained by the "rules of the game." An external logic brings about predictable political outcomes, regardless of who the players are. Politics is rational to the extent that it approaches the norm of mechanical efficiency.

In the self-actualization model, the "bottom line" is not being rational but being healthy. The fundamental issue is the psychological significance of politics for both the powerful and the powerless. This approach necessarily emphasizes the subjective side of political reality. It recognizes that we do not just react to an objective reality; we actively construct the theories that guide our conduct and produce our political institutions.

Politics can only be made comprehensible, therefore, in the context of people's total life pattern. Politics exists because people join together to coordinate inner needs with outer constraints. The notion that one can make sense of politics without close attention to the human values on which political life is based is one of the most limiting assumptions of rational choice theory.

The self-actualization approach differs further from its rival because it makes a connection between personal and political autonomy. As Thomas Jefferson said, changes in laws and institutions go hand in hand with the progress of the human mind. It will avail us nothing to alter the rules of the political game without simultaneously changing both our political values and our self-understanding.

To be a humanist, then, is to be political. It is to affirm that politics is a human process. The humanistic perspective provides not only a new vision of the possible human, but also a new look at our political life. It points to the dangers and opportunities politics offers for actualizing our potential as individuals, as groups, and as a species.

Both Maslow and Rogers tell us that as we become increasingly self-aware and autonomous, we tend to get involved with matters that take us beyond our personal lives. By so doing, we naturally come to value those qualities that make a civilized, humane society possible. The flowering of social consciousness within the human growth movement is therefore an integral part of our actualizing tendency. Humanistic psychology's political vision is being born. Let us give it a gentle, healthy birth.

❦ ❦ ❦

WALTER NORD, *A Marxist Critique of Humanistic Psychology*

The writings of Karl Marx have much in common with what modern writers have described as the essence of humanistic psychology. Like modern humanistic psychologists, Marx was concerned with defining the unique potential of humanity including awareness, choice, and intentionality. However, the potential contributions of his work for the ends sought by humanistic psychologists have not been realized, even though the work of Reich and Fromm, which clearly demonstrated the relevance of Marx's ideas to the problems studied by humanistic psychologists, has been available for some time.

In the 1930s and 1940s, well before humanistic psychology emerged as a special area of inquiry, Reich integrated Marx's socioeconomic analysis with elements of psychological thought to develop a "model" of social organization which would fully promote human development. Reich maintained that economic and social conditions experienced by the masses generated sexual inhibitions, fears of sexual impulses, and an authoritarian character structure. Consequently the masses were not fully capable of human development and freedom. In order to increase the capacity of the masses to exercise freedom, Reich proposed a radically new system of social organization which he called "work democracy." Work democracy was based firmly on many of Marx's thoughts about the development of humans as self-mediators.

More recently Fromm has discussed many of the basic parallels between Marx's work and modern humanism. However, despite the work of Reich and Fromm, at least in America, humanistic psychology has evolved without benefit of Marx's analysis and, for the most part, without consideration of the role of sociological and economic conditions in both the suppression and achievement of humanistic goals.

In this article I attempt to show the value of Marx's analysis for humanistic psychology in several ways. First, I summarize Marx's view as a possible vantage point from which to examine critically modern models of human development. Second, by comparing Marx's work with the main body of humanistic psychology, I point out a number of powerful sociological forces which have been neglected by humanistic psychologists. I argue that if humanistic psychologists continue to ignore these aspects of the social system, their efforts are unlikely to be a potent force toward humanistic ends. Finally, throughout, I point to some recent work by humanistic psychologists which has demonstrated the existence of a felt need for more macro-level analysis and action. I suggest that Marx's analysis may provide a valuable framework through which to integrate and to accelerate the development of these emerging concerns. However, these recent developments are, at most, a demonstration of the fact that humanistic psychologists are beginning to become aware of the importance of some of the issues Marx discussed a century ago. With the notable exceptions of Hampden-Turner and Anderson, none of these writers appears to have seriously proposed anything close to the sweeping social changes Marx saw as inevitable.

Marx's view of human development resembled currently popular models in important ways. For one thing, he envisioned a hierarchy of needs. As Feuer wrote, " . . . as soon as a need is satisfied . . . new needs are made . . . " In the third volume of *Capital,* Marx made it clear that he was envisioning some type of a hierarchical relation among these needs. He wrote:

> . . . With his [i.e., civilized man's] development of this realm of physical necessity expands as a result of his wants; but, at the same time, the forces of production which satisfy these wants also increase. Freedom in this field can only consist in socialized man, the associated producers, rationally regulating their interchange with Nature, bringing it under their common control, instead of being ruled by it as by some blind forces of Nature; and achieving this with the least expenditure of energy and under conditions most favorable to, and worthy of their human nature. But it nonetheless still remains a realm of necessity. Beyond it begins that development of human energy, which is an end in itself, the true realm of freedom, which, however, can blossom forth with this realm of necessity as its basis. The shortening of the working day is its basic prerequisite.

The satisfaction of material needs was a necessary condition for the development of human freedom.

Moreover Marx suggested that under appropriate conditions humans were oriented to act as "self-conscious mediators." In this sense Marx's position was consistent with White's discussion of competence motivation. Marx postulated that humans were the only animals capable of self-conscious activity. In fact, only when people exercised conscious control over the outcomes of their own activities would they be fully human. Without this control, humans were alienated; they did not become what they were capable of being. People, rather than controlling their own creations, were controlled by them.

However, unlike Maslow, White, and other modern writers who have focused mainly on what *individuals* can become, Marx emphasized the interdependence of people in achieving competence *vis à vis* nature. In this sense Marx's analysis parallels Hampden-Turner's model of psychosocial development. As I understand the gist of Marx's thought, it suggests that individual self-actualization could not occur without the actualization of the species.

Marx's emphasis on species actualization stemmed from his belief that human nature was created by humankind itself throughout history. Unlike many humanistic psychologists who appear to assume human nature is given and our task is to allow it to become manifest, Marx saw human nature itself as in process. There was no end state (except perhaps once communism had been achieved) at which one could say humans had realized their nature because it was constantly in process.

Human nature developed through the total configuration of relationships in the social system. Since the system was created by humans and it influences what human nature becomes, it can be said that human nature is created through the activity of human beings themselves. For what Marx called the full "species-man" to develop, humans had to be active, self-conscious agents in producing the social conditions which will lead to the end of alienation.

While Marx's view of human development represents a direct challenge to those humanistic psychologists who have seemed to assume human essence is relatively fixed, his position is quite consistent with what Greening terms existential humanistic psychology. For example in discussing self-actualization Greening wrote: "Man's ultimate essence is still to be created out of his existential choices in becoming." This perspective on human essence may orient humanistic psychology in more macro-oriented directions because it stimulates search to determine what the relevant choices are. Such inquiry is likely to focus on the sets of choices which have produced the existing social system.

At least one contemporary humanistic psychologist has begun to think along these lines. By pointing to Harman's work, I do not mean to imply that Marx and Harman were saying the same thing. While both recognized the need for important changes in the socio-economic system, the changes they envisioned differed markedly in both degree and in kind. For example, Marx saw the end of the capitalist system as a necessary condition for human development; Harman did not.

Nevertheless, Harman's emphasis on the need for education to develop the awareness and responsiveness needed by people to deal with macroproblems paralleled Marx's vision of an educational system. According to Zeitlin, Marx believed that education should be oriented toward developing full human beings rather than merely socializing them to be productive in existing organizations. Accordingly, the successful education required active participation by the learner; the good teacher was one who inspired self-education. Marx was extremely critical of the educational system of his time which he believed functioned to train people to accept the authority of the industrial system. He wished to have education develop people along many dimensions — to develop the whole person who would be prepared to act as a conscious mediator in exchanges with nature.

The cause of the most significant differences in their views of human development between Marx and most humanistic psychologists is Marx's sociological perspective. Many psychologists have tended to overlook the fact that man is a social being. Consequently, many contemporary models emphasize individual growth almost exclusively. Marx, however, stressed the need for a social system in which all members develop together. To him an appropriate social system was a necessary condition for human development.

From this perspective a humanistic psychology which omits attention to the features of the more macrosocial system appears severely limited. Glass has pointed out some of these omissions in describing a humanistic sociology to complement humanistic psychology. Glass wrote:

> A central task of humanistic sociology . . . would ask which institutions and social arrangements, supported by which values and norms, promote the capacity and ability of groups and individuals to make free and responsible choices in the light of their needs to grow, to explore new possibilities, and to do more than simply survive.

Marx's analysis included a thorough analysis of many of these aspects. Consequently his work provides an excellent foundation for the discovery of the social arrangements which must be developed if the goals of humanistic psychologists are to be achieved. Of course, these social arrangements may be far more difficult to create than most humanistic psychologists seem to assume; in fact radically different economic and social structures may be needed.

Marx and humanistic psychologists have engaged in similar polemics against the division of labor, the educational systems, and scientific methods of their respective times. Moreover, they have emphasized humanization and democratization of work as means to human psychological growth. However, with some notable exceptions, humanistic psychologists have focused their suggestions for change almost exclusively at the level of individuals and small social units. By contrast, Marx saw these microunits as products of forces operating at the level of the superstructure. From Marx's analysis, humanistic psychologists may be led to ask, Can humanistic goals be achieved without major changes in economic organization and the distribution of power? Marx's answer would, of course, be "No!"

Marx saw "real" human nature as a product of the existing social relations; he saw the competitive economy, alienation, private property, the division of labor, and social class as mutually supportive of and reinforcing to each other. He did not believe that humans could be treated as "ends" until this pattern of relationships was broken. After all it was this pattern which produced "real" human nature as it is. To break the cycle, it was necessary to introduce changes in the macrostructure. It was particularly important to change the components of the system which perpetuated the private ownership of the means of production.

In some ways Marx's view that human interrelationships are highly determined by variables operating at the level of the superstructure seems to be incorporated in Matson's 1973 statement of the purposes of the AHP Committee on Human Policies. Achievements of human potential depend on finding the aspects of the social system which are most important to change in order to produce and sustain a climate which facilitates the self-realization of all. Clearly, some humanistic psychologists are recognizing the need for macrolevel changes. Marx's work may provide a useful perspective to guide their search for leverage points from which social change can be most effective in producing a humanistic social system.

These leverage points may be quite different from those which have been taken as problematic by most humanistic psychologists. In particular, social classes, private property, the "competitive" and consumption-oriented economy, and the distribution of social power are all major, interrelated factors which help define the social relationships in which individuals function. These forces influence the real social goals (i.e., those goals to which resources are devoted) and are reflected in all elements of the social system including the processes of socialization, education, and work. Current emphasis on the growth of individual units needs to be replaced or complemented by attention to the interdependency of those parts. In fact the emphasis humanistic psychologists have given to individual growth may itself be seen as a product of existing social relations. In contrast a more social focus, produced by different cultural forces, would give far more emphasis to other values, such as the social ends stressed by Marx.

Marx's famous statement, "From each according to his abilities, to each according to his needs" represents a very different ultimate goal than the individual "self-actualization" sought by many contemporary humanistic psychologists. While some humanistic psychologists have stressed the importance of meaningful interpersonal relationships for human development, for the most part they have viewed the satisfaction of social needs as a step toward individual self-actualization rather than the acme of human development. In this sense, Marx's view represents an alternative set of priorities which is socially oriented as opposed to individually oriented. The degree to which American humanistic psychologists have taken individual development as an end, may indicate the cultural relativity of their work. Marx's social view provides a stimulus for questioning this choice of goals.

So far I have suggested that the writings of Karl Marx contain a framework which can be useful for enhancing progress toward humanistic goals by helping humanistic psychologists expand their analysis and question some of their latent assumptions. Moreover, his work may provide a framework to integrate some of the ideas of humanistic psychologists who are beginning to realize that the problems they have worked on at the level of the infrastructure are an expression of forces operating in the superstructure. I suggest that Marx's work provides a well-developed framework from which to seize upon the opportunity described by Anderson " . . . to make the highest development of human beings a deliberate social goal . . . " As Anderson argued, if we choose this course:

> . . . then the task before us is to think about the growth possibilities of all people, at all social and economic levels, and also to understand fully what it means when a species begins to become responsible for its own evolution.

Throughout this article I have been critical of many humanistic psychologists who have omitted attention to macrolevel social forces. In particular I have suggested that this lacuna is a major barrier to realizing humanistic aims because it leads the humanistic psychologist to underestimate the strength of a number of forces which influence human development. Such underestimation can be a factor associated with the production of radical sounding change strategies which are in essence quite conservative. Perhaps this point can best be made by looking at the writings of even as innovative a thinker as Maslow.

At many places Maslow seemed to recognize the need for change at the level of the superstructure. For example, at one point he noted that the creation of a democratic society requires change in economic, political, sociological, and educational activities. However, in the next sentence, instead of focusing directly on how these things could be changed, he retreated to talking about the role of social scientists as goal setters and researchers. Moreover in his article entitled "Power Relationships and Patterns of Personal Development," his entire treatment of power was limited to the socialization process. Again, Maslow in writing about how to produce change, focused almost exclusively at the psychological level. His major means of social change seemed no more sociological than therapy and personal growth groups. Moreover, Maslow, in discussing an era of social improvement, saw industry as a major vehicle to humanistic social change. However, his change strategy was nothing more radical than " . . . enlightened management to modify industry to permit human growth." While he did specifically note that such management could not occur in an authoritarian society, he did not discuss what structural changes were needed. Maslow's emphasis on microchange was consistent with his explicit belief in the need for slow rather than rapid change and his commitment to working for change at local levels.

My point is neither to put down Maslow nor to deny the importance of working at the microlevel; the microapproach is important. As Reich observed, Marxism is inadequate to the degree that many Marxists have failed to take the character structure of the masses into account. In fact, Reich's stress on developing "the masses" suggests that work at the microlevel is essential. However, to be maximally effective the microlevel efforts of humanistic psychologists may need to take new forms to appeal to a wider spectrum of the population. Although I have no data on the subject, it has been my impression that the current media used by humanistic psychologists have been much more effective in reaching members of the upper socioeconomic strata than they have been in reaching the working and lower classes. Hampden-Turner's observation that " . . . it is necessary for social scientists to understand how poor people construe social reality and how they perceive their dilemmas," suggests one concrete step that could be taken in beginning our quest for tactics to broaden the appeal of humanistic psychology to lower socio-economic groups.

However, even a broadened microapproach is not enough; this work must be complemented by macrolevel strategies. I wish to emphasize that despite clear recognition of the importance of structural variables, Maslow and other humanistic psychologists have been reluctant to take them as problematic. Consequently, their work is often dominated by a latent conservatism. Marx provided an alternative view — the individual is the ensemble of social relations. Without changes in these relations, human beings as a species, and hence as individuals, cannot develop their full potential. In short, much of humanistic psychology may be too psychological to be effectively humanistic.

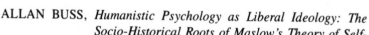

ALLAN BUSS, *Humanistic Psychology as Liberal Ideology: The Socio-Historical Roots of Maslow's Theory of Self-Actualization*

Humanistic psychology can best be understood within its cultural context. It is within this context that I advance the claim that humanistic psychology in general, and Maslow's theory of self-actualization in particular, have their genesis in liberalism.

My purpose in this article is to try and reveal both the nature and consequences of the link between humanistic psychology and the liberal tradition using Maslow's theory as a concrete case for analysis. This analysis is part of a larger goal to examine the social and historical basis of psychological theory and ideas.

Over a period of some thirty years Robert Nisbet has been arguing that the historical roots of classical sociological theory lie in the conservative response to modernity. Thus the writings of Marx, Weber, Durkheim, Tonnies, and others, may be seen as a quest for community in an age of increasing fragmentation, isolation, alienation, and bureaucracy. The latter are all due to forces of modernization such as the division of labor, and increasing rationalization or routinization of institutional services. During the nineteenth century, traditional society was crumbling under the heavy weight of rapid scientific, technological, and socio-political change, and the classical sociological theorists attempted to preserve the idea of community at a time when its continuing existence was in serious doubt. The rising tide of individualism (part of the growing liberal consciousness) seemed to show no sign of ebbing. Thus we can modify Nisbet's thesis slightly. Classical sociological theory can be seen as a conservative reaction to the growing liberalism which emphasized the autonomous individual.

Recently Westkott has argued that modern (as opposed to classical) sociology is also conservative in nature. However, in contrast to Nisbet's emphasis upon conservative theory, Westkott has argued that modern sociology draws its conservative tendencies from method. Its methodology, inherited from Comte, emphasizes the present and the process of collecting facts. This produces "a 'situational conservatism' that justifies the factual reality it records." Positivism as a method "is the denial of philosophy, theory, politics, and imagination." It creates a conservative disposition that reproduces, rather than criticizes, social reality.

Comte's methodology has also influenced the other social sciences. When the social sciences became the behavioral sciences, positivistic methodology became the common denominator that united mainstream sociology, psychology, political science, and anthropology. It did not matter that most behavioral scientists were themselves self-professed liberals. Their individual politics are separable from the political consequences of their collective professional practice. Westkott's criticism applied to any of the behavioral sciences adopting a similar methodology. In Hampden-Turner's words:

> their [behavioral scientists] conservatism is latent in the tools they employ. It comes about less by valuing conservatively than by the "value-free" selection of the less than human . . . He who is silent assents, and to describe the status quo with detailed and passionless precision is usually to dignify it.

Although humanistic psychology has been branded by Maslow as the alternative to behaviorism and psychoanalysis (i.e., as third force psychology) it can more accurately be considered as second force psychology, *as the liberal reaction to conservatism* (albeit conservatism in two different guises). Anderson has recently noted that the political consequences of both behaviorism and psychoanalysis are conservative in nature. In light of our previous distinction between conservative method and conservative theory, we can be somewhat more analytic than was Anderson regarding the sources of the common conservative effect of both behaviorism and psychoanalysis. Whereas the conservative element in behaviorism stems from its positivistic methodology, in psychoanalysis it is more rooted in theory. Thus Freud's deterministic, fatalistic, and pessimistic view of humanity offered little, other than trying to get along as best one could in a basically static, evil society. For Freud, the nature of society was derived from the nature of the individual, that is, from a biologically based, ahistorical view of humanity. Since human nature was basically irrational, destructive, and, of course, unchanging in his theory, there were no grounds for expecting improvement in the human condition, no plan for implementing social change. Humanistic psychologists reacted to a negative view of humanity that carried with it a latent conservatism. They certainly did not see in Freudian negativism any support for the idea of radical and revolutionary change that some have seen.

In summary, then, liberal humanistic psychologists rejected the conservative implications that both behaviorism and psychoanalysis seemed to entail. A mechanistic, deterministic conception of the individual left no possibility for an active, self-determining agent who could transform and change his/her situation. Behaviorism left no room for contemplation, speculation, or reflection about one's experience. Classical psychoanalysis offered little in this area as well, since one's experience and theorizing could ultimately never break through the prison of a deterministic past and predetermined future. To the liberal mind, freedom, liberty, and personal development or progress were ideals that were inconsistent with the conservative methodology of behaviorism and the conservative theory of psychoanalysis. It was on the basis of such liberal values that humanistic psychologists launched their critique of the two "traditional" psychologies. Thus humanistic psychology began as a radical and revolutionary liberal movement, much like the liberalism associated with the Enlightenment in which genesis also lay in criticizing the established order from a consideration of freedom, liberty, and individual progress.

In criticizing the conservative implications of both behaviorism and psychoanalysis, humanistic psychologists were really fighting a battle on two fronts: (a) attempting to deal with the very real problem of an alienated, determined, controlled, and objectified human existence; and (b) opposing the conservative ideology which had had the net effect of reproducing that reality. With respect to alienation, humanistic psychologists were reacting to the true content of both behaviorism and psychoanalysis. That is to say, the origins of both behaviorism and psychoanalysis can be seen as tied to a specific socio-historical condition and as such, they offer certain insights into that condition. A deterministic, mechanistic, and pessimistic conception of the individual was tied to a social reality which was indeed consistent with such an image. However, the error of both behaviorism and psychoanalysis was to accept current reality as absolute reality. Behaviorism in method, and psychoanalysis in theory, universalize and thus conserve and preserve a human condition that should be transformed. Their built-in conserving tendencies tend to perpetuate that social reality which spawned their being. Thus they are both ultimately ideological in the Marxian sense of that term.

Both behaviorism and psychoanalysis "reflect" social reality (the deterministic, alienated, mechanistic existence associated with advanced industrial capitalistic society), and this is their truth-content. Yet, at the same time, both also involve a distortion or an "inversion" of that social reality, which means both absolutize what is really an historically unique situation. This is their "falseness" dimension. For Marx, an ideology both "reflected" and "inverted" social reality and thus contained both truth and falseness.

While humanistic psychology as a liberal theory offers quite a different view of humanity than do the conservative theories of both behaviorism or psychoanalysis, it does not escape the latter's ideological fate. Although it started out with a revolutionary bang, humanistic psychology has ended up with a co-opted whimper. There can be little doubt that, historically speaking, third force psychology was a progressive movement. However, its critical foundations have gradually eroded away as it

has become institutionalized and housed with APA as the "official" oppositional wing. What was once an "out" group is now very much an "in"
group. The rhetoric of individual development and self-actualization has
been taken over by government, industrial, and organizational psychologists, and has been turned into an ideology which maintains the status quo.
What was once a theory of revolutionary liberal psychologists is now part
of the received doctrine of the liberal establishment — what might be
termed "conservative liberalism."

The excessive individualism contained in the doctrine of self-
actualization serves to mask the larger social questions surrounding society's structures and institutions. A theory that predisposes one to focus
more upon individual freedom and development rather than the larger
social reality, works in favor of maintaining that social reality. While several people have already noted the conformist implications of humanistic
psychology, thus far there has not been an adequate socio-historical interpretation of this dimension. What is required is situating the theory of
humanistic psychology within a larger social and political matrix, and,
more specifically, revealing the liberal foundations of the theory. The latter permits a deeper, more meaningful critique in the sense of pointing out
that it is necessary to transform the social props that support liberal
humanistic psychology in order to transcend its individualistic bias. In
other words, it is through praxis that more valid theory will develop (and,
being good dialecticians, our theory, such as the present critical effort,
should also inform our praxis). Let me now try and make the above rather
abstract ideas more concrete by focusing upon Maslow's theory of self-
actualization.

Having alluded to the link between humanistic psychology and liberalism, it is possible to become a little more specific about that relationship
by looking at the structure of Maslow's theory. Conceptually, there can be
little doubt that Maslow's psychological theory is founded upon, and
implies, the tenets of liberalism. Such themes in his writings as growth,
becoming, self-actualization, individual freedom, and tolerance, are all
the psychological embodiment of the liberal frame of mind which emphasizes optimism, pluralism, individual freedom, piecemeal progress, and

the gradual development toward perfection. Thus although Maslow rejected positivism as a methodology, he adopted a positive or optimistic, rather than a negative or critical approach. This way he shared the liberal disposition to concentrate on the "good," rather than on the "bad," and to attempt piecemeal social change through, for example, the education of individuals, rather than by transforming the deeper structures of society.

Maslow had a vision of the ideal liberal society in which freedom and individual development reigned supreme — a psychological utopia he called "Eupsychia." Thus in common with other liberal thinkers, Maslow shared the dual commitment to *(a)* finding out the "truth" — describing reality as it "really" is, and *(b)* hinting toward a social reality we ought to nurture into being. And the two tasks were often unconsciously fused. Maslow never did adequately distinguish between, and resolve to some degree of satisfaction, the "is' and the "ought." He attempted to pass his own theory off as based upon purely descriptive statements, rather than containing a hard normative core. Thus his theory lacks an explicit and self-conscious appreciation of its own value-laden nature, and more specifically, its affirmation of liberal values. The latter was the case in spite of the fact that Maslow gave considerable attention to the study of values.

In regard to Maslow's own values that guided his work, his original sample of self-actualizers, his own personal selection of individuals he considered to be self-actualized, appears to epitomize liberal values. According to Maslow, these people were democratic, autonomous, individualistic, and, true to the liberal penchant for piecemeal progress, preferred to work from within rather than from without the system on matters relating to social injustice.

Like classical nineteenth-century liberals such as Herbert Spencer, Maslow grounded his notion of individual progress upon the universal laws of biology. It was Maslow's absolute, ahistorical view of human nature, as anchored in his concept of the instinctoid, which was the foundation for his theory of self-actualization. His conception of human nature as primary, and the environment as secondary, was much like that of an earlier champion of liberal ideals — Rousseau. Rousseau's "natural man" would almost seem to have inspired Maslow's "concept of the psychiatrically healthy man, or the eupsychic man, who is also in effect the natural man." Thus for Maslow, "Man demonstrates *in his own nature* a pressure toward . . . more perfect actualization . . . The environment does not give his potentialities."

Whereas Freud's conception of an unchanging human nature was one that emphasized destruction, negation, and despair, Maslow's liberal essentialism was one of construction, affirmation, and hope. the important point here is that the structure of both Freud's and Maslow's view of humanity is identical (ahistorical, essential, unchanging, biological), although the content differs. Although he is not specifically discussing humanistic psychology, Lichtman's observations on various reactions to psychoanalysis are indeed appropriate:

> the tendency is to negate the Freudian *characterization* of human nature . . . [and] assert the view that the new set of attributes is *given fact* about human beings. Men and women are transformed into a *new* entity, but an *entity* nonetheless . . . What distinguishes human life, however, what constitutes its dignity and unique value, is our capacity to create ourselves in history . . . [T]he view of a fixed human nature is one of the basic mystifications to be opposed.

Thus the theories of both Maslow and Freud are ideological to the extent that they view human nature as an absolute.

Part of Maslow's view of human nature included a consideration of values and ethics. Maslow also attempted to ground his own values and ethics in biology and then passed them off as universal. As noted by Smith, this move is problematic for a truly humanistic approach, that is, an approach that rests upon choice, dialogue, and criticism within the context of a changing socio-historical reality.

Along with his emphasis upon an essential rather than an historical or transformable human nature, Maslow also stressed inner rather than outer freedom:

> Healthy individuals are not externally visible . . . It is an *inner* freedom that they have . . . they may be considered to be psychologically autonomous, i.e., relatively independent of culture. External freedom seems to be less important than inner freedom.

Here Maslow is following J. S. Mill's emphasis upon freedom or liberty in the internal, rather than in the external sphere. Mill's entire essay of 1859, *On Liberty,* is an exploration of the limits of society's constraint over the individual. The major theme that Mill defends is one in which there is "absolute nonintervention in the private sphere of human affairs." It is a position that Wolff has dubbed "Mill's Doctrine of the Liberty of the Inner Life," and would seem to find its psychological expression in Maslow's theory of inner freedom and self-actualization.

Finally in regard to the political content of Maslow's theory, we can note that in reading various political analyses of liberalism, it is very easy indeed to find passages that could have been penned by Maslow. Thus such classical liberal works as Mill's *On Liberty* written in 1859, and Hobhouse's *Liberalism* written in 1911, contain many references to the idea of individual development and self-actualization, although space does not allow us to consider relevant passages.

Important as the above observations are concerning the liberal foundations of Maslow's theory, we can go beyond a "mere" conceptual link between Maslow's concepts and the liberal tradition, and examine the deeper, socio-historical roots that nourished the specific form of liberalism that permeates his psychological categories. My strategy here is to single out the major underlying contradiction within Maslow's theory — *the tension between his democratic and elitist tendencies* — and place this contradiction within its socio-historical context.

❧

The major implicit contradiction with Maslow's theory has recently been made explicit by Aron. According to Aron, Maslow held two contradictory views of self. One view involved a democratic conception of self. It emphasized equality of rights, individual sovereignty, pluralism, and a toleration of others. This side of Maslow placed a premium upon individual choice and development and was based upon a relativistic notion of values. "Maslow's Other Child" involved what Aron has called an aristocratic or elitist view of the self. This elitist view of the self was derived from Maslow's judgment that, in reality, there are better values than others, better ways of living than others, better people than others. According to this side of Maslow, there are two distinct kinds, or what we might call classes, of people: *(a)* those who are self-actualizing, worthy of emulation, psychologically healthy, and in control of their lives (one percent of the general population according to Maslow); and *(b)* those who are non-actualizing, nonworthy of being emulated, psychologically unhealthy, and impotent vis-a-vis successfully charting themselves around life's obstacles. Maslow revered the former and disparaged the latter.

While Aron has detected and revealed the contradiction within Maslow's thought revolving around democratic versus elitist values, she has not explained its existence. Thus it is not enough to psychologize such a contradiction, and state that "Maslow committed an error in reasoning that cannot be rectified." It makes no sense to ask "Where in this wild dialectic is the *real* Maslow." since it is not necessary to choose between Maslow the democrat and Maslow the aristocrat. The "real" Maslow was both. The contradiction in his theory is not a conceptual one. There is no error in logic. Rather, the contradiction is a real contradiction. It is an historical contradiction rooted in a concrete social reality. *Maslow's contradiction is part of a larger contradiction — the contradiction between democratic theory and democratic practice within the modern liberal society.* A more adequate explanation of Maslow's psychological concepts (and their contradictory nature) must involve unearthing their social content and peeling away their surface layers, thus laying bare their historical origins.

Maslow's first systematic presentation of his views, *Motivation and Personality,* was published in 1954. This book contains revisions of several essays dating from 1941 onward, and was written over a period of time which witnessed some very significant political events revolving around the undermining of classical democratic theory. Several mass movements, all of which took a totalitarian turn (e.g., Naziism, Fascism, and McCarthyism), shook the very foundations of a classical liberal democratic theory which had considered the masses as the protectors of freedom and liberty. The growing post-war proletariat support for Communist parties in such western countries as France and Italy posed somewhat of a threat to classical liberal democratic theory. Rather than seeing the franchise and the further delegation of power to the masses as guaranteeing the preservation of democracy, there developed a growing realization that perhaps the masses could not be trusted to exercise such increased responsibility in a way which was consistent with preserving liberal values. During the early 1950s the lack of political sophistication of the common person was being increasingly documented by social scientists. Such findings helped to fuel the growing disillusionment amongst certain thinkers with classical liberal democratic theory, and the acceptance of elitist theories of democracy.

The tension between the theory and practice of classical democracy during this period could no longer be ignored. The historical setting that nurtured the development of democracy, that is, the small rural village where each individual was assured of a hearing, was no longer the prototype for the modern democratically run state. In an age of the nation-state there was little opportunity for direct participation of the masses. Along with nationhood, democratic government increasingly involved fewer and fewer decision-makers. Those who continued to espouse classical democratic theory were by now uttering rhetoric. The reality could no longer be ignored — democracy was increasingly becoming the purview of a very small but powerful elite. What Bachrach has called *democratic elitism* had replaced classical democratic theory.

As outlined by Bachrach, the flames of democratic elitism were fanned by the mass movements of the 1930s and 40s, and this liberal doctrine became a force to be reckoned with during the post-war aftermath. Whereas earlier liberals had believed that liberal values such as liberty, freedom, individual development, tolerance, and pluralism were to be defended and preserved through increasing the franchise and individual rights, post-war liberals began to take the exact opposite view. Liberalism was endangered by further democratization, and it needed a "power elite" to safeguard its existence.

We are now in a position to understand better the social basis of Maslow's theory of self-actualization, and the historical roots of the contradiction between the democratic and elitist views of self. Maslow's elite — the one percent of the general population who define and thus control what is meant by self-actualization — are the psychological embodiment of the social elite who are society's decision makers. *The structure of Maslow's psychological theory can be seen as incorporating the structure of his society. Maslow's hierarchical or "class" theory of self-actualization consists of social categories projected onto the individual.*

His is a liberal psychological theory that contains the real socio-historical contradiction between democracy and elitism — the contradiction that had evolved within the modern liberal democratic state. The tension in Maslow's theory of self-actualization between democracy and elitism — between the nonactualized masses and the actualized few — is part of the tension that liberal theorists were experiencing and trying to resolve in the 1940s and 50s. Whereas the latter attempted a conceptual solution involving a defense of democratic elitism. Maslow, as Aron has made clear, was never sufficiently conscious of the contradictory strains in his theory to attempt such a solution.

Thus, contrary to Hampden-Turner's argument that Maslow sought to synthesize "apparent"contradictions and transcend false dualisms, I believe that the democratic-elitist tension remains intact and below consciousness in his work. It is driven underground where it can serve an ideological function. And, even if Maslow had been self-conscious of the contradiction in his theory, an attempt to perform conceptual surgery by synthesizing the polarity would not have been the way out. False syntheses are no better than false dualisms. We should guard against applying dialectical thinking in a mechanical or undialectical manner. We need a truly critical approach. We need to turn the dialectic upon itself and adopt the perspective that Adorno has called "negative dialectics," in order to detect the actual contradictory and fragmentary social reality underlying our theory.

In other words, theory alone will not suffice to save Maslow's theory from its contradictory structure. Since the contradiction of which we are speaking is not a conceptual one but, rather, a real one anchored in a concrete socio-historical reality, its resolution requires transforming that social reality. Thus theory guiding praxis, and praxis, in turn, guiding theory, are necessary to resolve the contradictory democratic and elitist dimensions in Maslow's theory. The solution to Maslow's contradiction is part of a larger social solution which undermines the structural basis of democratic elitism and establishes a form of democracy with a broader base.

Re-establishing the very important core of classical liberal democratic theory, that is, a broad-based type of political participation, is absolutely necessary in order to achieve the kinds of goals that Maslow's theory of self-actualization is purportedly trying to achieve. Classical democratic theory "is based on the supposition that a man's dignity, and indeed his growth and development . . . is dependent upon an opportunity to participate actively in decisions that significantly affect him." Having the freedom to be an effective part of those collective decisions that affect one's life must be a prerequisite reality rather than a myth if Maslow's goal of wide-spread self-actualization is to be a realistic one. Democratic elitism, which sustains Maslow's self-actualized elite, must give way to mass self-actualization which, in turn, requires mass democracy. It is in this way that the structure of Maslow's psychological theory can inform our social praxis. Political action and psychological theory are thus connected dialectically.

Of course a plea for a return to the practice of classical liberal democratic theory is unrealistic in an age of the "global community," where increasing centralization of the decision making process has gone beyond the "mere" establishment of national governing bodies, to those with international powers. One must take account of the reality of C. Wright Mills' "power elite" in an age of increasing complexity, specialization, and bureaucracy. What, then, is a realistic, yet more democratic alternative to democratic elitism in the age of mass society? Bachrach's proposal for transcending democratic elitism would seem to provide at least a valuable hint in the direction of finding a social solution to the social contradiction that Maslow's psychological theory contains. According to Bachrach's "self-developmental theory of democracy," it is necessary to go beyond a nineteenth-century notion of political decision-making that restricts itself to government decision making. Thus "large areas within existing so-called private centers of power are political and therefore potentially open to a wide and democratic sharing in decision making." Thus greater effort should be made so that the common person can actively participate in those decisions that affect him/her in the factory and in the community — decisions that he/she considers important and vital, rather than tangential and irrelevant to day-to-day living.

In giving Maslow's theory of self-actualization a critical and dialectical reading, we are able to understand its liberal ideological foundations. Ideologically speaking, the validity of Maslow's theory derives from the contradictory social reality it "reflects" and supports — democratic elitism — a two-class theory of individual freedom and development. However, Maslow's theory is at the same time an "inversion" of that social reality to the extent that its psychological categories universalize an historically specific condition, namely, democratic elitism. Maslow's biologically rooted theory of self-actualization freezes human nature circa 1950 and makes an absolute out of two historically evolved classes of individuals. As such, it contains a hidden plea for social transformation once one appreciates that human nature is itself historical and that humanity can create and re-create its own nature through its making of history.

🌳   🌳   🌳

IV

THE END OF INNOCENCE

The discussions incorporated into this book have dealt with an underlying question of great practical import for our future: can psychology — especially that practice of psychology which calls itself "humanistic" — actively contribute to the political process, or can it only analyze the participants and interpret the results of that process? If as Floyd Matson notes, humanistic psychology is "the caring of minds and the nurture of minding," then it would appear that political involvement — through direct action, group support, media-exposure and timely intervention on behalf of human rights — is inescapable for therapists, theorists and clients alike. The AHP's Committee on Human Policies (1973), chaired by Matson and reported on in his first piece, committed humanistic psychologists to specific goals in the areas of economics, conflict resolution, the development of technology, equal rights for all and institutional reform.

Humanistic psychology may thus be considered not merely an analytical tool but a concrete way of "doing politics," of behaving politically. As Walt Anderson remarks at the beginning of his essay on "Politics and the New Humanism," there is no "distinction between psychology, sociology and political science which makes sense anywhere outside of a college catalogue. Any psychology is also a political ideology and a scientific methodology."

Matson's appeal for a "Civilization of the Dialogue" was originally issued nearly twenty years ago (1966); Anderson's call for a "human health" model in politics, more than ten years ago (1974). Their continuing relevance is assessed and contextualized in Elizabeth Campbell's "The End of Innocence." Campbell reviews the development of humanistic psychology over the past quarter century. Her essay is not only an appreciative retrospective, but also a forthright assessment of the foibles, mistakes and wrong turns taken by what is broadly called "the human potential movement." Campbell's optimistic conviction that humanistic psychology "has contributed a great deal to personal growth" is thus tempered by the realization that it "has had an indeterminate effect at the societal level."

Still, the resources brought to the tasks of politics and social transformation by humanistic psychology are many and impressive. Campbell concludes her confession of "the end of innocence" by listing some of them. Her words serve well as a challenge to complacency and an invitation to action:

> We can no longer dwell in a state of innocence and have a lot to learn about ourselves and our world. As humanistic professionals, we have a special responsibility to apply our knowledge and resources toward increasing our understanding and our ability to respond to the challenges of this in-between time. May we each find our own passionate path and be comforted by the fact that we are not alone.

This final section of the book is introduced by two contributions from Floyd W. Matson.

🌳   🌳   🌳

FLOYD W. MATSON, *Human Policies: Statement of Purposes*

If psychology is the study of mind, humanistic psychology is that and something more: the caring of minds and the nurture of minding. Those of us who practice psychology "humanistically" have two objectives: first, to identify and articulate the issues about which we care most and mind most. Our second objective is to explore all available means of making our concern manifest and effective in the world — that is, to translate principles into policies and humanistic theory into humane practice.

We are opposed, by definition, to all forms of tyranny over mind. But tyranny nowadays is often more subtle than stark, persuasive rather than coercive. For every act of overt exploitation or violence against the person, there are a thousand petty episodes of intrusion upon privacy, curtailment of freedom, control of personality, and violation of dignity — little murders of the mind which together add up to social menticide on a massive scale. We cannot hope, as a specialized group with limited competence and scarce resources, to expose and resist them all. What we can do, immediately, is to establish the priorities for an agenda of action, a program of humanistic intervention at crucial points in the culture, the society and the polity.

While we cannot be all things to all persons, or do all things for all victims, we can act — in various and appropriate ways — upon our commitment to social change in the interest of personal growth and cultural enrichment. One way to do this is to throw the weight of our resources and the force of our skills into the balance at critical moments in the career of psychological liberty — in legislative hearings and debates, in the public forum of mass-mediated controversy, before school boards and administrative agencies, and wherever an issue arises that is relevant to our purposes and proportionate to our capacities.

That is one way of putting our humanism on the line. Another way is to take the initiative in designing programs, proposing legislation, sponsoring research and conceiving alternatives in the direction of applied humanistic psychology. To be sure, given our modest capabilities, there will be limits to the scope of our participation and the impact of our best efforts. On the other hand, this association's reach should exceed its grasp — or what's a humanism for? A few preliminary and tentative suggestions toward a program of humanistic intervention are outlined below.

Believing that the rampant growth of technology has already reached pathogenic proportions and threatens to overrun human values if not humanity itself, we pledge our participation in the effort to redress the balance between man and machinery, between the needs of persons and the demands of efficiency, between creativity and technique. As humanistic psychologists, we are particularly alert to the laboratory exploitation and manipulation of human subjects as experimental guinea pigs in the service of dubious social norms, such as those implicit in the schemes of "psychotechnology" (Kenneth Clark) and the "technology of behavior" (Skinner). We are equally opposed to the abuse of psychological technique for commercial and political gain in the form of motivation research, subliminal advertising, and related devices of mental subversion. More positively, we propose to seek ways of bolstering the defenses of the human personality, in the roles of consumer and citizen, against the exponentially growing onslaught from communications technology and its masters.

We propose to explore feasible ways of contributing to the reduction or conciliation of conflict in those areas where its continuance is clearly destructive of the values of humanism. With regard to the most conspicuous example, conflict resolution in the international arena (war and rumors of war), we propose to pursue the precedent of the APA's Committee on Psychology in National and International Affairs, as well as the model for international dialogue set by the *Pacem in Terris* convocation under the auspices of the Center for the Study of Democratic Institutions. On the domestic front, we will propose the initiation of new projects and the support of ongoing efforts toward dialogical encounter between polarized community groups (e.g., police-ghetto residents, "old and new ethnics," etc.). Our aim is not to eliminate conflict, which is intrinsic to a dynamic society and doubtless essential to personal growth, but to convert it into a force for constructive social change, cultural diversity, and political pluralism.

The conventional economics of the private-enterprise corporate business system have demonstrably proved to be incompatible with the goals not only of humanistic psychology but of sound social policy. As Willis Harman has written, "Rational business decisions turn out too often to have resulted in irrational squandering of natural resources, fouling of the environment, technological disemployment, debasing of persons, and — in some dimensions at least — lowered quality of life." Accepting this judgment and seeking to reverse the cycle of economic aggrandizement and exploitation, we propose to sponsor and support alternative systems of marketing, management, and business operation such as: Charles Hampden-Turner's social marketing network, A. H. Maslow's program of "eupsychian management," and Harman's proposals for the reallocation of values and assumption of social responsibilities on the part of large-scale corporate enterprise. This commitment to internal reform and fabian-style persuasion does not, however, preclude an interest in the exploration of still more drastic alternatives to the contemporary pentagon of power — and the power of the Pentagon.

❧

We pledge support in principle of all genuine self-liberating movements on the part of significant cultural minorities, both ethnic (e.g., blacks, Chicanos, native Americans) and nonethnic (e.g., women, the poor, homosexuals, the blind) with the possibility of selective intervention and cooperation at points and in forms to be decided by the AHP on strict grounds of relevance, congruence, and competence (ours, not theirs). An essential tenet of humanism, in psychology as elsewhere, is respect for the right of persons to self-expression and self-actualization, which in social and political terms means equal access and full participation in community affairs and occupations — bar none. An example of pertinent humanistic research within this framework might be the critical examination of the recurrent theory of genetic inferiority and the ideology of IQ.

We propose to foster research and support experimental programs which give promise of advancing the liberation of learning from the confinement of the knowledge factory and the traditional view of school as social control agency and cultural induction center. At the college level, the AHP's Humanistic Psychology Institute provides a fully developed matrix for educational innovation and infiltration. At all levels the AHP's education network furnishes a potentially nationwide laboratory for exploration and experimentation. The creative work and provocative programs of numerous AHP members, balancing the cognitive and affective domains and smuggling ecstasy into education, constitute virtually an embarrassment of riches. The momentum is already there, and we are on our way toward the humanization of learning. Is it too much to say that the only thing we have to fear is the failure of nerve?

The precarious tradition of human rights, centering upon the concept of the person is nowhere more at issue than in the ambiguous procedures of legal surveillance, arrest, trial, conviction, incarceration, and the rest. As humanists, even as psychologists, we cannot evade the responsibilities of our commitment. Accordingly, we propose to lend our support in all feasible ways — with expert testimony and possibly with *amicus curiae* briefs as well as with research and persuasion — to responsible efforts aimed at the liberalization of legal norms regarding, for example, the rights of the accused (notably the indigent and "incompetent"), the rights of the convicted (i.e., prison reform), the treatment of the so-called mentally ill, the protection of citizen privacy against intrusion and surveillance (especially electronic), and many more. Against those who say that we are ill-equipped to right the wrongs of society and to rewrite its laws, we may reply that the limitations of competence — real as they are — deserve to be weighed against the motivations of conscience. It is for each of us, and all of us together, to find and strike the proper balance.

We propose to support legitimate welfare reforms conceived in the spirit of the 1956 amendments to the Social Security Act, which established the goals of self-care and self-support (the preliminaries to self-actualization) for all clients of public assistance. At the same time, we repudiate and will endeavor to defeat those spurious "welfare reforms" which have as their real purpose to make a crime of poverty, to eliminate the constructive programs of community action and client participation, and to turn the clock back to the Victorian workhouse if not to the Elizabethan poor laws. Our aims in this regard are, among others, to convert relief into rehabilitation, to equalize the conditions of competition for the handicapped and disadvantaged, and to reduce in some degree the fatal gap between power and innocence.

❦   ❦   ❦

FLOYD W. MATSON, *Humanistic Political Science and Humane Politics*

It was George Orwell, I believe, who first made our generation aware of the compelling relationship between political discourse and political behavior. He made his point most dramatically, of course, in the anti-utopian novel *Nineteen Eighty-Four* — in which words became the surgical instruments for mass menticide, a kind of verbal lobotomy practiced upon entire populations by those specialists from the Ministry of Truth whom I cannot help thinking of as the operant conditioners and positive reinforcers.

Orwell also made the same point with equal effectiveness in an essay entitled "Politics and the English Language," in which he demonstrated how the vocabulary of technical abstraction and official rationalization had already altered our perception of political acts and human crises. Perhaps the classic example of this subliminal modification of perspectives was Stalin's famous "solution" of the Kulak problem, which introduced the term *liquidation* to the language of politics. The very terminology of explanation in effect transformed the brutal slaughter of millions of peasants into an administrative exercise conducted with Stakhanovite precision.

But now I must qualify my earlier remark: that is not quite the classic example. The classic example — may it never be improved upon — was the solution of the Jewish problem by the laboratory technicians and "behavioral engineers" of the Third Reich. In light of the principle of linguistic determinism, it is less difficult to understand how millions of good Germans were able to blind themselves to the mass extermination going on virtually before their eyes. They were, in fact, protected by an armory of perceptual defenses — what Harry Stack Sullivan called the capacity for selective inattention. The events out there in front of them were filtered through the "pictures in their heads," and those stereotyped pictures were painted by the language of objective description and explanation. What the good burghers then perceived was not genocide but eugenics; not extermination but experimentation; not the torture and burning of countless men, women, and children, but the strategic solution of a problem in mathematics.

An instructive illustration of the transforming power of language, cited by Orwell in his essay, is the familiar phrase "pacification of the villages" — which, as I recall, he attributed to the Communists. Somehow I think Orwell would not have been surprised to learn that it is we, the adversaries of Communism and defenders of human dignity, who invoked the phrase recurrently to account for the burning and bombing of countless men, women, and children in Vietnam.

The style of our discourse, in short, not only reflects the style of our thought and experience; it also shapes it. This was the main thrust of the Whorf-Sapir hypothesis concerning language and culture; it has long been an axiom of the general semanticists; and indeed the concept is possibly as old as the magical veneration of the *Logos*. "In the beginning was the Word." It is noteworthy that whenever the ancients wished to clinch some disputed point with total finality, they had only to say: "It is written . . . " (The modern version of this conversation-stopper is, of course, "If you read it in the *Sun,* it must be true.")

I believe that there are two discernible styles or modes of discourse, two opposed vocabularies, which have contested for supremacy throughout the political tradition of the West. They are variously named; the Greeks knew them as the modes of *dialectic* and *rhetoric*. I prefer to identify them, following Martin Buber, simply as *dialogue* and *monologue*.

The dialogical mode of communication is that which is appropriate to questioning and questing, to learning and yearning, to meeting and understanding. It is the open-ended grammar of discussion and dissent, of contingency and toleration — and the toleration it implies most strongly is that which Else Frenkel-Brunswik used to call "the tolerance of ambiguity." This is the mode which existentialists from Kierkegaard to Jaspers have defined as "authentic communication," in opposition to the mere "talk" which is monologue. It is this connective tissue which permits Abraham Maslow to speak of the "isomorphic interrelationship between the knower and the known," and which has enabled Carl Rogers to develop his participative therapy of mutual respect and unconditional regard. In another but related field it designates that tradition of civility which has been celebrated by Joseph Wood Krutch, among others, as the heritage of Moral Discourse. And it is what Robert Maynard Hutchins for some decades affirmed as the Great Conversation and the Civilization of the Dialogue. I should like to quote Hutchins on this at a little more length:

"The Civilization of the Dialogue," he wrote, "is the only civilization worth having and the only civilization in which the whole world can unite. It is, therefore, the only civilization we can hope for, because the world must unite or be blown to bits. The Civilization of the Dialogue requires communication . . . It assumes that every man has reason and that every man can use it. It preserves to every man his independent judgment and, since it does so, it deprives any man or group of men of the privilege of forcing their judgment upon any other man or group of men. The Civilization of the Dialogue is the negation of force."

Opposed to this open society of the dialogue is the totalitarian system of the monologue. The monological mode of discourse is declined, as a grammarian might put it, in the objective or accusative case. Its purpose is not to commune but to command; its concern not to participate but to persuade. The monologue does not provide an avenue through which one seeks the truth; rather, it is the medium through which the Truth, once revealed and certain, is proclaimed and propagated.

The distinction between the dialogical and monological modes of communication may be personalized as the distinction between Socrates and Callicles (or Thrasymachus). In a later age it was the difference between Marcus Brutus and Mark Antony. In our own time it was the difference, almost exactly, between the two figures who dominated American public address during the 1950's: Adlai Stevenson and Joseph R. McCarthy. If the concept of dialogue embodies what Lippmann has termed "the public philosophy," the concept of monologue reflects what Richard Hofstadter has called *The Paranoid Style in American Politics*.

But this set of contrasts possibly oversimplifies the issue. For there is also abroad in the land a kind of white-collar paranoia, a soft-sell monologue, which is much more dangerous than the jungle jingoism of the McCarthys and Birchers. This is the discursive style which carries the sound, not of madness, but of purest rationality — the sound not of passion but of neutrality. And it is this well-bred monologue — the voice of "Science" itself, patient, detached, strategic, operational — which carries, if we attend to it, the message of our doom.

I am reminded, as I write these lines, of a portion of the memorable address delivered by William Faulkner (1949) on the occasion of accepting the Nobel Prize for literature. "It is easy enough," said Faulkner, "to say that man is immortal simply because he will endure; that when the last

ding-dong of doom has clanged and faded from the last red and dying sun-
set, that even then there will be one more sound: that of his puny inexhaustible voice, still talking. I refuse to accept this," he said. "I believe
that man will not merely endure, he will prevail. He is immortal, not
because he alone among creatures has an inexhaustible voice, but because
he has a soul, a spirit, capable of compassion, and sacrifice, and endur-
ance . . ."

Faulkner was talking about the difference between monologue and dialogue — between the inexhaustible voice, just talking, and the compassionate spirit, forever listening and sharing. He knew that we could never
be saved by rhetoric, but only by communion. But we have moved no
closer to that goal in the seventeen years since he spoke at Stockholm. In
the interim the very phrase he uttered as a declaration of faith — "I
believe that man . . . will prevail" — has become the desperate question
addressed to the world by Erich Fromm: "May Man Prevail?"

The answer may depend upon which voice he hears — which channel
he is tuned in to. And in the light of recent developments, both in the tower
and the abyss — in political science and in politics — there is very little
ground for optimism. The monological mode of discourse indisputably
dominates both arenas. This was indeed the contention fiercely argued by
Herbert Marcuse in his book bearing the notable title *One-Dimensional
Man*. There the political philosopher points to the emergence of "a pattern
of one-dimensional thought and behavior in which ideas, aspirations, and
objectives that, by their content, transcend the established universe of discourse and action are either repelled or reduced to the terms of this universe." Relating this trend to the rise of operationalism in physical science
and behaviorism in social science, Marcuse asserted that "the new mode
of thought is today the predominant tendency in philosophy, psychology,
sociology, and other fields." Beyond the academy, he maintained, "one-
dimensional thought is systematically promoted by the makers of politics
and the purveyors of mass information. Their universe of discourse is populated by self-validating hypotheses which, incessantly and monopolisti-
cally repeated, become hypnotic definitions or dictations."

This one-dimensional universe of discourse, sanctioned by the categories of its empirical science and formal logic, takes the form of a "technological rationality" which simply rules out of the forum as irrational and

irrelevant all that disputes its premises or questions its authority. Our society, said Marcuse, "bars a whole type of oppositional operations and behavior; consequently, the concepts pertaining to them are rendered illusory or meaningless . . . The operational and behavioral point of view, practiced as a 'habit of thought' at large, becomes the view of the established universe of discourse and action, needs and aspirations . . . Theoretical and practical Reason, academic and social behaviorism meet on common ground: that of an advanced society which makes scientific and technical progress into an instrument of domination."

The one-dimensional or monological mode of discourse — the language of technical rationality — was also the target of attack in another striking study: Anatol Rapoport's *Strategy and Conscience*. The thesis of Rapoport's book was that the cool-headed strategists of game theory, both in the academy and in the government, have led us down a one-way street of discourse, which must terminate, literally, in a dead end for civilization. The only possibility of escape is in reversing course, breaking through the barriers imposed by this mechanistic style of thought, and returning to the mode of moral discourse which reasons not in terms of strategy but in terms of conscience.

What is most remarkable about this argument is that its author, a distinguished mathetmatician, was one of the chief expounders of the game-theoretical approach to problems of political and international strategy. Not only did he have the insight to see the handwriting on the blackboard; he had the courage to repudiate it and warn against its tyranny. To Rapoport the issue of war and peace, of survival or extinction, was too important to be left to the strategic planners and rational policy-makers. Civilization has become a race between strategy and conscience — between the monological mode of objective calculation and value-neutrality, on the one hand, and the dialogical mode of "conscience-inspired thinking" on the other. Indeed, the central question of the book — concerning which the author was bitterly pessimistic — was whether a meaningful dialogue is possible between these radically opposite ways of thought and discourse.

One of the most hopeful signs of a change for the better in political science — of a breakthrough out of mechanism into humanism — is, I believe, just this shock of moral recognition on the part of more than a few prominent practitioners of hard-core social and physical science. Twenty years ago, three sociologists of my acquaintance published a textbook which they dedicated to all the members of the "Humanist Underground" in sociology. I am emboldened to think that more and more of these academic partisans have surfaced since then bringing with them into the light of day and of open discussion their revolutionary notes from underground.

What has encouraged and inspired them, I suspect, is the new mood — not so much of hope as of apprehension — which has been coming over their fellow scientists of behavior and strategy. Rapoport was clearly a case in point; another, still more impressive and indeed remarkable, was that of the late Norbert Wiener, the founding father of cybernetics

In that brilliant manifesto of the early computer age, *The Human Use of Human Beings,* published in 1950, Wiener revealed the full extent of his genius. He did so by transcending his own scientific categories — by moving beyond cybernetics, and against it. At a time when the awesome power of the new electronic "brains" was just beginning to be recognized, their principal creator had already looked far ahead into the cybernated future and returned with prophetic warnings of the anti-human use of non-human machines. "The hour is very late," he announced at the end of a key chapter, "and the choice of good and evil knocks at our door."

Wiener voiced his premonition dramatically through the recitation of three familiar fables: those of the Sorcerer's Apprentice, The Monkey's Paw, and The Genie in the Bottle. Each of these stories tells of a supernatural power capable of granting any wish and carrying out any order; but precisely because the force involved is not of this world, the terror of the tale is in the literal exactness — the relentless rationality — with which the commands are carried out. The very success of the nonhuman agency in executing its tasks carries with it the defeat and doom of its human master.

Wiener went on to point the moral emphatically: beware the temptation to abdicate to the great machine, or to the mechanistic mode of thought, the responsibility for decisions involving human purposes and values. He noted among other things the political extensions of the mathematical theory of games, which had come to exert a hypnotic fascination upon social scientists and decision-makers — rivalling that of the computer itself. "This great game," said Wiener, "is already being carried on mechanistically, and on a colossal scale . . . A sort of *machine a gouverner* is thus now essentially in operation on both sides of the world conflict, although it does not consist in either case of a single machine which makes policy, but rather of a mechanistic technique which is adapted to the exigencies of a machine-like group of men devoted to the formation of policy."

During the last years of his life, Wiener became increasingly concerned — even obsessed — by the danger of our elevating the Great Machine, the giant computer, into the status of an oracle. In warning us against this potential inhumanity, he came to appreciate the full significance of the human use of human beings — and to call for a social science and a political wisdom appropriate to that recognition.

Both Wiener, the scientist, and Rapoport, the mathematician, embodied to my mind the figure of the new and especially welcome convert to humanism — namely, the reformed mechanist-strategist-behavioralist who has peered deeply into the innermost recesses of the great machine, and there has glimpsed the germinating cell of a malignant possibility. Turning away in fright and remorse, they have joined the ranks of those of us who have long believed, with Hutchins, that the only civilization worth having is the Civilization of the Dialogue — and that the only science worth having is a science, not alone in the cause of operational truth, but in the cause of humankind.

WALT ANDERSON, *Politics and the New Humanism*

In trying to make sense of politics today we lack a fundamental sense of what it is all about, who we are, what we are trying to do and why. We need new ways of understanding political events and how we as individuals can relate to them.

My aim here is to present psychology as a perspective from which to consider political events and the way we study them in the social sciences. I do not think there is — or should be — anything remarkable about using humanistic psychology as an approach to politics because I do not think there is any distinction between psychology, sociology, and political science which makes sense anywhere outside of a college catalog. Any psychology is also a political ideology and a scientific methodology.

🍄

It does not do us much good to speculate about whether there might someday be a revolution in America. There is one going on, and the only thing which can prevent us from seeing it is attachment to a concept of revolution more appropriate to 1789 or 1917. Nor can we get far by agonizing about whether we should work inside or outside the system, because the system keeps changing all the time the debate goes on — and anyway there is really no inside or outside if we take a clear look at our evolving political culture. If we find a new perspective, look at political systems in terms of human evolution and at ourselves in terms of human growth, then perhaps we will be better able to understand the changes that are going on around us, and within us, and see new patterns of connection between the two.

Changes of great magnitude are occurring. I have heard the term "cultural revolution" used frequently to describe what's going on, and have found it useful. But a more apt term is "consciousness revolution" — this means that all of us are undergoing a basic transformation of awareness; moving toward a different way of experiencing ourselves; experiencing our relation to history, to other people, and to the world.

We can roughly compare this revolution to the Industrial Revolution, which was equally invisible in its early stages. It started, on a rather small scale, as a way people organized in relation to one another and to the production of goods. It was *not* basically mechanical; the machinery came later. Nor was it basically political, although everything political — and just about everything in the world — changed as a result of it. One specific consequence of the industrial revolution was its impact on political philosophy: it made it necessary for people who claimed to understand politics to pay attention to economics. Today, the consciousness revolution will require political scientists to pay attention to new factors, especially psychology and biology.

Humanistic psychology — a relatively new intellectual movement — offers us a perspective from which we can look at politics. Underlying this psychology is a view of human life — in fact of all organic life — as moving in the direction described by Carl Rogers in 1951, a direction of

> an increasing self-government, self-regulation, and
> autonomy, and away from heteronymous control, or
> control by external forces. This is true whether we are
> speaking of entirely unconscious organic processes,
> such as the regulation of body heat, or such uniquely
> human and intellectual functions as the choice of life
> goals.

Bugental has described this perspective as a "humanistic ethic," and lists as its identifying points: *(a)* centered responsibility for one's own life, *(b)* mutuality in relationships, *(c)* here-and-now perspective, *(d)* acceptance of nonhedonic emotions, and *(e)* growth-oriented experiences.

All of the above have a good deal more relevance to political change and to the practice of the social sciences than may be readily apparent. Bugental is talking about the idea of psychotherapy as a source of social change, which is considerably different from the "adjustment" goal of more conservative schools of therapy. He is also outlining some of the possible characteristics of a widespread cultural change he calls a "humanistic evolution." This is in sharp contrast to Freud, for example, who said:

> Our mind, that precious instrument by whose means
> we maintain ourselves alive, is no peacefully self-
> contained unity. It is rather to be compared with a mod-
> ern State in which a mob, eager for enjoyment and
> destruction, has to be held down forcibly by a prudent
> superior class.

In a historical sense we can see the emergence of Freudian theory as a recognition of the enormous demands placed upon the human instinctual system by the various forces of nineteenth-and twentieth-century Europe: Victorian morality, nationalism, the increasing bureaucratization and organization of life. Such demands, for Freud, were inherent in the process of civilization itself. "It is impossible," he wrote, "to overlook the extent to which civilization is built up upon a renunciation of instinct, how much it presupposes precisely the nonsatisfaction . . . of powerful instincts."

He did not believe that a life of gratification of those instincts offered any great promise. Research among primitive peoples, he said, showed that "their instinctual life is by no means to be envied for its freedom." The situation of the civilized human being was one of having "exchanged a portion of his possibilities of happiness for a portion of security." The task of the therapist was to facilitate this exchange, to aid the civilizing process by teaching people how to accommodate themselves to the demands of society, including those demands they had internalized. His only reply to a patient who wondered what value there could be in a therapy which made no basic change in the circumstances of life was that, "much will be gained if we succeed in transforming your hysterical misery into common unhappiness." Freud's life work was in the service of the reality principle. Philip Rieff, who sees him as essentially a moralist writes:

> Therapy prepares a mixture of detachment and forbearance, a stoic rationality of the kind Epictetus preached . . . To detach the individual from the most powerful lures in life, while teaching him how to pursue others less powerful and less damaging to the pursuer — these aims appear high enough in an age rightly suspicious of salvations. Freud had the tired wisdom of a universal healer for whom no disease can be wholly cured.

In Freud's pessimism and resignation we find the source of his political conservatism. A radical philosophy, a revolutionary program, contains some concept of a possible better future, a resolution of the present misery. Freud's view of society contains no such concept.

Freud's rejection of revolution does not arise from an opinion about its desirability or undesirability, but rather from a conviction that true revolution is simply not possible. External authority is a manifestation of psychological need, an expression of the inner structure of the individual psyche, and therefore no real change can be effected by striking out against institutions. If social authority stands in opposition to some psychological drives — and more primitive ones — it also exists in fulfillment of other, quite powerful, human needs. Thus Roazen wrote, in 1968:

> Patrick Henry's "Give me liberty or give me death" is, according to Freud, superlatively untrue to human experience. Man wants both liberty and restraint, and the tensions between conflicting needs comprise human tragedy. Freud's description of social restrictions, of the coercions of life, is so intensely real

> because he sees the extent to which outer authority is
> linked to our inner needs. Society is coercive precisely
> because its rules are internalized, are taken into the
> self; and at the same time society is useful in helping to
> keep some sort of a balance between various forces.
> Just as a child needs parental restrictions to handle his
> aggression, just as he needs to be stopped before the
> full horror of his murderous impulses becomes evident
> to him, so social restraints assist man in handling his
> aggression, both by providing vicarious forms of
> release, and by reinforcing his inner controls over
> drives which are alien to his inner security.

In contrast to philosophies which view political authority as a result of a conscious and deliberate agreement among members of a society, as a necessary consequence of God's order on earth, or as a reflection of the economic system, Freud sees it as the external manifestation of an internal conflict. This internal conflict is largely unconscious and fundamentally unchangeable.

Although Freud's system is based on a notion of evolution, it contains no prescription for future change, certainly no assertion that further progress is inevitable. Human development in his view seems to have reached a painful *detente* beyond which there is little hope of change. This is a great contrast to the view of Marx, whose system was also evolutionary (and who dedicated *Das Kapital* to Charles Darwin) but who offered, in fact, an inexorable dialectic of change and a utopian future of great freedom.

Freud offered no such promises but, instead, worked to devise ways that individuals could learn to live with themselves and with civilization. He gave the world the first system of psychotherapy which contained as an integral part of its intellectual foundation a theory of society and authority. He was the first person who fully recognized the impact of modern society upon the human instincts, and he does not seem to have seriously considered the possibility that modern society could be transformed. He chose to become a teacher of ways of adjusting to things as they are.

The psychoanalytic profession as it has taken form in America is consistent with Freud's view of its social function (i.e., it serves as a means of helping certain individuals adjust to the realities of modern civilization). It offers no program or rationale for fundamental political or social change.

There is no conclusive data on what, if any, changes in political persuasion are likely to result from psychoanalysis, but Arnold Rogow stated that

> The consensus of both psychiatrists and psychoanalysts is that successful psychotherapy, by promoting open-mindedness, relative freedom from intrapsychic conflicts, and a decrease in rigidity of belief, moves patients toward a moderate or middle-road political position if they were not already there at the commencement of treatment.

This is a revealing statement of an implicit value assumption about politics and mental health: namely, that the more healthy individual occupies a "middle-of-the-road" political position. This is consistent with a view of therapy as adjustment and with the values which are to be found in applications of Freudian theory to political analysis.

One of the first Americans to take serious note of the implications of Freudian theory for political science was Walter Lippmann, who used some of Freud's concepts in works published prior to 1930. But Lippmann did not attempt to develop a Freudian theory of political behavior; that task was taken up in the 1930s by Harold Lasswell, a political scientist who had made a comprehensive study of Freud's writings and had undergone a training analysis.

In *Psychopathology and Politics* Lasswell remained faithful to the basic Freudian theory of politics as a manifestation of "internal" personality structure. He dealt with political behavior as a *displacement* of private motives onto political objects.

> The most general formula which expresses the developmental f cts about the fully developed political man reads thus:
>
> $$p \ \} \ d \ \} \ r \ = \ P$$
>
> where p equals private motives; d equals displacement onto a public object; r equals rationalization in terms of public interest; P equals the political man, and $\}$ *equals transformed into.*

This formulation is an excellent statement of the Freudian theory of politics. The basic dynamic it describes is present in later psychoanalytically oriented work by Lasswell and others. It asserts that political behavior is in some degree an acting out of internal psychological conflicts which are repressed, unconscious, and irrational: people rationalize — create rational motives for their actions — but the motives they create are not the true sources of behavior.

Revolutionaries and revolutionary movements do not fare very well at the hands of Freudian political analysts. The internal theory of authority as expressed through Lasswell's displacement formula tends inescapably toward a view of any action against constituted authorities as an acting out of repressed hostility. Such an emphasis makes it difficult for the revolutionary to be taken seriously. His or her complaints against the power structure, however valid they may feel subjectively, are all too easily taken to be displacements: "The repressed father-hatred may be turned against kings or capitalists."

There have been persistent efforts dating back to the early years of the psychoanalytic movement to take Freud's insights in the opposite direction — to make the doctrine of repression the starting point for a program of political revolution and a transformation of human life.

The first of the Freudian revolutionaries was Wilhelm Reich, who in his stormy career managed to be expelled from both the International Psychoanalytic Association and the Communist Party. His troubles within the Freudian and Marxist movements stemmed from his attempts to tie the two together, an attempt which was unwelcome to the orthodox of both camps.

In 1929 Reich argued that psychoanalysis was a materialistic science, based on a description of conflict within the individual and society. Psychoanalysis, he said, was furthermore a revolutionary science: it located the source of sexual repression in bourgeois morality and thereby stated the case for a liberation of human instincts. At the same time, Reich granted that the movement seemed to be losing its sense of mission, and was degenerating into a business and a stylish fad. Later Reich criticized Freud himself for placing his science "at the disposal of a conservative ideology."

Reich felt that the European masses were incapable of acting according to the political and economic logic of their condition. Instead of becoming revolutionary, they had a tendency to become reactionary. He explained the mechanics of it in terms which were quite similar to Freud's theory of the internalization of authority. In Reich's explanation, great importance was attached to sexual suppression:

> The moral inhibition of the child's natural sexuality . . . makes the child afraid, shy, fearful of authority, obedient, "good," and "docile" in the authoritarian sense of the words. It has a crippling effect on man's rebellious forces because every vital life-impulse is now burdened with severe fear; and since sex is a forbidden subject, thought in general and man's critical faculty also become inhibited. In short, morality's aim is to produce acquiescent subjects who, despite distress and humiliation, are adjusted to the authoritarian order. Thus, the family is the authoritarian state in miniature, to which the child must learn to adapt himself as a preparation for the general social adjustment required of him later.

The interference with normal sexuality in the authoritarian family, then, was what maintained the authoritarian state. This is why "the authoritarian state gains an enormous interest in the authoritarian family: *It becomes the factory in which the state's structure and ideology are molded.*" And it is also the key to understanding the great flaw in the conventional, economically deterministic Marxist ideology: *"Sexual inhibition alters the structure of the economically suppressed individual in such a way that he thinks, feels, and acts against his own material interests."*

Since Reich's time there have been other reinterpreters of Freud, most notably Herbert Marcuse and Norman O. Brown. Each of these has found in Freudian theory a promise of human liberation, and both have attained great popular status as the philosophical mentors of rebellious youth. According to Theodore Roszak, "The emergence of Herbert Marcuse and Norman Brown as major social theorists among the disaffiliated young of Western Europe and American must be taken as one of the defining features of the counter culture."

Reich, Marcuse, and Brown share the belief that people are capable of being free and that adjustment to unfreedom is not the same things as mental health. The approach to political analysis that flows from this perspective is quite different from that of the orthodox Freudians. Reich summed this up succinctly: "What is to be explained," he said, is not why the starving individual steals or why the exploited individual strikes, but why the majority of starving individuals do not steal and the majority of exploited individuals do not strike."

Behaviorist psychologists such as Watson and Skinner have been quite willing to extend their theoretical formulations to large-scale architectonic propositions about cultural design, but they have tended to avoid identification with existing ideologies and have maintained that their concepts are above or beyond traditional political issues.

This has not discouraged the critics of behaviorism from drawing conclusions about its political content. For example, Floyd Matson, in a fairly representative summary of the case, wrote:

> Whether human conduct is conditioned or unconditioned it remains, on the behaviorist account, wholly determinate and predictable; and, in either event, it is open to manipulation by reconditioning . . . It seems extraordinary nowadays that such a doctrine could ever have been construed in any sense as democratic: its blindness to personal intention, its scorn of mind, its denial of any freedom of action or capacity for it, its tacit enlistment in the service of a kind of technocratic efficiency and regimentation — these characteristics of classical behaviorism appear rather to confirm the harsh judgment of Mannheim that it bears an unmistakable resemblance to fascism.

The judgment of Karl Mannheim to which Matson referred was based on a historical view of behaviorism as a response to the need of modern civilization for a more efficient principle of human organization. Behaviorism, said Mannheim, "is a typical product of thought at that stage of mass society in which it is more important, from the practical point of view, to be able to calculate the average behavior of the mass than to understand the private motives of individuals or to transform the whole personality."

The concern of behaviorism with the needs of society, and the shift of emphasis away from subjectivity, from inner experience, must inevitably produce a social, adjustment-oriented definition of mental health and pathology. For example, to quote Talcott Parsons: "Health may be defined as the state of optimum capacity of an individual for the effective performance of the roles and tasks for which he has been socialized. It is thus defined with reference to the individual's participation in the social system."

Richard Sennett, a sociologist who reviewed *Beyond Freedom and Dignity* in 1971, analyzed some of Skinner's specific proposals for social improvement and found his political stance to be neither fascistic nor technocratic, but simply, in a bland, middle-American kind of way, conservative.

> [Skinner] indicates a few purposes to which he personally would like to see the techniques put.
>
> First, behavior control appears to him a way to get people hard at work again in an age where indolence is rife . . .
>
> As a corollary to his belief in hard work, Skinner rails against the sexual and other sensual pleasures that he feels have become rampant today, and argues that such behavior needs to be redirected . . .
>
> Not surprisingly, Skinner also believes that the small group, the town, the village, the little neighborhood circle, is the scale at which behavior conditioning can operate morally . . .
>
> These beliefs should sound familiar. They are the articles of faith of Nixonian America, of the small-town businessman who feels life has degenerated, has gotten beyond his control, and who thinks things will get better when other people learn how to behave.

There is, certainly, a tendency for statements of the possibilities of behaviorist psychology to reflect the existing values of society, and this gives behaviorism a certain middle-of-the-road bias. For all the differences in philosophy and methodology that exist between Freudian and behaviorist psychology, they are rather similar in their tendency to operate as defenders of the social and cultural status quo.

Thomas Szasz charges that all psychiatry is in fact a form of social control, and that behavior-modification programs, usually imposed from above on institutional inmates, tend to become focal-points for the politicization of therapy.

It is common for behavior therapists to discuss their various techniques as remedial measures undertaken on behalf of, and upon the request of, the patient. In reality, however, consent is a rather more elusive concept; the quality of consent must be taken into account, for frequently the patient is being influenced strongly by someone else, such as the courts, a prison warden, employer, or family.

Let us now begin to look at humanistic psychology. Any science is in part shaped by what its researchers choose to study — by the things that, deliberately or not, they select to be in their line of vision. Abraham Maslow believed that psychologists had allowed themselves to become so preoccupied with mental illness that they had neglected almost entirely to form any meaningful concept of real health, of a fully functioning human being. "It becomes more and more clear," Maslow wrote, "that the study of crippled, stunted, immature, and unhealthy specimens can yield only a cripple psychology and a cripple philosophy."

Maslow developed a theory of human *health,* and eventually became convinced that the study of healthy (self-actualizing) people was producing not only a better conceptualization of mental health, but a whole new psychology, a radically different vision of humanity. One of his statements about self-actualizing individuals is very important to this discussion:

> Such a person, by virtue of what he has become, assumes a new relation to his society and indeed, to society in general. He not only transcends himself in various ways; he also transcends his culture. He resists enculturation. He becomes more detached from his culture and from his society. He becomes a little more a member of his species and a little less a member of his local group.

The idea that healthy human growth tends toward deenculturation adds a new dimension to some of the basic concepts of political philosophy, such as obligation and authority. It also opens up new areas for empirical research: behavioral political scientists have done a good deal of research on socialization, but they have made no comparable investigation of any process of *de*socialization. Maslow clearly means that the "transcendence of culture" is a kind of desocialization: self-actualizing people simply outgrow much of what they have been taught about society and their relation to it.

Maslow merely mentioned this particular facet of the character structure of self-actualizing people as one of several points to be considered.

Personally, I find it to be a revolutionary idea: it says that there exist within our society a significant number of people — some of our wisest and strongest, in fact — who are "in" the society in a fundamentally different way from the rest of us. The attitude of these people toward some of the things which civilizations traditionally rest upon (cultural norms, laws, etc.) seems to be that they are all right if you keep them in their place.

One important point about Maslow's work is that although he found his self-actualizing subjects to be quite capable of radical social action, such action is not a result of deprivation, which is commonly assumed to be the main source of revolutionary social change, nor is it the action out of personal pathology according to the Freudian model. Instead, the altruistic, creative behavior of self-actualizing men and women is, in Maslow's view, the natural satisfaction of complex biological needs which emerge when the lower physiological and psychological needs have been satisfied. Maslow was convinced that the failure to recognize these higher needs (metaneeds) contributed to the "frustrated idealism" experienced by many young people, particularly students:

> This frustrated idealism and occasional hopelessness is partially due to the influence and ubiquity of stupidly limited theories of motivation all over the world. Leaving aside behavioristic and positivistic theories — or rather, non-theories — as simple refusals even to see the problem, i.e., a kind of psychoanalytic denial, then what is available to the idealistic young man and woman?
>
> Not only does the whole of official nineteenth-century science and orthodox academic psychology offer him nothing, but also the major motivation theories by which most men live can lead him only to depression or cynicism. The Freudians, at least in their official writings (though not in good therapeutic practice), are still reductionistic about all higher human values. The deepest and most real motivations are seen to be dangerous and nasty, while the highest human values are essentially fake, being not what they seem to be, but camouflaged versions of the "deep, dark, and dirty." Our social scientists are just as disappointing in the main. A total cultural determinism is still the official, orthodox doctrine of many or most of the sociologists and anthropologists. This doctrine not only denies intrinsic higher motivations, but comes perilously close sometimes to denying "human nat-

ure" itself. The economists, not only in the West but also in the East, are essentially materialistic. We must say harshly of the "science" of economics that it is generally the skilled, exact, technological application of a totally false theory of human needs and values, a theory which recognizes only the existence of lower needs or material needs.

Maslow did not go far in the direction of stating the social or political theories which might be derived from his work, but two main propositions come through clearly. These are *(a)* that, contrary to Freudian theory, the needs of people and the needs of civilization are not *necessarily* antagonistic, and *(b)* that the possibilities of a society's development are contingent upon the ability of its structures and its members to recognize and encourage higher human needs and the potential for self-actualization. These two propositions are workable guidelines, I believe, toward the development of humanistic politics, and a humanistic political science.

Gestalt therapy talks a great deal about responsibility, but this has a meaning rather different from the traditional moral exhortation to take responsibility for oneself. The gestaltist is convinced that all people already are responsible for most of what is happening to them, but simply unaware of how they manipulate the environment and simultaneously block their own awareness of what they are doing. In their book *Gestalt Therapy,* Perls, Hefferline and Goodman wrote:

> The attitude of the passive-suffering projector . . . we believe is typical of modern dissociated men. It is imbedded in our language, our world-attitude, our institutions. The prevention of outgoing motion and initiative, the social derogation of aggressive drives, and the epidemic disease of self-control and self-conquest have led to a language in which the self seldom does or expresses anything; instead, "it" happens. These restrictive measures have also led to a view of the world as completely neutral and "objective" and unrelated to our concerns; and to institutions that take over our functions, that are to "blame" because they "control" us, and that wreak on us the hostility which we so carefully refrain from wielding ourselves — as if men did not themselves lend to institutions whatever force they have!

The idea of a close relationship between authority and awareness is one of the major contributions of gestalt. It gives us a clinical perspective on a psychological principle that seems to be understood by a growing number of political activists. The principle can be stated this way: *individuals who are under the control of an authority not only surrender their own power to that authority, but to some extent surrender also their awareness of being controlled.* A political corollary to this could be stated: *to become fully aware of being dominated is itself a step toward ending domination.* This principle appears to be influencing a good deal of contemporary radical action. Women's liberation forces especially are aware of the tremendous potential of "consciousness-raising" — bringing the power relationship out into the open — as a technique for social change.

Fritz Perls, a short time before his death, told gestalt therapists that they had a certain kind of historical mission, which was to make a real revolution possible:

> . . . so far we only have a rebellion. We don't have a revolution yet . . . If there is any chance of interrupt- ing the rise and fall of the United States, it's up to our youth and it's up to you in supporting this youth. To be able to do this, there is only one way through: to become real, to learn to take a stand, to develop one's center . . .

For Perls, then, the work of gestalt was a person-by-person revolution, freeing individuals from their own inner tyranny and fragmentation, pav- ing the way for profound social change.

Hopefully, the psychological foundations of social control are erod- ing, and the kind of enforced morality we have always known and accepted in America will no longer be possible. To talk of political revolution as we have known it becomes irrelevant to our times. Nobody will have to over- throw the state; we will simply outgrow our need for many of its functions.

The encounter movement, too, presents a political challenge. Two of its characteristics are the conviction that alternative styles of interpersonal relationship are truly available and the determination to make personal openness a political issue. It is nothing less than an attempt to transform the whole society's style of interpersonal relating. Like gestalt therapy it aims not at the institutional superstructure but at the person-to-person foundation of society.

An important source of philosophical influence in humanistic psychology comes from outside Western culture. Many of the concepts and values and techniques of Eastern systems such as Zen, Yoga, and Sufism have found their way into psychological theory, therapy, and encounter-group practice.

Zen, for instance, is hardly a religion in the Western sense; it is primarily a technique for the development of consciousness. And when we deal with Zen as a psychological system we come again to the concept of internalization of social norms. Zen goes much further than Freudian and gestalt theory, however, and asserts that all perceptions of reality, even the very sense of self, are products of social conditioning. This, too, is not entirely alien to Western thought. Fromm (1970), for example, states that:

> Every society, by its own practice of living and by the mode of relatedness, of feeling, and perceiving, develops a system of categories which determines the forms of awareness. This system works, as it were, like a *socially conditioned filter;* experience cannot enter awareness unless it can penetrate this filter .

Is it possible to become deconditioned, to throw away the social filter, and what are the larger political implications of such a process? Zen is a training process aimed at a specific goal, the *satori* experience. Equivalent terms for *satori* in English are enlightenment, awakening, liberation. Both Fromm and Watts believe that Zen liberation is essentially a release from the psychological conditioning of the society. Fromm asserted that:

> In its historical development each society becomes caught in its own need to survive in the particular form in which it has developed, and it usually accomplishes this survival by ignoring the wider human aims which are common to all men. This contradiction between the social and the universal aim leads also to the fabrication (on a social scale) of all sorts of fictions and illusions which have the function to deny and to rationalize the dichotomy between the goals of humanity and the goals of a given society.

If this is true, then obviously an awakening from the socially conditioned consciousness is an experience which profoundly transforms one's relationship to the political order, and the word "liberation" as a synonym for *satori* takes on a political meaning. The individual so liberated is still subject to the laws of the state, of course, but the state's roots in consciousness have virtually disappeared.

Zen also sheds some light on the assertion that the prevailing political order enforces not only certain patterns of economic and social interaction, but also a fundamental definition of reality, a world-view and value system which is the basis for all power, *and which is defined, not simply as patriotism, but as sanity.*

Humanistic psychology can best be understood as a search for some kind of common transcultural meeting ground on which human beings can recognize one another and communicate. In this context, Zen, which teaches that all people contain within themselves a true and unconditioned consciousness which can be trained to break through and make contact with its environment, offers an important contribution.

When we view politics within the Freudian paradigm, we see society as a huge stage for the acting out of internal conflict, a hopeless war between the deep inner needs of individuals and the needs of the system. The behaviorist movement did not offer any such dramatic new paradigm — in part because it was essentially a restatement of what had been a dramatic new paradigm in the seventeenth century: the image of the universe as a smoothly-spinning machine, guided by hard and discoverable natural laws. But although the behaviorist movement produced no single new political theory, it has tended to convey a fairly coherent view of political behavior stressing power and economic motivations, to view society as a kind of vast machine, and to deal with individuals in terms of their social roles and group memberships.

Just as Freud believed that his discoveries about the unconscious brought an entire new world-view into existence, so do humanistic psychologists believe that their discoveries about the growth and integrative possibilities of men and women are not simply additional psychological data but the basis of an entire redefinition of humanity.

All of the humanistic theories that we have discussed seem to indicate that the process of personal growth, especially as it moves into the higher reaches of human potentiality, includes some kind of a transformation of the individual's relation to the social order, cultural norms, laws, ideology, and institutions. Third force psychologists have not attempted to work out a systematic theory of consciousness and politics, to devise some kind of an intellectual apparatus to make it clear how the kind of personal development that they are (as theorists) studying and (as therapists) helping to bring about, may affect American society (or how American society may affect it).

Charles Hampden-Turner holds that the social sciences as they stand conspire to force us to think of humanity in terms that are essentially conservative. This is not the deliberate product of ideological conservatism — in fact most of the social scientists are political liberals — but rather the unexpected yet inevitable result of the use of "scientific" methodology. As he wrote in 1971,

> Their social conservatism is *for others*, the object of investigation. Moreover their conservatism is latent in the tools they employ. It comes about less by valuing conservatively than by the "value-free" selection of the less than human . . . He who is silent assents, and to describe the status quo with detailed and passionless precision is usually to dignify it.

Thus academic political science was taken completely off guard by the protest movements of the 1960s and the liberation movements of the 1970s and still has trouble dealing with evidence of idealistic behavior or seriously considering the possibility that any really fundamental change can or will take place in American society. Hampden-Turner argues that the social sciences in general have so successfully directed their attention to men and women as cogs in the power-driven, wealth-manipulating system that they can not see people as capable of any truly creative or idealistic social action.

"The establishment" or "the power structure" can be viewed as an established consciousness, a psychological power structure. All social institutions rest upon how people think and feel, how they comprehend the *meaning* of being human, how they experience the self, how they perceive their relationship to the environment and to each other. The state, in short, is a state of mind.

In spite of all the efforts of psychiatrists to maintain that their profession is an objective, ideologically neutral science, political issues seem to be turning up in it with increasing frequency. On one hand there are those who agree with Dr. Ewald Busse, who was president of the American Psychiatric Association in 1971-1972:

> It is my opinion that psychiatric services should not be the tool for restructuring society or solving economic problems or for determining new human values. Psychiatric services should be continued as patient oriented activities designed to reduce pain and discomfort and to increase the capacity of the individual to adjust satisfactorily . . .

On the other hand Dr. Raymond Waggoner, a past president of the same association, says:

> I plead for a psychiatry that is involved with fundamental social goals. I plead for a psychiatry that will eschew isolation altogether and assume its proper leadership role in advancing the total health of our nation. I plead for a psychiatry that is at once concerned with individual liberty and communal responsibility and I ask of psychiatrists that they be not only pragmatists but also dreamers with a vision of the future.

This is a fairly mild argument, and yet it represents what I consider to be the basic cleavage between working to maintain the system, and working to clear the way for human growth, wherever that may lead.

The issue becomes clearer as we look at more extreme statements. J. McConnell, a behavior-modification psychologist advocating massive use of psychological techniques to deal with crime wrote, in 1970:

> . . . We'd assume that a felony was clear evidence that the criminal had somehow acquired a full-blown social neurosis and needed to be cured, not punished. We'd send him to a rehabilitation center where he'd undergo positive brainwashing until we were quite sure

he had become a law-abiding citizen who would not
again commit an antisocial act. We'd probably have to
restructure his entire personality.

I have described this as an extreme statement, but it would be more
accurate to call it a particularly blunt expression of values that are widely
held. At the other extreme is a new movement calling itself Radical Therapy, which takes the position that the task of therapy must be social
change, and that any form of encouragement of adjustment is concealed
social control. As M. Glenn put it,

> Therapy is change, not adjustment. This *means*
> change — social, personal, and political. When peo-
> ple are fucked over, people should help them fight it,
> and then deal with their feelings. A "struggle for men-
> tal health" is bullshit unless it involves changing this
> society which turns us into machines, alienates us
> from one another and our work, and binds us into rac-
> ist, sexist and imperialist practices.

It is characteristic that those who are farthest from the centers of power
are most convinced that therapy is inherently political, while those who
are in control usually maintain that it is not. Certainly there can be an
enormous amount of political power concealed behind the supposedly
neutral, objective, or scientific act of defining mental illness. It is a power
which can only be effectively exerted by those who already *have* power.
Dissenting psychologists can talk about pathology in the acts of leaders,
but the leaders are not subsequently subject to the various acts of
control — psychiatric diagnosis, behavior therapy, commitment —
which are the fate of thousands of people at lower levels of society. Thomas
Szasz asserted that, "There is no such 'condition' as 'schizophrenia,' but
the label is a social fact and the social fact a political event." In fact, he
argued that the existence of such a thing as "mental illness" has never been
proven with enough certainty to justify the enormous persecution of all
those who happen to get branded with such a designation:

> What we call modern, dynamic psychiatry is nei-
> ther a glamorous advance over the superstitions and
> practices of the witch-hunts, as contemporary psychi-
> atric propagandists would have it, nor a retrogression
> from the humanism of the Renaissance and the scien-

> tific spirit of the Enlightenment, as romantic tradition-
> alists would have it. In actuality, Institutional
> Psychiatry is a continuation of the Inquisition. All that
> has really changed is the vocabulary and the social
> style. The vocabulary conforms to the intellectual
> expectations of our age: it is a pseudomedical jargon
> that parodies the concepts of science. The social style
> conforms to the political expectations of our age: it is a
> pseudoliberal social movement that parodies the ideals
> of freedom and rationality.

Most humanistic psychiatrists and psychologists prefer to steer clear
of the "medical model," and most humanistic therapies strive to reduce
the authoritarian character of the therapist — this is fundamental to
Rogerian counseling, to gestalt work in which the patients are expected to
take responsibility for themselves, to encounter work in which the leader
is also a participant.

Now, it is undoubtedly true that, so far, the emphasis in humanistic
psychology has been upon individual, personal growth, and that when
humanistic psychologists have addressed themselves to the possibility of
bringing about widespread *social* change, they have often tended to
emphasize the incremental results of individual growth (such as the cumulative effect of many people undergoing some kind of personal transformation through therapy or encounter group experience). There has been
less of an inclination to consider the possible ways of changing institutions
or to understand institutional change as a way of facilitating personal
growth for great numbers of people.

Yet humanistic psychology does offer guidelines for looking at institutions — and changing them and creating them — in terms of human needs
and human development. These are most highly developed in the works of
Maslow and Hampden-Turner: Maslow's hierarchy of needs and
Hampden-Turner's model of psychosocial development, both address
themselves directly to the question of how social arrangements can facilitate (or obstruct) the growth of human beings. They offer propositions
which are testable according to the empirical standards of contemporary
social science research, and they lead rather easily to ideas about public
policy. They also lead toward a different idea of what politics *is*. To get at

what I mean let me cite a few general statements about politics by leading political scientists. Robert Dahl said, "A political system is any persistent pattern of human relationships that involves, to a significant extent, power, rule, or authority." Heinz Eulau suggested that "what makes man's behavior political is that he rules and obeys, persuades and compromises, promises and bargains, coerces and represents, fights and fears . . . " And of course there is Harold Lasswell's oft-quoted definition of politics as a matter of "who gets what, when, and how."

These definitions all tell us something about politics, and they also tell us something about the range of vision of the definers, what it is that they have chosen to see.

But suppose we try defining politics as the ways people organize themselves in order to attain the greatest satisfaction of human needs possible within the environment. When we look at politics this way we naturally turn our attention to the things which obstruct human development. The most important single limiting factor is the idea which any society has about what the possibilities of human development actually are. A stunted or narrow conception of the human potential, especially when deeply built into cultural norms and reinforced by a society's art and science and philosophy, is as powerful a form of tyranny as any political institution. By stunted or narrow conception I mean any lopsided view which focuses on certain human needs-safety or esteem, for example — to the exclusion of others, or a truncated value system such as our own which sees the acquisition of a great amount of material goods and social prestige as evidence of the upper limits of human growth.

The historical importance of humanistic psychology is that it offers us a new and more expansive vision of human growth at a time when the shortcomings of the old vision have become most evident. Humanistic psychology is a challenge to our commonly held beliefs about what people are, how they grow and change, and what they may become. Humanistic psychology is significant only insofar as it pushes and tugs at fundamental ideas.

It seems to me that if we are guided at all times by some kind of image of the upper reaches of human development, then our way of considering matters of public policy will be fundamentally different. We will not be trying — as in the case of welfare — to remove a potential source of crime, or even to make certain individuals more "socially productive," but rather to release the fullest possibilities of human development. Guided by such a perspective, we would certainly create policies far different from the ones we now have. Our politics, like our psychology, has lost touch with a concept of human health. We think mainly in terms of acute social ailments and first-aid remedies, rarely in terms of the fullest possibilities of human growth and how societies may facilitate it.

I fear that our political science has supported this kind of thinking (take a look again at the above definitions of politics) by making the most outrageous symptoms of political sickness (e.g., the inequitable distribution of goods and services, the conflicts for power and special advantage, the manipulation of the public by office-holders and office-seekers) seem like the norms of civilized life. This "realism" has conspired to banish the search for a more sane and nourishing social order to the realm of "idealism," and thus deprive it of intellectual legitimacy.

But the search — because it, too, expresses a deep and very real human drive — goes on anyway. And we have available to us now a somewhat different conception of human life, which forms the unifying framework of humanistic psychology. It also forms the theoretical basis for the many methods of humanistic therapy and encounter group work. These experiences have touched the lives of thousands of people, and have undoubtedly accounted for some degree of social change. But their application is still fairly limited. We have not — nor has any society in history — made it an effort of high priority to understand the processes and possibilities of human growth and to translate that understanding into social policy.

If we should choose to make the highest development of human beings a deliberate social goal, then the task before us is to think about the growth possibilities of all people, at all social and economic levels, and also to understand fully what it means when a species begins to become responsible for its own evolution. As we consider such questions, the humanistic perspective becomes not merely psychological, but political; we are not talking about principles of research or therapy, but about principles of social action and institutional change. Our new vision of the possibilities of human existence becomes a set of guidelines for building a human community. It is no longer the concern merely of writers and clinicians and social scientists but a *res publica*, a public thing.

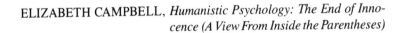

ELIZABETH CAMPBELL, *Humanistic Psychology: The End of Innocence (A View From Inside the Parentheses)*

I have been asked to review the development of humanistic psychology from the 1960s to the present and to suggest professional applications and strategies for the 1980s. When asked to take on this task, I was less than certain I wanted to attempt such a sweeping survey. I was faced with my own ambivalences regarding the accomplishments of humanistic psychology. However, I have given the subject a good deal of thought, time, and energy over the last twenty years. The challenge was too appealing to ignore.

Like many of you, I have been trying to understand what is happening in the world and how humanistic psychology fits into the broader scheme of society. As Executive Officer of AHP, I was dealing daily with the issues of relevance. I also have been scrambling through the surfeit of information regarding the fate of our planet. I have been exploring general systems theory, futures research, the new sciences, including Pribram, Prigogine, and Sheldrake. I have read the more popular analyses of the state of the world, including Toffler's *Third Wave,* Capra's *Turning Point,* and Naisbitt's *Megatrends.* I have attempted to broaden my understanding by looking at structural analyses including studies by the Institute for World Order, World Watch reports on environmental crises, and Club of Rome reports warning of resource depletion. I have also looked at sustainable society economic and ecological studies, including those by Henderson, Berry, Sales, and Schumacher. I have been impressed by Barnet and Muller's biting analysis of the multi-national corporations, *Global Reach.* I have not ignored the SRI reports, especially Markley and Harman's *Changing Images of Man,* nor the arguments for a pluralistic society presented by Hawken, Ogilvy, & Schwartz in *Seven Tomorrows.* Not to leave out transpersonal psychology, I have discovered Ken Wilber and read all his books.

However, try as I might, the more I study and observe, the less sure I become of what's happening. I now find myself with old anchors and certainties dissolving without new truths rushing in to hold my picture of the world together, at least in familiar forms. So I might subtitle this presentation, "A view from inside the parentheses."

Of all the catch phrases and slogans describing where we stand in history, I like "time of the parentheses." I first heard it from Jean Houston who describes us as "people of the parentheses." Recently, John Naisbitt in *Megatrends* concluded,

> We are living in the time of the parenthesis, the time between eras. It is as though we have bracketed off the present from both the past and future, for we are neither here nor there. We have not quite left behind the either/or America of the past — centralized, industrialized, and economically self-contained . . . But we have not embraced the future either.

I looked in Webster's dictionary to see if additional light might be shed on the meaning of parenthesis, and found, "A word, phrase, or sentence, by way of comment or explanation, inserted in, or attached to, a sentence grammatically complete without it. It is usually marked off with curved lines, commas, or dashes." This definition gives me cause to ponder the significance of such a time and position. I find the following characteristics of this view from inside the parentheses:

First, there is a great deal of uncertainty and ambiguity about this placement. Are we really a comment inserted or attached, or are we the needed transition from what's behind to what's ahead? There is pressure inside these lines, experienced as a push from behind and a pull forward. There is a definite sense of urgency; something needs to be done, comment made, explanation given. There is a strong tendency to act; do anything, just as long as we do it fast.

This uncertainty and ambiguity creates a good deal of stress, and this is the second characteristic. The problem is that there is not much agreement about what should be done. Quite honestly, there is a lot of confusion inside this space, and it gets quite uncomfortable. Theories, models, and explanations abound. If anything, we suffer from overload, too many versions of reality. We appear to have a deep yearning for truth, but just whose truth are we to believe?

I am puzzled by the folks who seem assured they see the path ahead clearly, with such claims as "We are approaching the crest of the Third

Wave," or "We have entered the Age of Aquarius and transformation is guaranteed," or on the other hand, those who are sure our fate is sealed and the coming dark ages are at hand. Maybe some few advanced explorers have crossed beyond these curved lines and do indeed see which reality is in store for us. If so, I don't think we have gotten the message yet. I rather suspect most predictors are still standing where we are, "seeing through a glass darkly," and we misread their visioning and speculations because we need structure so desperately.

Another characteristic of this view from inside the parentheses is that it is no easier to look behind than to look ahead. We don't have the comfort of trusting our past experience to guide us, for as we look behind, the bridges are rapidly burning, and the old certainties are crumbling. There is no simple return to the good old days, nor can we rely on old problem-solving methods. True, there are many proposals suggesting solutions, including those who believe the solution lies in returning to a more human scale, or on the other hand, to trusting the new technologies to revolutionize our lives. Perhaps there is truth in both these paths and several others, but there is too much complexity in the issues to be sure what is happening. No wonder people seek a simple answer, some structure to give meaning to their lives.

I ask your patience as I look at the field of humanistic psychology from an "inside the parenthesis" perspective. Will you join in a spirit of self-examination and searching as we review together both humanistic psychology and the state of our world, and seek some understanding of how we may be of service to our fellow human beings? (1) First, I'll look at where we find ourselves; (2) Second, I'll look backward and raise some questions about our intentions and actions in humanistic psychology during the past two decades; (3) Third, I'll attempt to assess the resources and skills we have to offer the world and look at the contributions we might best make; and (4) Finally, I'll raise the question, "How do we proceed from here?"

In searching for a theme to pull my thoughts together, I came to the essence of where I believe we are, both as a culture and as a movement. I call it the end of innocence. Perhaps never before has there been such a species-wide consciousness raising as during the past few years. We have had some rude awakenings, particularly in our Western world, regarding our human capabilities and limitations. What we are experiencing is a systemic breakdown and it is increasingly clear that no emergency treatment is sufficient, no bandaid action will suffice. Included in our common understanding are the following:

(1) We have become a global village. The interdependency of all nations is now acknowledged. As Buckminster Fuller has pointed out, we are all on Spaceship Earth and we were left without an operation manual. It has been trial and error, and now our margin for error has been reduced. Some people prefer the image of Gaia, mother earth groaning with the many wounds we have inflicted upon our home, our source of life.

(2) Our spaceship appears headed toward self-destruction. There is environmental overload; depletion of limited resources, overpopulation, pollution, poverty, poison of the air we breathe, of water, of food, and our delicate ecosystem is endangered.

(3) There is the threat of worldwide economic collapse. Developing nations face an increasingly widening gap in their standard of living: developed countries are threatened with prolonged recession/depressions. Economic realities underscore the increasing interdependency of the planet.

(4) The world is fraught with social upheavals, social structures are crumbling, power struggles are shaking the institutions and cultural traditions of both developed and developing nations. New norms have not emerged.

(5) Perhaps most frightening, our world has become a global powder keg. A worldwide explosion could be set off even by accident. We are thinking the unthinkable. Willis Harman recently put it this way:

> I find myself thinking back to my experience during World War II, when the peril and the urgency were apparent, and tens of millions of people set their usual lives aside to deal with the present danger. I feel the society to be in far more peril now than it was in 1941, and yet there is little sense of the need to set our usual lives aside to undertake a common task. This is understandable, of course, because in 1941 the enemy was clearly "out there."

And he adds, "Yet the awakening is beginning to happen."

The fact that we are in a period of great transition and urgency does seem to be commonly realized, and we are sensing that the scope of this transition is larger, the stakes higher, than we have experienced in our short human history. As Capra emphasizes in *The Turning Point,* we are experiencing the convergence of several major transitions. A unique feature of this particular transition is the acceleration of change which is the cumulative effect of our technology which has made it possible for us to be aware of this escalating change and has precipitated the end of innocence.

There is not much common agreement about the dynamics of this transition, except to agree that it is indeed upon us, and many are calling it if not the major transition in human history, at least ranking near the top. In 1969, U. Thant said we have perhaps ten years to reverse the trends. William Irwin Thompson warned us more than a decade ago that we are "At the Edge of History" where old relations between culture and nature are breaking up. Buckminster Fuller has suggested we are facing "Utopia or Oblivion," and the Club of Rome reports have suggested we are "Mankind at the Turning Point."

Neither is there any general agreement about whether change will be slow and incremental, or quick; either a cataclysmic collapse into a dark age, or an evolutionary leap to new levels of integration, or whether we are already into a postindustrial, information age.

How are we to respond to this new awareness? We have been brought to understand the incredible interrelatedness of everything, and it won't do to try and fix the parts. There are many ways people find to avoid dealing with the issues, but I'll not review those here. I'm assuming we are all searching for appropriate responses.

Quoting again from Willis Harman:

> If transformation is required, a key task for each of us is reexamination of our belief systems. Most of us here have done that in one respect, in the psychological dimension. But it is necessary to go further in the social dimension. We have to search out and remove the basic contradictions in our own belief systems, because those are contributing to the insanity of the nuclear arms race, the world economy plundering the planet on which it subsists, and all the rest.

Of course, this is what we have been about for the past twenty years. But

Harman is suggesting we have to go beyond our individual psychological theories and into social dimensions. He goes on to name three fundamental obsolete concepts we have taken for granted which must be replaced:

(1) War as a legitimate and inevitable means for settling international disputes.
(2) Mass-consumption, full-employment society as a goal.
(3) The supremacy of economic logic and institutions.

I would add another concept especially relevant to humanistic psychology: the concept that personal transformation inevitably leads to social transformation. Structural issues that are deep and pervasive will not necessarily dissolve by personal development. All of the above obsolete concepts lead to short-term, tunnel vision with disastrous results.

We do know that premises and values are changing. Harman states that over the past decade perhaps a fifth of the adult population in the United States have shifted to a set of premises far different from the materialist, positivist, relativist, skeptically agnostic premises that prevailed in the 1950s. The emerging premises are more transcendentalist and holistic, and the value priorities associated with them are more humane, more ecological, more spiritual.

We are also becoming conscious of our responsibility for life on this planet, our role in making it what it is and the challenge to participate consciously in its future. This is what I call the end of innocence. Ruben Nelson, a Canadian futurist says, "The healing of our society, ourselves and this earth, is not merely a function of our good intentions . . . We must not only intend t＞ do, but we must actually do the right things." He stresses that there is an important intermediate step between discovering significant trouble and our taking action to correct it — namely, understanding the trouble, its nature, origin, and implications. In North America, he suggests, we like to see ourselves as "action oriented" and our inclination is to "get on with it." The danger, of course, in being so single-mindedly action oriented is that we leap too quickly from the perception of problems to fiddling with their solutions. Little time is spent developing skills by means of which we can select, attend to, and make sense of the symptoms of our conditions.

We are responsible for the effects of our actions. Nelson says we live in a society which suffers from the "Aswan High Dam Complex," characterized as "well intended, well attempted, but ill directed." The actual effects of our actions are often damaging and not at all what we intended. I quote from him:

> At the heart of our struggle towards not merely well-intended but appropriate behavior is our need for an accurate and adequate description of our situation and our condition. We need to move towards an understanding of ourselves, and of the many inconsistent things going on in and around us, that is sufficiently powerful and persuasive to allow us to find our bearings, to form life-giving intentions, and then to govern ourselves accordingly.

He suggests that a consensus is slowly growing that the deep malaise has to do less with hard issues of resource shortages, than with the soft issues of our imagination and the patterns of our society which reflect and reinforce our imagination. We are now coming to understand that there is a deep, permanent, and rich interpenetration among thought, consciousness, action, and environment.

Jack Landau in a recent editorial statement in the journal *Revision* concerning artists and the future described our common predicament: "We are all of us caught between our good intentions and the chain of unintended evil consequences, between short-term and long-range survival. We are afraid that what we do today may in fact doom us tomorrow." A good example of this has been the history of U.S. foreign economic aid policy. We find to our dismay that the massive economic aid program has not only *not* reversed the growing gap between rich and poor, but has actually in many cases contributed to its increase.

There are no instant, easy solutions. Another awakening that comes with the end of innocence is a growing recognition that there are no cheap fixes, no quick and easy solutions, in spite of our tendency to want to make the world work. This does not mean we should give up visioning, but neither should we be looking for simple solutions. Ruben Nelson asserts that the task of refashioning our world will be measured in generations, not merely in years:

> We have a long period of time in which our prime
> agenda must be the development of an understanding
> of ourselves and our world which is sufficiently power-
> ful to allow us to act in hope with reasonable confi-
> dence. Meanwhile, precisely because we are coming
> to understand the depth of our confusion and are begin-
> ning to glimpse the innumerable ways we betray our
> best intentions, we will do as little as possible.

I have become very cautious of single solutions or explanations. An example of what I consider "too easy" explanations comes from John Naisbitt in his best-seller, *Megatrends*. Naisbitt says the Information Age is revolutionizing our lives and he identifies nine trends relating to and resulting from this phenomenon, including high tech/high touch, moving from national economy to world economy, from centralization to decen-tralization, from hierarchies to networking. He places heavy emphasis on the fact that we have become a global market with the increasing interde-pendency of nations due to our flow of resources, goods, and materials. He asserts that change occurs when there is a confluence of both changing values and economic necessity — not before.

That we are deeply enmeshed in the process of a global redistribution of labor and of production I do not doubt, and due to the collapse of what Naisbitt calls the "information float" (the time it takes for information to circulate through a system), we have a truly global economy because for the first time we have instantaneously shared information. This sounds terrific. However, Naisbitt does not mention another trend; the tremen-dous growth of the multinational corporations during the past forty years. The global corporation is now to a large extent controlling the world mar-ket; made possible by advances in the technology of centralization, and based largely on the sophisticated control of communications. If you want to get a very different view of what this attempt at integrating a world system is about, read Richard Barnet and Ronald Muller's *Global Reach*. They point out that the average growth rate of the most successful global corporations is two to three times that of most advanced industrial coun-tries, including the United States. The most revolutionary aspect of the planetary enterprise, they assert, is not its size but its world view. It mea-sures its success and failures not by the balance sheet of an individual subsidiary, or its social impact in a particular country, but by the growth in global profits and market shares. Its fundamental assumption is that the growth of the whole enhances the welfare of all the parts. In the last fifteen years it has been substantially easier to make profits abroad than in the U.S. economy. The result has been that U.S. corporations have been shifting more of their total assets abroad. The top 298 U.S.-based global corporations studied by the Department of Commerce earn 40% of their entire net profits outside the United States. The global corporation view is a need to plan, organize, and manage on a global scale. The global corporation is transforming the world political economy through its increasing control over three fundamental resources of economic life: the technology of production, finance capital, and marketing.

You will question Naisbitt's optimistic conclusions regarding our global economy after reading Barnet and Muller's *Global Reach*.

I have dwelled upon this issue of responsibility because I believe it is the primary issue we must face as humanistic psychologists, both in examining our lives and what contribution we may have to offer. We are, indeed, at the end of our innocence.

I am not going to add to the many analyses of the 1960s and 1970s, nor give you a chronology of the history of humanistic psychology. Rather, I will review some applications and contributions of humanistic psychology and raise questions about the effects of our actions by looking at major criticisms of the movement. To do this, I have to begin with myself as participant/observer in the humanistic psychology movement for the past twenty years. I had intended to tell something of my story, the early years at Esalen and the growth centers, and the early networking in AHP. However, I would never get to more important issues if I get into reminiscences of the "good old days." I will say this voyage of self-discovery has been a stormy passage, with still no end in sight. As all of us know who started on such a path, we are not always filled with joy, light, and love. We are not often told at the beginning that there is no going back. There may be arrested development, and we may get stuck at points along the way, but there is really no going back. While I maintain a basic faith in the tenets of Third Force Psychology, I'm afraid our actions have often fallen short of our aims, and our good intentions have not always resulted in what we expected.

In assessing what our contributions have been, it is important to recognize humanistic psychology as a small thread in a broad cultural pattern, the shape of which we are just beginning to see. John Naisbitt's high tech/high touch explanation notes that the human potential movement developed simultaneously with TV and by implication was primarily a response to that high technology. His point may be well taken that high tech does stimulate a high touch response, but in my estimation, Naisbitt's analysis is too slick and too simple.

Humanistic psychology *is* based on a very simple premise, and not a new one; that people matter and that their potential is hardly tapped and that psychology should focus on those issues and dimensions of greatest importance to humans. It asserts that given a nourishing environment, humans have the potential to develop as a self-determining, self-actualizing, self-transcending healthy persons; if denied such an environment, these potentials do not develop. We have asserted that these human needs/rights should be given priority, and that they have been denied in the rapidly changing technological world. Further, humanistic psychology speaks of personal transitions, even transformations, and encourages personal growth and development. Basic to personal growth is learning to take responsibility for oneself rather than being a victim. This is especially important in times of cultural transition. For good and for bad, our therapies and personalities have touched many lives in the United States, Canada, and other countries. We have focused on the individual and the primacy of human needs, and the measure of our success during the past two decades must be seen in individual lives.

I know of no way to measure quantitatively the impact of humanistic psychology on people's beliefs and behavior. While there are reports indicating changing values, it is most difficult to determine causal factors. There is much disagreement, even within the ranks of humanistic psychology, regarding the effects of our therapies. I will ask this question when I look at criticisms of the movement.

Rather than examine the impact of humanistic psychology on individual behavior, I want to consider the applications of humanistic psychology as an indicator of our accomplishments. While this is no easier a task than looking at individual change, it may provide a broader lens through which to view ourselves. I am going to refer to a study I did in 1973-1974. The purpose of that study was to forecast major trends in the humanistic psychology movement in the United States during the decade 1975-1984. The intention was to investigate the probable impact of humanistic psychology on U.S. society. The question posed was, "What likely contribution will the humanistic psychology movement make toward the realization or increasing likelihood of an emerging self-determining, self-actualizing, positive image of the future of humans in the next ten years?"

Admittedly, this was a large and difficult question, not to mention presumptuous. Nevertheless, it does raise issues and questions of relevance that seem appropriate to look at now that the end of that ten years has arrived.

The research method used involved 36 in-depth interviews, primarily with leaders in the field of humanistic psychology. A few were included who had written extensively about the future, or had been important in the futurist movement. Persons were chosen who represented various views and fields within the humanistic movement — education, therapy, academic psychology, science, growth centers, body therapists, and leaders of AHP. Seven overall trends were identified by participants:

(1) The humanistic psychology movement will develop maturity, which includes a shift from the initial protest state toward affirmation of the humanistic approach, including an increasing interest in developing a unified theory of humanistic psychology.

(2) There will be a trend toward synthesis and integration of a holistic approach to human behavior, with a shifting of emphasis from the highly emotional toward an integrative, holistic approach which includes cognitive, affective, physical, and spiritual dimensions.

(3) There will be a shifting of emphasis away from personal growth toward social and political responsibility. There will be increasing concern for the person in relation to his/her environment.

(4) There will be a trend toward increased acceptance of humanistic psychology in the culture; the scope of the field will continue to broaden, and increased emphasis will be placed on applied humanism.

(5) There will be increased research in humanistic psychology and related fields, and increasing concern with developing methodologies for a new science adequate to the study of the whole person. Expanded research in areas not previously explored will continue to bring in infor-

mation which may revolutionize the conception of human potential. Also, there will be an increased interest in transpersonal psychology.

(6) There will be increased acceptance of humanistic psychology within the field of psychology and increased dialogue between the various schools of psychology; however, not without conflict.

(7) There will be increased community within the humanistic psychology movement. Communication networks will expand among those with similar interests.

Regarding specific applications, four areas were identified as important fields for application of humanistic approaches — education, medicine, mental health and professional psychology, and political action. The participants felt there would be increased application of humanistic psychology in the fields of education and medicine, most effectively in medicine. They also predicted a continuing trend toward the deprofessionalization of psychology and an increased influence of humanistic psychology in the mental health professions. However, no significant increase in the application of humanistic psychology in the area of political action was seen. The consensus was that the movement has no political clout, our people have not been politically oriented, are too soft about power issues, and humanistic psychology has not created an atmosphere for political action. Also, we were seen as having a great deal of naiveté about political power and social change.

While there was no indication that humanistic psychology would become dominant in any of these fields, there was felt to be a general trend toward increased acceptance of humanistic approaches.

When I completed the study, the predictions seemed rather modest. Looking backward, they seem indicative of general trends and, to the extent these have been realized, provide a small indicator of the contributions of humanistic psychology. Each of the trends might be debated, with some people supporting the claim that humanistic psychology has made significant contributions and others disclaiming that it has had any significant impact beyond its small number of adherents. Indeed, it is difficult to evaluate whether these trends have made much impact on the culture at large. Certainly there were notable omissions in the study. The centrality of the nuclear issue was not foreseen; the importance of alternative "soft" technologies was not predicted, nor were the significant changes in the work place. Further, the acceptance of humanistic psychology has no doubt been affected by the economic hardships of the worldwide recession and the backlash of the New Right.

My personal conclusion is that humanistic psychology has contributed a great deal to personal growth and development and has had an indeterminate effect at the societal level. My main point is that it is now time to apply the learning we have accumulated about personal growth and development to societal issues and problems.

Another way to assess the contribution of humanistic psychology is to review major criticisms of the movement. I will dwell on some of these criticisms as a way of asking questions regarding our responsibility for the effects of our actions. My intent is not to defend nor deny, so I will not answer the critics, but rather focus our attention on issues we need to keep before us.

Probably the most serious charge is that humanistic psychology has encouraged a narcissistic, selfish, and hedonistic trend, often labeled the "Me Generation." The claim is that people become so involved in their personal development they do not look at the real issues in the world. They hide behind a false and pollyanna picture of the world as they would have it be. This issue is of great concern to leaders within our ranks as well as outside critics. Michael Marien recently expressed this as "Transformation as Sandbox Syndrome." Rollo May has addressed his concern with our tendency to see only what we want to see and thereby block out half the world. He said, "We are in a great danger when we close our eyes to half the reality in human existence. We are dangerous if we lull people into thinking that evolution, or progress, or inspiration, will get us over these problems."

Perhaps you have been following the dialogue between Rollo May and Carl Rogers which began in the summer of 1982 in a series of exchanges in the *Journal of Humanistic Psychology*. May charges that there is danger of the movement becoming "a community of like-minded persons" meaning those "who are so lost in self love that they cannot see and relate to the reality outside themselves, including other human beings." Rogers responds that he finds the opposite is true in groups he has experienced. They lead to social action of a realistic nature. Maurice Friedman pointed out that their basic disagreement concerns the nature of good and evil, with Rogers seeing good and evil as opposites, and May seeing what we call evil as itself containing the possibility of the good if it is given direction, or as leading inevitably to destructiveness if it remains unrecognized and undirected.

We each have to search our own experiences and beliefs to sort out the validity of this criticism. Therapists and teachers must ask themselves to what degree they have unintentionally aided in an "adjustment" to the world and encouraged people to think only of themselves.

Another criticism relates to the reckless use of powerful technologies. A few years ago, Richard Farson, a critic within our ranks, looked at the dangers of our eager applications of powerful technologies and questioned the virtue and responsibility of such work, especially the more dogmatic and totalitarian of these methods. He pointed out that a primary contribution Carl Rogers has made is to give us an ethical basis for relationships. Farson is one of the more gentle critics. Koch, Nord, and Wooton are more severe. The question of responsibility for the use of these technologies is still an important issue. If we acknowledge we are at the end of innocence, we have to accept responsibility for the technologies we use. How responsible have we been about their use?

The two criticisms just discussed are probably the most important issues concerning the effect of our actions. Several other criticisms are worthy of mention.

There is the charge that the therapies are ineffective. The proliferation of techniques and claims for everything from sexual delights to spiritual enlightenment have surely created a credibility gap between our promises and what is delivered.

Another charge is that people may become "true believers." How obnoxious are those who express their enthusiasms for new found potentials and paths, especially when they insist these cannot be explained, but have to be experienced. The similarity to dogmatic religious sects, where only prescribed behavior is tolerated, has been pointed out. I see the continuing danger of assuming we are the brightest, most enlightened, the leading edge.

Another serious charge is that of elitism; a white, middle-class phenomenon. It is true this movement has been primarily a self-help group of middle class, mostly white Westerners. This does not mean that the values of humanistic psychology only apply to us, but we have been blessed with the luxury to explore levels beyond survival.

Another charge is that humanistic psychology is a fuzzy-headed approach, and that its advocates do not support their assertions with adequate research or clear thinking. I believe there is a growing body of theory and research that speaks for itself, which I don't have time to review here. However, there are still wild assertions and unfounded claims that do not lend credibility to the field.

A final charge is one we sometimes laugh at, but perhaps should take seriously. This is that we are part of the Aquarian Conspiracy aiming to wipe out the good old American way. The New Right is not to be taken lightly, and some of you are probably experiencing the effects of this charge, especially those of you in education. There is no doubt humanistic psychology has challenged some of the prevailing beliefs and values, and to some it is seen as threatening.

I have spent so much time on these charges because as a professional, I believe it is important to look at these criticisms seriously, and to the degree they are true, sort out our role in contributing to them. At least by acknowledging the two-edged sword of our actions, we will gain humility as we approach the tasks before us.

Let us not spend more time rehashing the achievements and failures of humanistic psychology. We have our lessons to learn from these experiences, and we now can take a more sobering and humble look at what we have to offer in these perilous times.

Willis Harman has suggested three contributions we can make in this time of global-level dilemmas. The first is in the realm of values and meaning. While our society knows how to approach almost any "How to?" question, it is more unsure when faced with the question, "What for?" When you can accomplish almost any technical task imaginable, if willing to commit resources, then what is worth doing?

A second contribution he suggests is to help in understanding what traditional societies have to offer the world. We need to consider soberly whether the planet could eventually support one Western industrial monoculture and if that would be desirable. The alternative is an ecology of diverse cultures, supported by a global order significantly different from the presently dominant world economy.

A third contribution is understanding resistance to seeing problems and solutions. The analogy to psychotherapy is a useful one. The client is overwhelmed by problems. He or she is ambivalent about them, seeking a solution yet obstructing at the same time. Resistance shows up in a tendency to seek simple explanations in which the solution lies in change out there; to feel the person has no option or is impotent, to seek salvation in authority, to do almost anything except see the roots of the problem in the need for a change of mind. The analogy to the problems of society is evident.

I will add another to this list. I believe humanistic psychology can contribute to developing the *will to survive* and our success or failure will depend not on outside critics, but on our ability to determine goals and objectives that are both visionary and practical, our heads neither in the sand (or sandbox) nor in the clouds. We can do this with a clear sense of our responsibility for our actions.

I further believe that the next step is one of *social responsibility,* understanding that my needs and rights are interconnected with everyone. So personal growth and responses to change become linked with societal transition. Ted Roszak said it best in his book *Person/Planet,* with his statement that the needs of the person are the needs of the planet. We always hoped and intended that a self-actualizing individual by definition would become socially responsible and transfer learnings about self and others into the world.

I have made a list of resources I find we as humanistic practitioners bring to the tasks ahead:

Humanistic psychology holds a hopeful view of people, in their ability to be self-determining, self-actualizing, and capable of making choices;

It promotes human growth and transformation;
It gives priority to human needs;
It is holistic and insists on looking at total systems;
It honors the subjective, the intuitive in the study of humans;

> It supports self-disclosure, trust, openness as ways
> of being in the world;
> It supports risk taking, is heuristic, believes there is
> no one right way.

These values seem appropriate for the tasks ahead. And we can add to these values certain skills which have been developed within the field of humanistic psychology:

> —Personal growth technologies. A wide range of therapies and teachings have facilitated personal development and have established benefits.
> —Interpersonal skills. Group dynamics from encounter groups to the most sophisticated methods have been developed and have influenced individuals, businesses, churches, and other organizations.
> —Transpersonal dimension. The acknowledgement that humans are in relation to the universe, not apart, has fostered meditation and encouraged spiritual paths.
> —Systems. Skills for working with systems have been developed, including families and organizations.
> —Theory/Research. There is a growing body of research to support expanded methods for studying persons, including interdisciplinary studies.
> —Self-help models have proliferated and have developed mutual support systems. There is a large body of information and skills available in this area, from community, neighborhood self-help groups to holistic health.

In addition to specific values and skills, we also have our supreme resource: people. Read Marilyn Ferguson's *Aquarian Conspiracy* for a sense of the extent of people involved. There are professionals and paraprofessionals from all fields who grasp the significance of this transitional period. Networks are growing with large numbers of people who have gone through personal development and are ready to contribute to what some are calling the "We Decade" of the 1980s.

So here we stand, our innocence shed, with all the good intentions and concerns for our future, acknowledging our deep confusions while honoring the values, skills, and resources we bring to the tasks ahead.

In this time of parentheses, what seems most important to me is how we approach our changing world. Given the uncertainties about our responsibilities and the effect of our actions, what kind of stance do we take? Jack Gibb in his recent work calls for individuals to find their own "passionate path." I want to suggest several stances that seem appropriate to the time and invite you to add to this list:

(1) Do we, as Donal Michael has suggested in *On Learning to Plan, and Planning to Learn,* become learners, acknowledging that we don't know and act tentatively, learning from our errors and living with ambiguity?

(2) Should we follow Jonas Salk's advice in *Survival of the Wisest* and act as if we have the wisdom; to proceed and perhaps gain the wisdom along the way?

(3) Should we adopt the warrior stance in the Don Juan sense, remaining alert and ready to move adroitly in any necessary direction?

(4) Should we see ourselves as nurturers, healers of a wounded planet?

(5) Should we be visionaries, concentrating on positive images and visions for our future, thereby contributing to self-fulfilling prophesies?

(6) Should we take a stance as co-creators, acknowledging our responsibilities and choice in creating our future?

(7) Should we seek attunement, be still and wait for spiritual guidance, and as suggested by the third Zen patriarch, "Do not search for the truth, only cease to cherish opinions"?

I think it makes an important difference what kind of stance we choose, and that we do it consciously. Obviously, our choice depends on our beliefs and values. We are again back to looking for guidelines, for maps to help chart these unknown waters. We must each explore the models and guides that are available, some new and some old, understanding them as best we can, without necessarily accepting one way as the true one, but rather approach them as aids, dimly lighting our path. We will probably find more than one path, and more than one appropriate stance. There are a variety of models and theories that offer frameworks for viewing change, including general systems theory, psycho-dynamic and developmental models, mythic and historical models, spiritual teachings, ecological and evolutionary models, feminine models, new economic and political models, and the new sciences, both biological and physical.

While all these models offer structures to help comprehend change, they do not tell us for sure what is ahead. There are positive signs that provide a basis for optimism, yet we continue to live daily under the threat of the mushroom cloud. When people are on the streets, hungry and cold, with little hope of employment in our own country; when the suffering of people around the world is increasing, we cannot avoid the responsibility of addressing human needs.

Ten years ago I attempted to forecast trends in humanistic psychology. Today I am less able to do so. However, I composed a modest ten-point proposal a while ago suggesting approaches to strategies for humanistic psychology in the 1980s. I have just revised this to a more modest eight points, and I offer them for your consideration:

> (1) A healthy self-examination is in order. This is what I've been attempting to do here. This begins with a personal examination of beliefs and actions — Do I model what I talk about? What are my consumption patterns? What stance am I moving from? It broadens to looking at the effects of our actions collectively.
>
> (2) Assess our skills carefully. What do we have to offer, both to individuals, and in the area of addressing structural issues?
>
> (3) Address structural issues that are basic to human survival, including: (a) peace, disarmament, human world order, alternative security strategies. This is the most urgent issue and is eliciting the most response. Perhaps it will provide a model for addressing other primary human survival issues; (b) human rights issues: support self-empowering movements, new age politics, liberation movements; (c) redistribution of world resources: address issues of world poverty, starvation; and (d) environmental issues: support conservation, alternative energy sources, and the concept of stewardship.
>
> (4) Build support systems. We need a new sense of community for nourishment and revival and to know that we are not alone. Networking has become an important linking mechanism.
>
> (5) Massive education effort, a consciousness-raising effort to first inform ourselves on what is going on in the world, and second, to present humanistic ideas to the public, especially researching new modes of learning.

(6) Collaborative efforts. Join with others who have similar values and objectives, via networking, coalitions, and building an informal, empowering constituency capable of being heard, to lobby and to inform the public of issues.

(7) Hold a positive vision of the possible future, while grappling with hard realities. This involves developing a strategic vision to support positive change.

(8) Finally, whatever we do, let's do it with a great deal of humility. Let us approach the tasks ahead in a spirit of trust, faith and surrender, more yin than yang, in a sense of stewardship and willingness to admit and acknowledge our ignorance. Let us be aware of the pitfalls, and help pick one another up. I believe we can consciously help what is gestating, we can be open to new patterns, we can help others find these changes less threatening. We can learn to move more freely in this time of parentheses.

To summarize and clarify what I've said: I am not saying humanistic psychology has made no significant contribution to our society. We have given a psychological basis and framework for change and transformation. We have seen people's lives change as a result of our therapies and teachings. Also, I do not underestimate the current indicators of positive change. I only ask that we look carefully at the broad societal implications. Neither am I saying we should stop being visionaries. To the contrary, the visioning and imaging are crucial, as are the innovative models of learning.

What I am saying is that it is time to ask ourselves "What business are we in?" and to reconceptualize our role in society. To do this we must start with conscious self-evaluation and learn to take responsibility for the effects of our actions. I believe our major challenge, our business, is to apply the skills and resources accumulated in humanistic psychology in the broad arena of social change.

If we can accept the responsibility of being "people of the parentheses," without an overblown sense of our own importance and without being overcome by uncertainty and fear, we have a contribution to make. We can no longer dwell in a state of innocence and have a lot to learn about ourselves and our world. As humanistic professionals, we have a special responsibility to apply our knowledge and resources toward increasing our understanding and our ability to respond to the challenges of this in-between time. May we each find our own passionate path and be comforted by the fact that we are not alone. The number of people consciously dedicated to creating a positive and sustainable world community is growing.

JACQUELINE DOYLE, *The Political Process: Working Statement*

A political system which does not live by its stated values degenerates. Unkept political promises and secrecy in decision-making have undercut the confidence of the electorate. The body politic is ill. It has trafficked too long in distrust. The people are disaffected, feeling powerless to be heard, to influence the political process. A grassroots protest, signifying health, is welling up: a protest against deceit in politics, against runaway technology, against raped environments, against interpersonal violence, against economic imbalance and discrimination. In this protest rest the seeds of hope: a renewed clarity of values and purpose.

Reform movements have always relied on the invention of new forms or structures to create new directions. Today, however, there is less need for new form in politics than for new content, expressed in terms of human values and a humane political process.

The body of ideas expressed in the brief statement which follows represents a reform movement of another sort. As humanists and psychologists, we are addressing change at the interpersonal level of politics rather than structural change. We are moving from a history of theory and practice in personal growth and change to a responsible consideration of social change.

We seek a new political process equal to the task of governing wisely and fairly a planet of co-operative peoples interested in mutual survival through sharing of the earth's resources. The new co-operative solutions sought will not emerge through the outworn mechanisms of threat and coercion. Needs for control and governance certainly exist. Displays of power and force will not generate the mutual confidence and support needed between nations, communities or people.

The challenge of this new age lies in a process of transforming fear and mutual suspicion into trust between peoples. How is this massive task to be undertaken? Through a process of re-education of the people, beginning with the modeling of new forms of leadership in government.

We can suggest directions for the invention of a healthy political process:

1. *Employ ecological assumptions:* All of the elements necessary for the resolution of the current problem between people already exist. The solutions will become apparent when we remove the blocks to their recognition. Each element or person in the environment is intrinsically valuable to balance. For our preservation, we must actively fight discrimination: it denies us information.

2. *Share responsibility and power:* Through very broad and active mechanisms or participation, we heighten the speed and totality of feedback, correction and innovation of the political process. We need to build and connect local networks to the complex representative, democratic forms of governance. The creation of these networks, complete with facilitators trained in sharing listening and speaking skills, must become a national priority.

3. *Practice truth:* Truth is the most radical instrument available to us in changing our politics and our lives. It contains all the information sought. We are not referring here to popular truth, but to complex and complete truth on pertinent matters. This includes the admission that we do not know the answers: admissions to confusion, fatigue and lack of knowledge from leaders and "experts". Inherent in this practice is necessary training of the listener and speaker in the management of frustration, stress and anxiety. This education should begin in public elementary schools and continue to be made available to adults.

4. *Train "new competencies":* We need political leaders with the capacity to tolerate ambiguity and uncertainty, the ability to hear and honor multiple truths simultaneously, in addition to the above skills. We strongly urge value-confrontation as training.

5. *Encourage self-help and self-responsibility:* Through fiscal rewards and support for leadership, consultation and housing of homogenous problem-solving groups.

6. *Establish local conflict-resolution centers:* Mediation skills must be spread widely across and within cultures.

We are suggesting a broad-scale social experiment, never before attempted. It is unknown whether we, as a species, are equal to the challenge ahead. Leadership in this exploration will require courage, humility, and requests for guidance. We must all learn together.

NOTES AND SOURCES

The original form of most pieces collected in this book included the system of references which has become standard in many academic and professional journals. Quotations, for example, were usually identified by a parenthetical reference within the text (e.g., (Rogers, 1951, p. 6)) which led the reader to an alphabetically arranged bibliography printed at the end of the article. In some of the pieces, footnote numbers were used, with the notes printed at the bottom of the page or collected at the end of the piece. Here, considerations of uniformity and a desire to keep the texts themselves as readable as possible, have led to the decision to gather all references and notes at the end of the volume. These are listed sequentially as they appear or are alluded to in the texts.

I: GOOD AND EVIL

ROLLO MAY, *The Problem of Evil: An Open Letter to Carl Rogers*

Rogers, C. "Notes on Rollo May," *Perspectives* 1981, 2/1. "A recent Gallup poll . . . :" reported in *Newsweek,* October 5, 1981, page 35.

Rogers, "Notes on Rollo May," page 16.

May, R. *Love and Will.* New York: Norton, 1969.

Rogers, C. *A Way of Being.* Boston: Houghton Mifflin, 1980.

Cousins, N. "Thoughts at Year's End," *Saturday Review,* December 1981, page 12.

Rogers, *A Way of Being,* page 356.

Yankelovich, D. *New Rules.* New York: Random House, 1981, page 184.

Milgram, S. *Obedience to Authority.* New York: Harper and Row, 1969, page 178.

Zimbardo, P. G.; Banks, W. C.; Haney, C.; and Jaffee, D. "The Mind is a Formidable Jailor: A Pirandellian Prison," *New York Times Magazine,* April 8, 1973, pages 38 ff.

"Veterans Administration Hospital:" Rogers, C.; Gendlin, E.; Kiesler, D.; and Truax, C. *The Therapeutic Relationship with Schizophrenics.* Madison: University of Wisconsin Press, 1967.

Rogers, Gendlin, Kiesler and Truax, *The Therapeutic Relationship with Schizophrenics,* page 503.

Raskin, N. "Becoming — a Therapist, a Person, a Partner, a Parent," *Psychotherapy: Therapy Research and Practice,* 1978, 15/4, page 367.

Rogers, Gendlin, Kiesler and Truax, *The Therapeutic Relationship with Schizophrenics,* page 503.

Raskin, N. "Becoming . . . ," page 366.

May, *Love and Will,* page 129.

Yankelovich, D. *New Rules.* New York: Random House, 1981.

May, *Love and Will,* page 131.

CARL ROGERS, *Some Social Issues Which Concern Me*

Hauser, P. "Population," in Foreign Policy Association, ed., *Toward the Year 2018.* New York: Cowles Education Corp., 1968.

The Next Ninety Years. Proceedings of a Conference sponsored by California Institute of Technology, Pasadena, CA., 1967.

Ward, B. "Speech to Members of 'California Tomorrow'," San Francisco, 1967.

Calhoun, J. "Population Density and Social Pathology," *Scientific American* 1962, 206/2, 139-150.

Rogers, C. *Becoming Partners.* Marriage and Its Alternatives. New York: Delacorte, 1972.

Rogers, C., "Interpersonal Relations in the Year 2000," *Journal of Applied Behavioral Science,* 1968, 4/3, 265-280.

Personal reports from Dr. Norman Chambers and Dr. Lawrence Carlin, both of the Center for Studies of the Person, La Jolla, CA.

MAURICE FRIEDMAN, *The Nuclear Threat and the Hidden Human Image*

Friedman, M. "Comment on the Rogers-May Discussion of Evil," *Journal of Humanistic Psychology* 22/4, 93-96.

Friedman, M. *Problematic Rebel:* Melville, Dostoievsky, Camus. Chicago: University of Chicago Press, 1970.

Friedman, M. *The Hidden Human Image.* New York: Delacorte Press, 1974.

Friedman, M. *To Deny Our Nothingness.* Contemporary Images of Man, 3rd edition. Chicago: University of Chicago Press, 1982.

Friedman, M. *Contemporary Psychology: Revealing and Obscuring the Human.* Pittsburgh: Duquesne University Press, 1984.

Wiesel, E. *One Generation After.* New York: Random House, 1970.

Friedman, M. *The Confirmation of Otherness:* In Family, Community and Society. New York: Pilgrim Press, 1983.

II: INNOCENCE AND GROWING UP

JAMES LAFFERTY, *Political Responsibility and the Human Potential Movement*

Satir, V. *Self Esteem.* Millbrae, CA: Celestial Arts, 1970.

May, R. *Love and Will.* New York: Dell, 1969, pages 288-289; italics added.

Perls, F. *In and Out of the Garbage Pail.* New York: Bantam, 1969, pages 268-269; italics added.

Berne, E. *Games People Play.* New York: Dell, 1964, page 184; italics added.

Anderson, W. "Politics and the New Humanism," *Journal of Humanistic Psychology* 14 (1974/4), page 23 (italics added); page 25.

MICHAEL MARIEN, *The Transformation as Sandbox Syndrome*

"Aquarian Conspiracy:" Marilyn Ferguson, *The Aquarian Conspiracy.* Personal and Social Transformation in the 1980s. Los Angeles: J. P. Tarcher, 1980.

"Green Menace:" Green parties such as Les Vertes, Die Grünen, and the UK Ecology Party are now established minor political parties in Europe. Despite characteristic disorganization, they are at or near the point of being wooed by the major parties.

"Sandbox Syndrome:" The Sandbox Syndrome is not confined to New Age groups, but can be found in many minority political groups of both the Right, the Left, and "beyond Right and Left" (which New Age groups purport to be), as well as in established organizations. For purposes of this exploratory essay, Sandbox behaviors will be described only as they apply to "transformationalists."

"1977 Harris Poll:" Duane Elgin, *Voluntary Simplicity.* New York: William Morrow, 1981, page 128. An example of the leading questions asked: "By 66 percent to 22 percent, the public chooses 'breaking up big things and getting back to more humanized living' over 'developing bigger and more efficient ways of doing things.' "

"Stanford Research International:" Elgin, *Voluntary Simplicity,* page 132. Based on work with Arnold Mitchell at SRI, Elgin estimates that, in 1980, roughly 6 percent of the U.S. population is "wholeheartedly exploring a life of voluntary simplicity," and that such a lifestyle "could well grow to be the dominant orientation for as much as a majority of the adult population of many Western developed nations by the year 2000." No justification is given for this exuberant extrapolation. Although the SRI data have been frequently and acritically cited by many New Age writers, they are not based on a rigorous survey, but on "best guesses based upon our immersion in all of the relevant data that we could find" (Elgin letter to Marien, September 7, 1979).

"Consciousness II:" For historical buffs, Consciousness II is the establishment mindset as characterized in a 1970 best seller by Charles A. Reich, *The Greening of America* (New York: Random House). Ferguson's *Aquarian Conspiracy* might be usefully compared as a 1980s version of Reich's book.

"childish state of innocence:" Rollo May, *Power and Innocence,* New York: W.W. Norton, 1972. May describes innocence as the virtue of not having power — a way to confront one's powerlessness by making it a seeming virtue. He distinguishes between the authentic innocence of childlike attitudes and the childishness of pseudoinnocence, often associated with utopianism and the urge to make things simple and easy.

"books by Lester R. Brown, etc.:" Abstracts of recent books and articles by most of these writers are available in *Future Survey Annual 1980-1981,* ed. Michael Marien (Bethseda, MD: World Future Society, 1982). Note especially the section on Decentralization/Eco-Humanism, pages 109-117.

"Hamiltonian corporate view:" This argument, still applicable today, is made in detail by Herbert Agar, *Land of the Free* (Boston: Houghton Mifflin, 1935), who poses a choice between the true American Culture of self-government, equality, freedom and humanity, and a debased form of the Civilization of the West (finance capitalism and ownership by the few).

"Point (c):" May, *Power and Innocence,* page 110, eloquently states that "our narcissism is forever crying out against the wounds of those who would criticize us or point out our weak spots. We forget that the critic can be doing us a considerable favor."

"Point (d):" Charles Hampden-Turner, *Radical Man. The Process of Psycho-Social Development* (Cambridge, MA: Schenkman, 1970), page 327. Developmental radicals, in contrast to dogmatic radicals, need the insights of all their political opponents (page 329). Also see May, *Power and Innocence*, pages 109-110, who points to the necessity of opponents for all important truths.

"Point (i)" William Ryan, *Blaming the Victim* (New York: Pantheon, 1971, argues that the ideology of victim-blaming is a primary barrier to effective social change. Also see Dana Ullman, "Responsibility and Holistic Health," *Holistic Health News* (Berkeley Holistic Health Center), Spring 1980. Ullman has pointed out that "blaming the victim" (including self-blame) is another important characteristic of the Sandbox Syndrome (Ullman letter to Marien, July 30, 1982).

"(2) Connect . . . :" Fritjof Capra, *The Turning Point. Science, Society, and the Rising Culture* (New York: Simon and Schuster, 1982), page 36.

"Point (c):" Byron Kennard, *Nothing Can be Done, Everything is Possible* (Andover, MA: Brick House Publishing, 1982), page 83.

"Point (e), Gardner:" John W. Gardner, *The Recovery of Confidence* (New York: Norton, 1970), page 29.

"Point (e), avoiding illusions:" Abraham H. Maslow, *The Farther Reaches of Human Nature* (New York: Viking, 1971), pages 308-309.

"Point (c):" The first three paradigms are explored in somewhat greater detail by Michael Marien, "Toward a Devolution of Services," *Social Policy* 9/2 (1978): 26-35.

"(5) . . . various scientific traditions:" Bruce Holbrook, *The Stone Monkey. An Alternative Chinese-Scientific Reality* (New York: William Morrow, 1981). Holbrook argues that the Chinese Polar-Complete world view is clearly superior to the Absolute-Fragmental paradigm of Western science. Although he does not suggest the compromise of a synthesized world science, such a synthesis would seem to be ultimately likely and desirable. Also see Ziauddin Sardar, "Why Islam Needs Islamic Science," *New Scientist*, April 1, 1982, pages 25-28, for a parallel argument from another scientific tradition.

MICHAEL MARIEN, *Further Thoughts on the Two Paths to Transformation: A Reply to Ferguson*

"A leaderless . . . network" (quote from Ferguson): Marilyn Ferguson, *The Aquarian Conspiracy: Personal and Social Transformation in the 1980s* (Los Angeles: J.P. Tarcher, 1980), page 23. This is the opening sentence of the first chapter.

"Broader than reform . . . " (quote from Ferguson): Ferguson, *The Aquarian Conspiracy*, page 23.

Arnold Mitchell: *The Nine American Lifestyles. Who We Are and Where We Are Going* (New York: Macmillan, 1983).

Theodore Caplow: *Toward Social Hope* (New York: Basic Books, 1975).

Resource Manual: Virginia Coover *et al.*, *Resource Manual for a Living Revolution* (Philadelphia: New Society Publishers, 1981).

"a hundred names:" Michael Marien, "One Hundred Answers," *Resurgence* 98 (May-June, 1983), 24-29.

Hadley Cantril: *The Pattern of Human Concerns* (New Brunswick, New Jersey: Rutgers University Press, 1965), page 304.

Anthony Downs: "They Sell Sizzle, but their Predictions Fizzle," *Wall Street Journal*, April 6, 1983. Also see Donald N. Michael, "Aquarians Riding Third Wave," *The Wharton Magazine*, Winter 1980-1981, 10-11.

"evolution from T-I to T-II:" This fundamental distinction is thoroughly explored by Bertram M. Gross, *The Managing of Organizations* (New York: Free Press, 1964), Chapters 19-24.

Rudyard Kipling: "Cities and Thrones and Powers," *Puck of Pook's Hill*, 1906.

III: THE PROBLEM OF A POLITICAL ELITE

MILDRED HARDEMAN, *A Dialogue with Abraham Maslow*

Maslow, A.H. "Notes on Being-Psychology," *Journal of Humanistic Psychology* 1962, 2, 47-71.

ABRAHAM MASLOW, *Politics 3*

Huxley, A. *Letters of Aldous Huxley,* edited by Smith Grover. London: Chatto and Windus, 1969, page 524.

Moynihan, D. "Commencement Address, Notre Dame University, June 1, 1969," reprinted in *The American Scholar*, 1969, 573-583.

ADRIANNE ARON, *Maslow's Other Child*

Smith, M.B. "On Self-Actualization: A Transambivalent Examination of a Focal Theme in Maslow's Psychology," *Journal of Humanistic Psychology* 1973, 13, 17-33.

"hippies . . . self-indulgence:" The substitution of self-indulgence for self-actualization might be characteristic of Maslow's middle-class followers as well, in the sense that those who gravitate toward sensitivity training are not seeking to correct a deficit in their lives (i.e., to satisfy depletion drives, but rather to indulge themselves by satisfying enhancement drives. They pay high tuitions for the luxury of sensitivity training, in hopes of finding respite from "boredom, feelings of worthlessness, lack of excitement, and other indicators stereotyped as the symptoms of affluent suburbia" (K. Back, *Beyond Words. The Story of Sensitivity Training and the Encounter Movement.* New York: Russell Sage Foundation, 1972, page 37). It is noteworthy that the advent of the growth movement has not ushered in an apocalypse of self-actualization in the suburbs.

Maslow, A.H. *The Farther Reaches of Human Nature.* New York: Viking, 1971, pages 344; 159; 7.

"But to speak of the hippies . . . unknown to them:" One hundred and forty hippies in San Francisco, Berkeley, and Santa Cruz, California, were asked to name people they most admired. In over 300 responses Maslow's name appeared not once.

Maslow, A.H. "Peak-experiences as Acute Identity-experiences," *American Journal of Psychoanalysis*, 1961, 21.

Maslow, A.H. *The Farther Reaches of Human Nature*, pages 185; 110; 192 (italics added).

Maslow, *The Farther Reaches of Human Nature*, pages 19; 26.

Maslow, *The Farther Reaches of Human Nature*, pages 187; 19.

Maslow, *The Farther Reaches of Human Nature*, pages 294-295.

Maslow, *The Farther Reaches of Human Nature*, pages 185; 294 (italics added).

"If the model of Eupsychia . . . between the two:" By a convenient but intellectually indefensible process Maslow avoids dealing with the subject by shifting back and forth between two concepts of Eupsychia. In one the population consists exclusively of self-actualized people and a democracy is posited as suitable, for the *demos* are simultaneously the *aristoi,* and therefore democracy and aristocracy fuse. In the other, self-actualized people live with their inferiors and conflicts therefore arise. When the conflicts become too heavy, Maslow switched back to the monolithic community of the self-actualizers.

Maslow, A.H. *Motivation and Personality.* New York: Harper, 1954, page 350.

"the rock concert at Altamont:" At the Altamont concert in December 1969, 300,000 fans from the counterculture sat passively and watched a gang of Hell's Angels murder a spectator in front of the stage where Mick Jagger was performing.

Maslow, *The Farther Reaches of Human Nature*, page 289.

"Consider . . . free love:" Quotations from hippie subjects are from work in progress by the author, using tape-recorded interviews made by David Whittaker and William A. Watts in the San Francisco Bay Area in 1967 and by the author in Santa Cruz county, California, in 1973. The Watts-Whittaker data were collected under the auspices of the Center for Research and Development in Higher Education, University of California, Berkeley. Where subjects are named the names are fictitious.

"Acceptance:" Maslow, *The Farther Reaches of Human Nature*, pages 112 ff.

"eulogies on the modern corporation:" In *The Farther Reaches of Human Nature,* Maslow writes: "Let us not fall into the delusion of thinking of a relatively less well-managed large corporation as having 'bad conditions' — these are not bad at all. Let us remember that 99 percent of the human species would give several years of their lives to get a job in the worst-managed large corporation we have in the whole country." Cf. also his implicit transfer of responsibility for conditions from the corporation to the employee, through the notion of *acceptance.* If workers are dissatisfied with the corporate structure, all they need do is scale down their expectations (presumably by remembering that 99 percent of the human race would gladly trade places with them!) so that what they've *got* becomes identical to what they *want.* Thus, like the woman who feared and resented her husband's maleness but learned to be "religiously awed by it to the point of ecstasy" by changing not her husband (i.e., he continued mistreating her) but *her acceptance of him,* so too the worker can train himself to see "a glory" rather than "an evil" in the corporate organization (see Maslow, *The Farther Reaches*, page 113). I might add in passing that the corporate clients of sensitivity training are not unaware that A.H. Maslow is probably the best friend to have come along for them since the Corporate Tax Law.

Koch, S. "The Image of Man Implicit in Encounter Group Theory," *Journal of Humanistic Psychology*, 1971, 11, 109-127.

Maslow, *The Farther Reaches of Human Nature*, page 273.

CHARLES HAMPDEN-TURNER, *Comment on 'Maslow's Other Child'*

Aron, A. "Maslow's Other Child," *Journal of Humanistic Psychology* 1977, 17/2, 9-24.

Aron, "Maslow's Other Child," page 16 (italics added).

STEPHEN WOOLPERT, *A Comparison of Rational Choice and Self-Actualization Theories of Politics*

Downs, A. *An Economic Theory of Democracy*. New York: Harper and Row, 1957.

Riker, W. *The Theory of Political Coalitions*. New Haven: Yale University Press, 1962.

Riker, W. "Theory and Science in the Study of Politics: A Review," *Journal of Conflict Resolution*, 1965, 9, 375-379.

Riker, W. "The Future of a Science of Politics," *American Behavioral Scientist*, 1977, 21, 11-38.

Riker, W. and Ordeshook, P. *An Introduction to Positive Political Theory*. Englewood Cliffs, New Jersey: Prentice-Hall, 1973.

Ball, T. "From Paradigm to Research Programs: Toward a post-Kuhnian Political Science," *American Journal of Political Science*, 1976, 20, 151-177.

Maslow, A.H. "A Theory of Human Motivation," *Psychological Review*, 1943, 50, 370-396.

Maslow, A.H. "Resistance to Acculturation," *Journal of Social Issues*, 1951, 1, 26-29.

Maslow, A.H. *Motivation and Personality*. New York: Harper and Row, 1954.

Maslow, A.H. *The Farther Reaches of Human Nature*. New York: Viking, 1971.

Rogers, C. *Client-Centered Therapy*. Boston: Houghton Mifflin, 1951.

Rogers, C. "Toward a Modern Approach to Values: The valuing Process in the Mature Person," *Journal of Abnormal and Social Psychology*, 1964, 68, 160-167.

Rogers, C. "Toward a Science of the Person," in T. Wann, ed., *Behaviorism and Phenomenology*. Chicago: University of Chicago Press, 1964.

Rogers, C. "A Humanistic Conception of Man," in R. Farson, ed., *Science and Human Affairs*. Palo Alto, CA: Science and Behavior Books, 1965.

Anderson, W. *Politics and the New Humanism*. Pacific Palisades, CA: Goodyear, 1973.

Bay, C. "A Human Rights Approach to Transnational Politics," *Universal Human Rights*, 1979, 1, 19-42.

Burns, J. *Leadership*. New York: Harper and Row, 1978.

Davies, J. *Human Nature in Politics*. New York: John Wiley, 1963.

Gurtov, M. *Making Changes*. Oakland, CA: Harvest Moon, 1979.

Hampden-Turner, C. *Radical Man*. Cambridge, MA: Schenkman, 1970.

Knutson, J. *The Human Basis of the Polity*. Chicago: Aldine, 1972.

Matson, F. *The Broken Image*. New York: George Braziller, 1964.

Roszak, T. *Person/Planet*. Garden City, New York: Doubleday, 1977.

Satin, M. *New Age Politics*. New York: Delta, 1978.

"Human growth . . . fulfillment of potential:" Rogers, "A Humanistic Conception of Man."

Maslow, A. *The Farther Reaches of Human Nature*.

Riker and Ordeshook, *An Introduction to Positive Political Theory*, page 11.

Riker and Ordeshook, *An Introduction to Positive Political Theory*, page 21.

Riker, *The Theory of Political Coalitions*, page 28.

"The differences in the subject matter . . . psychological meanings:" Richman, H., ed. *Wilhelm Dilthey: Pattern and Meaning in History*. New York: Harper and Row, 1961, pages 37 ff.

"The next major difference . . . individuals involved:" Lukes, S., "Methodological Individualism Reconsidered," in A. Ryan, ed., *The Philosophy of Social Explanation*. Oxford: Oxford University Press, 1973.

Riker, *The Theory of Political Coalitions*, page 22.

Riker, "The Future of a Science of Politics," page 31.

Riker, "Theory and Science in the Study of Politics: A Review," page 379.

"Ghandi and Nixon . . . :" Burns, *Leadership*.

"It reflects not only situational factors . . . :" Knutson, *The Human Basis of the Polity*.

Matson, *The Broken Image*, page 249.

Allport, G., "The Composition of Political Attitudes," *American Journal of Sociology* 1929, 35, 220-238.

"Lockean . . . Leibnitzean model:" Allport, G. *Becoming: Basic Considerations for a Psychology of Personality.* New Haven: Yale University Press, 1955.

"Perception is a transaction . . . physical object:" Bohm, D., "Quantum Theory as an Indicator of a New Order in Physics. Part B: Implicate and Explicate Order in Physical Law," *Foundations of Physics,* 1973, 3, pages 139-168; Pribram, S. *Languages of the Brain.* Englewood Cliffs, New Jersey: Prentice-Hall, 1971; Pelletier, K. *Towards a Science of Consciousness.* New York: Delta, 1978.

"The idea of an external world . . . is rejected:" d'Espagnat, B., "The Quantum Theory and Reality," *Scientific American,* November 1978, pages 128-140.

"By deepening our self-understanding . . . our actions:" Gergen, K., "Social Psychology as History," *Journal of Personality and Social Psychology,* 1973, 26, pages 309-320.

"That is why self-actualizers . . . other people:" Maslow, "Resistance to Acculturation."

"They symbolize the competing . . . juncture in history:" Buss, A., "The Emerging Field of the Sociology of Psychological Knowledge," in A. Buss, ed., *Psychology in Social Context.* New York: Irvington, 1979.

Matson, *The Broken Image,* page 247.

WALTER NORD, *A Marxist Critique of Humanistic Psychology*

Reich, W. *The Mass Psychology of Fascism.* New York: Farrar, Straus and Giroux, 1970.

Fromm, E. *Marx's Concept of Man.* New York: Ungar, 1961.

Fromm, E. "Introduction," in A. Schaff, ed., *Marxism and the Human Individual.* New York: McGraw-Hill, 1970.

Hampden-Turner, C. *Radical Man.* Cambridge, MA: Schenkman, 1974.

Hampden-Turner, C. *From Poverty to Dignity.* Garden City, New York: Anchor Press, 1975.

Anderson, W. *Politics and the New Humanism.* Pacific Palisades, CA: Goodyear, 1973.

Feuer, L.S., ed. *Basic Writings on Politics and Philosophy: Karl Marx and Friedrich Engles.* Garden City, New York: Doubleday, 1959, page 249.

Marx, K. *Capital,* Volume 3. New York: International Publishers, 1967, page 820.

White, R.W., "Motivation Reconsidered: The Concept of Competence," *Psychological Review* 1959, 66, pages 297-334.

"Marx postulated that humans . . . :" For the most part Marx used the word "man" to refer to people in general. However, in accordance with the policy of this publisher, I will use "human" or "people" in making such references. For the most part, in his references to "man" in his writings on human essence and alienation, Marx was discussing mankind as a species, rather than as individuals.

Maslow, A.H. *Motivation and Personality.* 2nd Edition. New York: Harper and Row, 1970.

Hampden-Turner, *Radical Man.*

Greening, T.C. *Existential Humanistic Psychology.* Belmont, CA: Brooks/Cole, 1971, page 9.

Harman, W.W., "The Future of the Existential-Humanistic Perspective in Education," in T.C. Greening, ed., *Existential Humanistic Psychology.*

Harman, W.W., "Humanistic Capitalism: Another Alternative," *Journal of Humanistic Psychology,* 1974, 14, 5-32.

Zeitlin, I.M. *Marxism: A Re-Examination.* New York: Van Nostrand Reinhold, 1967.

"Many psychologists . . . man is a social being:" Glass, J.F., "The Humanistic Challenge to Sociology," *Journal of Humanistic Psychology,* 1971, 11, 170-183.

Glass, "The Humanistic Challenge," page 179.

"However, with some notable exceptions . . . :" Bugental, J.F.T., "The Third Force in Psychology," *Journal of Humanistic Psychology,* 1964, 4, 19-26; Glass, "The Humanistic Challenge," 1971; Hampden-Turner *Radical Man,* 1974; Harman, "Humanistic Capitalism," 1974; Matson, F.W., "AHP Committee on Human Policies: Statement of Purposes," *Journal of Humanistic Psychology,* 1973, 13, 15-18.

Matson, "AHP Committee on Human Policies," 1973.

"While some humanistic psychologists . . . human development:" Peterman, D.J., "Toward Interpersonal Fulfillment in a Eupsychian Culture," *Journal of Humanistic Psychology,* 1972, 12, 72-85.

Anderson, *Politics and the New Humanism,* page 145.

Maslow, A.H., "Power Relationships and Patterns of Personal Development," in A. Kornhauser, ed., *Problems of Power in American Democracy.* Detroit: Wayne State University Press, 1957.

Reich, *The Mass Psychology of Fascism.*

Hampden-Turner, *From Poverty to Dignity,* page 87.

ALAN R. BUSS, *Humanistic Psychology as Liberal Ideology*

Buss, A.R., "The Emerging Field of the Sociology of Psychological Knowledge," *American Psychologist,* 1975, 30, 988-1002.

Buss, A.R., "Development of Dialectics and Development of Humanistic Psychology," *Human Development,* 1976, 19, 248-260.

Buss, A.R., "Galton and the Birth of Differential Psychology and Eugenics: Social, Political, and Economic Forces," *Journal of the History of the Behavioral Sciences,* 1976, 12, 47-58.

Buss, A.R., "Piaget, Marx, and Buck-Morss on Cognitive Development: A Critique and Reinterpretation," *Human Development, 1977, 20,* 118-128.

Buss, A.R., "Critical Notice of Izenberg's Psychohistory and Intellectual History," *History and Theory, 1978, 17,* 94-98.

Nisbet, R.A. *The Quest for Community.* New York: Oxford University Press, 1953.

Nisbet, R.A. *The Sociological Tradition.* New York: Basic Books, 1966.

Nisbet, R.A. *Tradition and Revolt.* Historical and Sociological Essays. New York: Random House, 1968.

Westkott, M., "Conservative Method," *Philosophy of the Social Sciences, 1977, 7,* 67-76.

Hampden-Turner, C. *Radical Man.* Garden City, New York: Anchor Books, 1971, pages 17-18.

Anderson, W., "Politics and the New Humanism," *Journal of Humanistic Psychology,* 1974, 14, 5-26.

"They certainly did not see in Freudian negativism . . . revolutionary change that some have seen:" Brown, N.O. *Life Against Death.* The Psychoanalytic Meaning of History. Middletown, Connecticut: Wesleyan University Press, 1959; Jacoby, R. *Social Amnesia:* A Critique of Contemporary Psychology from Adler to Laing. Boston: Beacon Press, 1975; Marcuse, H. *Eros and Civilization:* A Philosophical Inquiry into Freud. Boston: Beacon Press, 1955; Reich, W. *The Mass Psychology of Fascism.* New York: Farrar, Straus and Giroux, 1970 (originally published, 1933); Robinson, P.A. *The Freudian Left.* New York: Harper and Row, 1969.

"Thus they are both ultimately ideological . . . Marxian sense of that term:" Lichtman, R., "Marx's Theory of Ideology," *Socialist Revolution,* 1975, 5, 45-76.

"The rhetoric of individual development . . . and organizational psychologists:" Harman, W.W., "Humanistic Capitalism: Another Alternative," *Journal of Humanistic Psychology,* 1974, 14, 5-32.

"While several people have already noted the conformist implications . . . :" Adams, H., "Toward a Dialectical Approach to Counseling," *Journal of Humanistic Psychology,* 1977, 17, 57-67; Beit-Hallahmi, B., "Humanistic Psychology: Progressive or Reactionary?", *Self and Society,* 1977, 5, 97-103; Glass, J.F., "The Humanistic Challenge to Sociology," *Journal of Humanistic Psychology,* 1971, 11, 170-183; Nord, W., "A Marxist Critique of Humanistic Psychology," *Journal of Humanistic Psychology,* 1977, 17, 75-83.

Maslow, A.H. *Motivation and Personality.* New York: Harper, 1954, pages 353-362.

"He attempted to pass . . . a hard normative core:" Smith, M.B. *Social Psychology and Human Values.* Chicago: Aldine-Atherton, 1969, p. 169.

Maslow, *Motivation and Personality,* pages 160; 340.

Lichtman, R., "Marx and Freud, Part 2: Antagonistic Themes," *Socialist Revolution*, 1977, 7, 59-84; page 81.

Smith, M.B., "On Self-Actualization: A Transambivalent Examination of a Focal Theme in Maslow's Psychology," *Journal of Humanistic Psychology*, 1973, 13, 17-33.

Maslow, *Motivation and Personality*, page 351.

"The major theme that Mill defends . . . :" Wolff, R.P. *The Poverty of Liberalism*. Boston: Beacon Press, 1968, page 7.

Mill, J.S. *On Liberty.* New York: W.W. Norton, 1975; originally published in 1859.

Hobhouse, L.T. *Liberalism.* Oxford: Oxford University Press, 1964; originally published in 1911.

Aron, A., "Maslow's Other Child," *Journal of Humanistic Psychology*, 1977, 17, 9-24; pages 14-15.

Bachrach, P. *The Theory of Democratic Elitism: A Critique.* Boston: Little, Brown, 1967, for the reference in the sentence which begins "Such findings helped to fuel . . . "

Hampden-Turner, C., "Comment on 'Maslow's Other Child,'" *Journal of Humanistic Psychology*, 1977, 17, 25-31.

Adorno, T.W. *Negative Dialectics.* New York: Seabury, 1973.

"Classical democratic theory 'is based . . . significantly affect him.':" Bachrach, *The Theory of Democratic Elitism*, page 98.

Bachrach, *The Theory of Democratic Elitism*, page 102.

IV: THE END OF INNOCENCE

FLOYD W. MATSON, *Humanistic Political Science and Humane Politics*

Maslow, A.H. "Isomorphic Interrelationships Between Knower and Known." In F.W. Matson and A. Montagu, eds., *The Human Dialogue: Perspectives on Communication.* New York: Free Press, 1966, pages 195-206.

Krutch, J.W. *The Measure of Man.* New York: Grosset Universal library, 1953, Chapter 10.

Hutchins, R.M. *Freedom, Education, and the Fund.* New York: World and Meridian, 1956.

Faulkner, W. "Nobel Prize Acceptance Speech." Stockholm: The Nobel Foundation, 1949.

Fromm, E. *May Man Prevail?* New York: Doubleday, 1961.

Marcuse, H. *One-Dimensional Man.* Boston: Beacon Press, 1964, pages 12, 14, 15-16.

Rosenberg, B.; Gerver, I.; and Howton, F.W., eds. *Mass Society in Crisis: Social Problems and Social Pathology.* New York: Macmillan, 1964.

Wiener, N. *The Human Use of Human Beings.* Garden City, New York: Doubleday Anchor Books, 1954, pages 182, 186.

WALT ANDERSON, *Politics and the New Humanism*

Rogers, C. *Client-Centered Therapy.* Boston: Houghton-Mifflin, 1951, page 201.

Bugental, J. "The Humanistic Ethic — The Individual in Psychotherapy as a Societal Change Agent." *Journal of Humanistic Psychology,* 1971, Volume 11/1, 11-25.

Freud, S. "My Contact with Josef Popper-Lynkeus." In *Character and Culture,* from Collier Books edition of *The Collected Papers of Sigmund Freud.* Translated by J. Srachey. New York: Crowell-Collier, 1963. Originally published, 1932, page 303.

Freud, S. *Civilization and Its Discontents.* Translated by J. Strachey. New York: W.W. Norton, 1961. Originally published, 1930, pages 44, 62.

Freud, S., and Breuer, J. *Studies on Hysteria.* Translated by J. Strachey. London: Hogarth Press, 1955. Originally published, 1893, p. 305.

Rieff, P. *Freud, The Mind of the Moralist.* New York: Viking, 1959, p 327.

Roazen, P. *Freud: Political and Social Thought.* New York: Knopf, 1968, p. 157.

Rogow, A. *The Psychiatrists.* New York: G.P. Putnam's Sons, 1970, p. 72.

Lippmann, W. *A Preface to Politics.* New York: Mitchell Kennedy, 1913.

Lippmann, W. *Public Opinion.* New York: Harcourt, Brace and World, 1922.

Lasswell, H. *Psychopathology and Politics.* Chicago: University of Chicago Press, 1930, p. 76.

Reich, W. *The Function of the Orgasm.* New York: Noonday Press, 1942, p. 195.

Reich, W. *The Mass Psychology of Fascism.* New York: Farrar, Straus, and Giroux, 1970, p. 30.

Reich, W. *The Mass Psychology of Fascism.* New York: Orgone Institute Press, 1946, p. 26.

Roszak, T. *The Making of a Counter Culture.* New York: Doubleday Anchor, 1969, p. 84.

Reich, W., 1946, p. 15.

Matson, F. *The Broken Image.* New York: George Braziller, 1964, page 60.

Mannheim, K. *Man and Society in an Age of Reconstruction.* New York: Harcourt, Brace and World, 1940, page 213.

Parsons, T. "Definitions of health and Illness in the Light of American Values and Social Structure." In E. Jaco, ed., *Patients, Physicians and Illness.* Glencoe, Illinois: Free Press, 1963, page 176.

Sennett, R. "Review of B. Skinner, *Beyond Freedom and Dignity,"* *New York Times Book Review,* 24 October, 1971, Page 1.

Szasz, T. *Law, Liberty and Psychiatry.* New York: Macmillan, 1963.

Maslow, A. *Motivation and Personality. New York: Harper and Row,* 1954, page 180.

Maslow, A. *Toward a Psychology of Being.* Litton Educational Publishing, 1968, page 11.

Maslow, A. "A Theory of Metamotivation: The Biological Rooting of the Value-Life," *Journal of Humanistic Psychology* 1967, Volume 7/2, 93-127; page 110.

Perls, F.; Hefferline, R.; and Goodman, P. *Gestalt Therapy.* New York: Delta, 1965, page 215.

Perls, F. *Gestalt Therapy Verbatim.* Moab, Utah: Real People Press, 1969, page 3.

Fromm, E.; Suzuki, D.; and DeMartino, R. *Zen Buddhism and Psychoanalysis.* New York: Harper Colophon, 1970, pages 98 and 99.

Hampden-Turner, C. *Radical Man.* Cambridge, Mass.: Schenkman, 1971, pages 17-18.

Halleck, S. *The Politics of Therapy. New York: Science House,* 1971, pages 11, 12; quotations from Busse, Waggoner.

McConnell, J. "Criminals can be Brainwashed — Now." *Psychology Today,* April 1970, page 74.

Glenn, M. "Introduction" to J. Agel, ed., *The Radical Therapist.* New York: Ballantine, 1971, pages x-xi.

Szasz, T. *The Manufacture of Madness.* New York: Delta, 1971, pages 27, 84.

Dahl, R. *Modern Political Analysis.* Englewood Cliffs, New Jersey: Prentice-Hall, 1963, page 6.

Eulau, H. *The Behavioral Persuasion in Politics.* New York: Random House, 1963, pages 4-5.

ELIZABETH CAMPBELL, *Humanistic Psychology: The End of Innocence (a view from inside the parentheses)*

Barnet, P. and Muller, R. *Global Reach.* The Power of the Multinational Corporations. New York: Simon and Schuster, 1974.

Berry, W. *The Unsettling of America.* Culture and Agriculture. New York: Avon Books, 1977.

Brown, L. *The Twenty-Ninth Day.* New York: W.W. Norton, 1978.

Capra, F. *The Turning Point.* New York: Simon and Schuster, 1982.

Falk, R. *A Study of Future Worlds.* New York: Free Press, 1975.

Falk, R.; Kim, S.; Mendlovitz, S., eds., *Toward a Just World Order,* Volume 1. Boulder, Colorado: Westview Press, 1982.

Galtung, J. *The True Worlds: A Transnational Perspective.* New York: Free Press, 1980.

Hawken, P.; Ogilvy, J.; and Schwartz, P. *Seven Tomorrows: Toward a Voluntary Tomorrow.* New York: Bantam, 1982.

Henderson, J. *The Politics of the Solar Age*. Alternatives to Economics. Garden City, New York: Doubleday, 1981.

Laszlo, E. and One Hundred Contributors. *Goals for Mankind*. New York: E.P. Dutton, 1977.

Markley, O.W. and Harman, W. *Changing Images of Man*. New York: Pergamon, 1982.

Meadows, D.H.; Meadows, D.L.; Randers, J.; and Bettrens, W. *The Limits to Growth*. New York: New American Library, 1972.

Mesarovic, M., and Pestel, E. *Mankind at the Turning Point*. New York: New American Library, 1974.

Pribram, K.H. *Languages of the Brain*. Englewood Cliffs, New Jersey: Prentice-Hall, 1971.

Prigogine, I. *From Being to Becoming*. Time and Complexity *in the Physical Sciences*. San Francisco: W.H. Freeman, 1980.

Sales, K. *Human Scale*. New York: Coward, McCann and Geoghegan, 1980.

Schumacher, E.F. *Small is Beautiful*. Economics as if People Mattered. New York: Harper and Row, 1973.

Sheldrake, R. *A New Science of Life*. The Hypothesis of Formative Causation. Los Angeles: J.P. Tarcher, 1982.

Toffler, A. *The Third Wave*. New York: Bantam, 1981.

Wilber, K. *No Boundary*. Boulder, Colorado: Shambhala, 1979.

Wilber, K. *The Spectrum of Consciousness*. Wheaton, Illinois: Theosophical Publishing, 1977.

Wilber, K. *The Atman Project*. Wheaton, Illinois: Theosophical Publishing, 1980.

Wilber, K. *Up from Eden*. Garden City, New York: Doubleday, 1981.

Wilber, K. *The Holographic Paradigm and Other Paradoxes*. Boulder, Colorado: Shambhala, 1982.

Wilber, K. *A Sociable God*. New York: McGraw Hill, 1983.

Wilber, K. *Eye to Eye*. The Quest for a New Paradigm. Garden City, New York: Doubleday, 1983.

Naisbitt, J. *Megatrends*. Ten New Directions Transforming our Lives. New York: Warner Books, 1982, page 249.

Fuller, B. *Utopia or Oblivion*. The Prospects for Humanity. New York: Bantam, 1969.

Harman, W. "AHP and Global Issues." *AHP Newsletter,* October, 1982, page 15.

Thompson, W.I. *At the Edge of History*. New York: Harper and Row, 1972.

Harman, W., 1982, page 14.

Harman, W., 1982, pages 14-15.

Nelson, R.F.W. *Beyond the Slap of the Beaver's Tail.* Understanding the Threats to our Future. Address to the Way Through the Future, Kingston, Ontario, Canada, March 11, 1977. Available from Square One Management, Ottawa.

Nelson, R.F.W. *The Illusions of Urban Man.* Ottawa, Canada: The Ministry of State for Urban Affairs, 1978.

Nelson, R.F.W., 1977, page 20.

Naisbitt, J., 1982.

Barnet and Muller, 1974.

Marien, M. "The Transformation as Sandbox Syndrome." *Journal of Humanistic Psychology,* Winter, 1983.

May, R. "The Hazards of AHP," *AHP Newsletter,* October, 1982, page 16.

May, R. "The Problem of Evil. An Open Letter to Carl Rogers," *Journal of Humanistic Psychology* 22 (Summer, 1982), 10-21.

Rogers, C. "Notes on Rollo May," *Journal of Humanistic Psychology* 22 (Summer, 1982), 8-9.

Rogers, C. "Reply to Rollo May's Letter to Carl Rogers," *Journal of Humanistic Psychology* 22 (Fall, 1982), 85-90.

Friedman, M. "Comment on the Rogers-May Discussion of Evil," *Journal of Humanistic Psychology* 22 (Fall, 1982), 93-96.

Farson, R. "The Technology of Humanism," *Journal of Humanistic Psychology* 18 (Spring, 1978), 5-36.

Koch, S. "The Image of Man Implicit in Encounter Group Therapy," *Journal of Humanistic Psychology* 11 (Fall, 1971), 109-128.

Nord, W. "A Marxist Critique of Humanistic Psychology," *Journal of Humanistic Psychology* 17 (Winter, 1977), 75-84.

Wooten, L. "Albert Speer: How to Manage an Atrocity," *Journal of Humanistic Psychology* 21 (Fall, 1981), 21-38.

Harman, W., 1982.

Roszak, T. *Person/Planet.* Garden City, New York: Doubleday, 1978.

Ferguson, M. *The Aquarian Conspiracy.* Personal and Social Transformation in the 1980's. Los Angeles: J.P. Tarcher, 1980.

Gibb, J. "The Hibernation," *AHP Newsletter,* February, 1983.

Michael, D.N. *On Learning to Plan and Planning to Learn.* San Francisco: Jossey-Bass, 1973.

Salk, J. *The Survival of the Wisest.* New York: Harper and Row, 1972.

WALT ANDERSON, Politics and the New Humanism (JHP 14 [4]:5-26, Fall, 1974)

ADRIANNE ARON, Maslow's Other Child (JHP 17 [2]:9-24, Spring, 1977)

ALLAN R. BUSS, Humanistic Psychology as Liberal Ideology (JHP 19 [3]:43-55, Summer, 1979)

ELIZABETH CAMPBELL, Humanistic Psychology: The End of Innocence (JHP 24 [2]:6-29, Spring, 1984)

JAQUELINE DOYLE, The Political Process: Working Statement (AHP Newsletter)

MARILYN FERGUSON, Transformation as Rough Draft (JHP 23 [1]:16-18, Winter, 1983)

MAURICE FRIEDMAN, The Nuclear Threat and The Hidden Human Image (JHP 24 [3]:65-76, Summer, 1984)

CHARLES HAMPDEN-TURNER, Comment on 'Maslow's Other Child' (JHP 17 [2]:25-30, Spring, 1977)

MILDRED HARDEMAN, A Dialogue with Abraham Maslow (JHP 19 [1]:24-28, Winter, 1979)

JAMES LAFFERTY, Political Responsibility and the Human Potential Movement (JHP 21 [1]:69-75, Winter, 1981)

MICHAEL MARIEN, Further Thoughts on the Two Paths to Transformation. A Reply to Ferguson (JHP 23 [4]:127-136, Fall, 1983)

MICHAEL MARIEN, The Transformation as Sandbox Syndrome (JHP 23 [1]:7-15, Winter, 1983)

ABRAHAM MASLOW, Politics 3 (JHP 17 [4]:5-20, Fall, 1979)

FLOYD W. MATSON, AHP Committee on Human Policies: Statement of Purposes (JHP 13 [3]:15-18, Summer, 1973)

FLOYD W. MATSON, Humanistic Political Science and Humane Politics (JHP 7:80-86, 1967)

ROLLO MAY, The Destiny of America (AHP Newsletter 22-23, May, 1980)

ROLLO MAY, The Problem of Evil: An Open Letter to Carl Rogers (JHP 22 [3]:10-21, Summer, 1982)

WALTER NORD, A Marxist Critique of Humanistic Psychology (JHP 17[1]:75-83, Winter, 1977)

CARL ROGERS, The Person (AHP Newsletter 8-9, May, 1980)

CARL ROGERS, Notes on Rollo May (Perspectives 2 [1]:16, Summer, 1981)

CARL ROGERS, Some Social Issues which Concern Me (JHP 12 [2]:45-60, Fall, 1972)

STEPHEN WOOLPERT, A Comparison of Rational Choice and Self-Actualization Theories of Politics (JHP 22 [3]:55-67, Summer, 1982)